Women Of The West

Spokane Indians Mr. & Mrs. Stevens & their daughter Maimie, dressed in ceremonial clothe

"Our Home."

The dugout of an unidentified family near McCook, Nebraska, in the 1890s.

Work is love made visible.

Arizona Mary, a woman engaged in ox teaming, ca. 1890.

To those women of the West whose stories will never be told.

Women Of The

W. W. Norton & Company

New York • London

West

by Cathy Luchetti
and Carol Olwell

Miriam Davis Colt's book *Went to Kansas* was published in 1862 by L. Ingalls & Co. and reprinted by Readex Microprint Corporation in 1966 as part of their Great Americana series.

The source of our material on Bethenia Owens-Adair was her autobiography *Dr. Owens-Adair, Some of Her Life Experiences,* published in 1906 by Mann and Beach, Portland, Oregon.

Material from the life of Sarah Winnemucca was drawn from her book *Life Among the Piutes; Their Wrongs and Claims*, by Sarah Winnemucca Hopkins, edited by Mrs. Horace Mann (Boston: For Sale by Cupples, Upham and Co., G. P. Putnam's Sons, New York, and by the author), 1883.

First published as a Norton paperback 2001
by arrangement with Antelope Island Press

Library of Congress Cataloging in Publication Data

Luchett, Cathy Lee, 1945–
    Women of the West.
Bibliography: p.
    1. Women—West (U.S.)—Bibliography. 2. Women—West (U.S.)—Correspondence. 3. Women—West (U.S.)—History.
I. Olwell, Carol, 1944–   II. Title.
HQ1438.W45L8   305.4'0978   81-13035
                                    AACR2
ISBN 0-393-32155-X
ISBN 978-0-393-32155-5

W. W. Norton & Company, Inc.,
500 Fifth Avenue, New York, N.Y. 10110
www.wwnorton.com

W. W. Norton & Company Ltd.
15 Carlisle Street, London W1D 3BS

11

Permission to publish selected excerpts of the diaries of Mary Richardson Walker has been granted by the Huntington Library, San Marino, California.

Permission to publish portions of the diary of Anna Harder Ogden has been granted by The Bancroft Library, Berkeley, California, and by her son, Paul Ogden.

The letters of Pauline Lyons Williamson have been published with the permission of the New York Public Library, New York. They are from the Lyons/Williamson Collection, Schomburg Center for Research in Black Culture, The New York Public Library; Astor, Lenox and Tilden Foundations.

Permission to publish the journal of Priscilla Merriman Evans from *Heart Throbs of the West* and *Our Pioneer Heritage,* both edited by Kate B. Carter, has been granted by the Daughters of the Utah Pioneers.

The words from the *Life of Sister Mary Catherine Cabareaux, S.N.D.* are reproduced herein by permission of the Sisters of Notre Dame de Namur, Office of Provincial Archives, College of Notre Dame, Belmont, California 94002 and ©1981, Sisters of Notre Dame de Namur.

Permission to publish the diary of Keturah Penton Belknap has been granted by Mrs. Donald A. Belknap, whose husband was given the diary by his mother, Mrs. Jane Belknap, who in turn received the work from its original owner, Reva Barrett. Mrs. Roberta Harband has also granted permission to publish that portion of Keturah's diary which she contributed to the original manuscript. A portion of the diary, edited by Glenda Riley, was previously published in *The Annals of Iowa* 44 (Summer 1977): 31–51.

Permission to use the material from the life of Helen J. Stewart has been granted by the Nevada Historical Society.

Permission to reprint selected letters of Elinore Pruitt Stewart has been granted by the Houghton Mifflin Company, who own the rights to the book from which these letters were drawn: *Letters of a Woman Homesteader,* Copyright 1913 and 1914 by The Atlantic Monthly. Copyright 1914 and 1942 by Elinore Pruitt Stewart.

Table of Contents

Mrs. Smith & wildcat she killed near Glenrock, Wyoming.

Camp of Alaskan prospectors, ca. 1900.

Camp of Klondikers, 1897. It was not uncommon for people to winter in tents such as these.

Preface

From my early years in Texas, I remember stories of the old Goodnight-Loving cattle trail which ran north, along the outskirts of town. It ran through the brushy mesquite, past grazing herds of longhorn steers, through the oil fields, where the heavy metal of the petroleum industry threatened to obscure all that remained of the past. Though nearly erased from the earth, that trail still bore a strange kind of excitement for me: its name had a ring of adventure; its history bespoke the dozens of families who tried to raise cattle in the desert a hundred years ago. Yet it was also a path out—to Dallas, Santa Fe, and further on, to Denver.

There were other memories, too; stories my grandmother had passed along about my own relatives emigrating west in Conestoga wagons. Two families, with bedding, buckets, Bibles, and high hopes on their way to Oregon. Perhaps they had passed along that very trail—I never knew if they had or not. They had settled, claimed land, raised families. Among them was my great-great-grandmother, a bird-like woman whose response to running a farm while raising seven large sons was to get suddenly angry late at night, remembering some impudence, then to march into the offending boy's room and whale him with a birch rod while he was asleep. A handy method of discipline, I always thought!

There were dozens of stories like this, and in hearing them, it seemed to me that she and the other women in my family were a spirited lot. They cooked, sewed, complained, nurtured—all the while living their lives under unbelievably hard circumstances. It never occurred to me to question their absence from history as taught in school. At the time we learned only about the men who defended the Alamo, the men who rode roughshod into Mexico to claim more land for the United States, the men who forged across the mountains and opened the Northwest Passage.

History seldom tells the stories of the eight hundred thousand women who also came West, lively stories of courtship, love, inventiveness, humor, skulduggery, passion.

To present all these stories would have entailed the labor of a lifetime, but when my collaborator presented her idea of making a book about the women of the West that included a dozen or so of the strongest, most poignant, and most diverse stories along with a vast selection of photographs, it seemed a perfect opportunity to give at least a few of these women a voice.

We do not intend for this book to be an academic history based on the political and social events of the settling of the West, but a document of personal experience. It does not pretend to cover the numerous nationalities and religions present in the West during this period, nor does it address the dozens of wonderfully diverse occupations women began to pursue. Instead this book is about those women who have not had a place in academic history. These women were still a quiet part of the American West; their stories show as clearly as possible the quality of their daily lives. We wanted this book to be a tribute to them. As great granddaughters of men and women pioneers, it has been our honor and joy to bring these stories to light.

Cathy Luchetti

Public School House, Teacher and Pupils, in Live Oak county, Texas, 1887. Photo by Brack.

Notes on the Photographs

My great-grandmother Zillah Player Riser was born shortly after her mother crossed the Platte River in 1851. Some family accounts even suggested it was "several minutes" after the crossing. Records list her place of birth as "on the plains near Lincoln, Nebraska," or "crossing the plains." I've often wondered what that trip must have been like, especially from her mother's point of view, and how that crossing differed from the one Zillah's grandparents made in 1847. Sometimes I have wished that I could have been there, could have known them and their fellow travelers, known the bustling activity, the sounds and smells of camp life, and seen the whole country revealed in their passing. Another part of me has been grateful not to have watched children and adults die of injury and disease, or to have witnessed, and been a part of, the slow extermination of Indian peoples and cultures.

Through the years, in reading other books on the West, I've looked for a glimpse of the world and of life through my great-grandmother's eyes. There are wonderful documentations of railroads being built, towns constructed, mines excavated, and cavalries drilled, but hardly anywhere were there photographs of what women were doing all the while. In most books, when a woman did appear, her presence was often barely noticeable and seemed hardly worth mention, as in the photograph on the opposite page.

The contribution of women to the West is, however, worth more than noting—it should be acclaimed. To this end, I spent a year driving more than twenty thousand miles while visiting the major photographic archives of sixteen western states. My friend Cathy Luchetti spent that same year sequestered in the Bancroft and other libraries, researching, reading, writing, and assembling the text of this book. We wanted to offer a sense of life as lived by western women between 1840 and 1915 through their actual words—their letters, diaries, and journals—and through photographs portraying daily life.

Such photographs of women actually doing things have been hard to find. This is partly because the work that women were doing was not considered important enough by many to record. (Indeed, who today photographs women cooking, vacuuming, or doing the dishes?) Also, the photographic processes first developed—daguerrotypes, tintypes, and ambrotypes—required long exposure times and complicated processing, conditions that did not lend themselves to a rapid, spontaneous reporting of life. Finally, the style of photography most popular in the nineteenth century was not the informal, "true to life" image. What most people wanted, and were willing to pay for, was the formal, posed portrait, with men and women dressed up in their Sunday best, staged against an artificial backdrop.

For these reasons, we have not been able to offer a photographic documentation of *everything* women did: either prints could not be found, or they were in too poor a condition to be reproduced. Not one photograph could be found of the handcart pioneers pulling their belongings across the plains, although nearly three thousand people in ten separate trips did exactly that. Even pictures of wagon trains in transit are very rare. Due to the prevailing racism of the times, photographic records of black and Asian pioneers are practically nonexistent. The daily activities of Catholic nuns in most orders were not allowed to be photographed until after the turn of the century—instead, Catholic archives are full of the formally posed group portraits of nuns, photographs of the buildings in which they worked and the people whom they served. A far better record of Indians exists—it is so broad, in fact, that their tribal and cultural diversity would require volumes to describe.

Where possible we have concluded each of the eleven life stories in this book with a photograph of that woman; its omission means simply that no picture could be found. Names, dates, and places have been included in photographic captions when they were available; unfortunately, in many cases, they were not.

To thoroughly illustrate the life of women in the West we would need to include material from the lumber camps, railroads and mines, military posts and frontier towns, for women were witnesses to and participants in all aspects of life in the West. We felt this was a scope too great for one book, and so, in selecting the photographs we chose to concentrate on the more quiet and unobtrusive—though no less important—side of life, to show how hard these women worked, and how much they gave.

Carol Olwell

Gold discovery on Porcupine River, Alaska.

Notes on the Editing

Each woman included in this book has a distinct literary style influenced by her education, profession, ethnic background, and her general outlook on life. Some of the women who left these diaries, letters, and journals had an audience in mind as they wrote; others were less concerned with future historical value than with merely keeping track of their lives. Some wrote simply and directly; others wrote in a more convoluted style. Some of the journals are intimate, confiding; some elicit pity; some are inspiring. Because of the striking differences between these works, and the wide divergence of styles, it was necessary to edit each manuscript for clarity as well as content.

Some works represent the author's entire effort, while others are only segments of larger works, either published or still in manuscript form. In the case of longer journals, such as those by Mary Richardson Walker and Bethenia Owens-Adair, there was no choice but to edit for length. Shorter reminiscences, or groups of letters such as those by Pauline Williamson, are printed almost in their entirety.

Our use of paragraphs—particularly in the journal of Sister Mary Catherine—was simply an aid to the reader. She was a well-educated woman whose narrative was flawlessly written—whether she wrote on board a pitching ship or in the privacy of her bunk in the Oregon forests. But there was never a pause in her outpourings, never a place to rest the eye, and it became necessary to create paragraphs throughout her story. She also made liberal use of exclamation marks, which someone deleted in later transcriptions. These we have replaced in order to be more faithful to the original material and spirit of her work.

Miriam Colt wrote in retrospect of her trip to Kansas. Hers was a florid Victorian style, and the self-consciousness of her writing may have resulted from the fact that she hoped to publish her work. We chose excerpts that show the events of her journey rather than her more flowery metaphysical passages. Semi-colons and dashes end nearly every sentence of her narrative; we frequently substituted periods.

Mary Richardson Walker kept a journal of her entire life—twelve full volumes from which the chapter in our book is excerpted. She was a well-educated woman, and though a missionary, religion did not seem to give her the release she sought. Instead, her journal became her best companion. She wrote so honestly about her feelings and her life that it was painfully difficult to shorten her story. The disparate events in her life can be traced by the dates of her entries—we have tried not to interfere with excessive editorial comment. Most of her Victorian spellings stand as she wrote them: "tho" and "buffalow" seem perfectly easy to comprehend without modernizing the spelling.

Bethenia Owens-Adair wrote a book describing her life experiences, from which her chapter in this book is excerpted. Because her book was written in retrospect, the tone is even and flowing, and the grammar impeccable. There was little we had to adjust in her story, save the length.

Priscilla Merriman Evans was a handcart pioneer who accompanied her husband from Wales to Salt Lake City, Utah. Whether she kept her journal during the trip itself, or wrote it after her arrival is unknown, but there are two slightly different versions of her story recorded by Kate B. Carter for the Daughters of the Utah Pioneers. Both versions appeared in Carter's series of books on the West: *Heart Throbs of the West* and *Our Pioneer Heritage*. Because one version embellished the other we chose to combine them, rearranging some paragraphs and, in a very few instances, slightly altering the sentence structure.

Keturah Belknap's story was by far the most difficult to edit. It came to us in typescript; someone in the family had earlier transcribed the original manuscript from Keturah's hand. The journal began when Keturah was a young girl and progressed through her adult life. This particular manuscript was unique because her spelling was erratic, periods were seldom used, and capitalization often occurred in mid-sentence. Yet the overall affect was one of freshness and charm. As the manuscript progressed, the sentences became more organized, the spelling more standard. Possibly her grammar improved through continual reading of the Bible, or perhaps the transcriber began to edit. We decided to leave her material as we found it, only adding extra spacing to indicate breath pauses, rather than to substitute conventional punctuation.

The story of Sarah Winnemucca was excerpted from her book, *Life Among the Piutes; Their Wrongs and Claims*. An original copy of this book is in the archives of the College of Notre Dame in Belmont, California, where Sarah was briefly a student. Her story was written in retrospect, and although there is some confusion as to time and place (for example, in her narrative she mentions her second husband before she accounts for meeting him), the story generally proceeds chronologically. The allegation has been made that Mrs. Horace Mann contributed slightly more than editing to the book, but Sarah Winnemucca has always been credited with its authorship. Although we have edited freely in order to reduce the length of the story, the only change in style has been to eliminate the frequent "oh!" which began many of her sentences.

Pauline Williamson's letters came from a collection that was apparently kept by her parents, to whom she was describing her attempt to make her living in Oakland and in San Francisco, California. The photocopied letters were quite legible, except for those times when she had more to say than one page would hold, and so she would turn the page and write vertically across the horizontal lines of script. The result was a spidery mosaic of cross-hatched letters which enabled her to conserve paper, but were bewildering to read. Other letters exist in the collection which are not reprinted here. There were some omissions within the text of her letters, but no editorial changes.

Elinore Pruitt Stewart's story is also encompassed within the text of numerous letters which she wrote to a past employer, Mrs. Coney. Initially the letters were intended only for Mrs. Coney, but Elinore's skill with words and description became so recognized that in later years she wrote for publication. Our segment of her story comes from *The Letters of a Woman Homesteader*. We have reprinted her words unchanged, except in one case where her Scots husband-to-be, Mr. Stewart, says "gey duir trip." Unintelligible to us, we decided to edit it out of the text. Otherwise, only indentations for paragraphs have been added for the reader's convenience.

The letters and daybooks of Helen J. Stewart, which had been donated to the Nevada Historical Society by Carrie Townley Miller, were in such fragile condition that photocopying was prohibited. Instead, Ms. Miller loaned us her own hand-written tran-

Letter writing after hanging out the wash.

scriptions—particularly helpful since the Stewart material was quite extensive. Because of the erratic nature of this material— ranging from personal letters, poetry and short stories to daybooks, ledgers and ranching accounts—it has been necessary throughout to explain to whom she was writing and, if possible, what had preceded each event and precipitated the correspondence. Helen Stewart's material covers nearly the length of her adult life— beginning when she was Archie's bride on the ranch in Nevada and ending in the twentieth century when she was an elderly woman barely able to write, but determined enough to peck out her messages by typewriter. Her style is consistent throughout and she needed little editing for grammar.

Anna Harder Ogden began her journal at the age of twenty-one. She was then earning a living as a servant, but was eager to find a husband and anxious to better her station in life. Her journal is alternately ebullient and morose, perhaps because of her youthful emotionalism. Her journal has at times, a scattered, unfocused quality which we have tried to minimize through selective omissions. Every entry also bore the time of day and night when it was written, which we eliminated to provide a smoother transition from one entry to the next. Otherwise, the only editorial change we made was to shorten the journal to fit the book.

In the hope of retaining as much authenticity as possible, we have used Victorian spellings of such words as "staid" and "thot" since they were widely used during the time these women wrote. Other words that seem difficult to read because of their spelling have been changed to their modern form. Any antiquated words that still appear in the dictionary—such as "clout" for a bunch of rags, or "swale" for a marshy area—stand without explanation. Any that do not have dictionary definitions or need further explanations are followed by a brief, bracketed note.

Throughout, our intention has been to keep a low editorial profile, to explain only where necessary and to limit our modern interpretation of these stories. We have not introduced the feminist questions of our times, nor our own political views, because we felt it would be unfair to use the lives of others—who might have felt quite differently from the way we feel—for those purposes. Instead, we have tried to create a book that does its best to let these women speak for themselves.

One of the original criteria of the book was to present not only white American pioneers, but also the writings of minority women who lived during the time. Unfortunately, a year's research turned up very little minority writing: only two stories suited the purposes of this book. We can only hope that in time the basements, attics, and private archives throughout the country will begin to yield up these important documents. Without them, we will continue to be limited in our understanding of the experience of all the women of the West. In lieu of these journals, we have briefly sketched the history of minority women on the frontier. It is a meagre offering, considering the vastness of their impact and the large numbers in their population, but until more primary information is available, it will have to do.

Unidentified woman, probably living in Washington state.

The Quin family, San Diego, California, 1899.

The Richard Leigh family in the 1880s.

The Shores family near Westerville, Nebraska, 1887.

The Barak Livingston family near Anselmo, Nebraska, 1888.

21

Unidentified family, Custer Co., Nebraska, 1887.

Unidentified family, Southwest Custer Co., Nebraska, 1892.

Unidentified family, Southwest Custer Co., Nebraska, 1892.

The Robins family's dugout near West Union, Nebraska, 1886.

The Reinhardt Porath family, near Mason City, Nebraska, ca. 1888.

Unidentified family, Southeast Custer Co., Nebraska, ca. 1888.

The Ball family near Woods Park, Custer Co., Nebraska, 1886.

The France LaDuke family near Berwyn, Nebraska, ca. 1888.

The exterior & interior of Mr. & Mrs. Batholomew's sod house built 1899, Kansas.

Introduction

Myth and misunderstanding spring from the American frontier as readily as rye grass from sod, and—like the wiry grass—seem as difficult to weed out and discard. They emerge from a time in our history when hundreds of thousands of Americans rushed across the continent, forsaking their past lives for land, gold, opportunity, and adventure in the western territories. From this tumult the western epic hero was born—a rugged individualist who moved further west at the first sign of a neighbor's smoke and who was only marginally committed to home, hearth, and family. Daniel Boone, Davy Crockett, Jedediah Smith: these were the men of folklore and legend.

If the legends included women, then they too were of the mythical sort—either staunch, bonneted women who stood at sunset etched in bold relief against the prairie, or frolicsome harlots, splendid in lace and fancy goods, able to please for a dollar or love for nothing if the right man came along.

Yet somewhere between these extremes lie the real lives of the real women who traveled this vast frontier. They were not the women as recorded or explained by scholars, nor the women who obligingly took their places in the shadows of history while their men fought wars, passed legislation, homesteaded, found gold, loved, and died. Instead, they were individuals who make themselves known to us through their own words in their letters, their diaries, and their journals.

Their history, too, is recorded in photographs—faded prints of gaunt, sunburned faces peering from the wagon backs, or somberly clad women stirring lye soap over an open fire. The truth of the westward migration stares out, as well, from the speculative, squinting eyes of tow-headed children who spent long days helping their parents in the fields, tying long strings to the corn, then pulling each string over and over again to startle the crows and shake them out. It went without saying that if the crows got fat the children would starve, and these children—with their hard bright eyes and flour-sack shirts—knew it.

Equally eloquent are the photographs of men and women posed before their soddie houses. Dressed in their Sunday best, their children lined up like ninepins beside them (often with scarcely a quarter-inch difference between them in height), the settlers' very presence on the land marked them as both victims and victors. Their soddie houses were cool in summer and warm in winter, but a single leak in the roof would send streams of dirty brown water down over the blankets and bedding below. As they lived year after year on the Midwestern plains, they had to contend with scourges that were Biblical in scale—infestations of grasshoppers, bedbugs, and fleas; blizzards, tornadoes, and drought. History has seldom illuminated their trials. Their lives remain for the most part unknown.

Even more obscure are the lives and stories of the minority

Woman making soap in Oregon, ca. 1908.

Indians. Women wrote more personal descriptions. They marveled at the scenery and noted in detail the character of their traveling companions. They described what was worn, what was said, and what was accomplished. They rejoiced in births, and mourned the dead, but also sought to avoid minute descriptions of the pain and hardship encountered along the trail. (Thus the strangely wooden references to children falling under wagon wheels or passing away from disease.) Though often narrow-minded and unwittingly bigoted, these accounts also reveal women who reached out with compassion to others in need. Their stories were strong and make a compelling human document.

As these women wrote, they often paused in retelling incidents that, to them, were simply beyond description. Sudden encounters with half-clad Kiowas or Pawnees, bawdy Mexican bullwhackers, trail herders, coolies, gamblers, or gunslingers were startling experiences which each woman handled according to her ability. When Helen Carpenter observed a "queer little human being" for whom she knew no name until she "remembered some pictures in the old school geography, and then . . . decided he must be a Chinaman,"[2] she was no different than scores of hitherto untraveled, insular Americans whose crossing of the continent promised to be the single most memorable experience of their lives.

The first wagons to set forth found uncluttered trails, resplendent with lush prairie grass and unsullied campsites. But by 1850, so many Conestoga wagons were leaving St. Joseph, Missouri, that the plains were dotted with their white billowing covers and teams traveled twelve abreast. Along the Platte River the crush of humanity resulted in campsites befouled with the litter and waste of earlier parties. Between 1840 and 1848 only 18,847 individuals had traveled into Oregon, California, and Utah. By 1860, an additional 296,259 had made the journey, resulting in such unpleasant trail conditions that Charlotte Pengra was compelled to report in her journal "an unendurable stench that rose from a ravine that is resorted to for special purposes by all the Emigration."[3] Lavinia Porter cried to her husband that "if you do not drive me to a cleaner place to camp and sleep tonight I will take my blanket and go alone."[4]

Limited water supplies and scant privacy rendered even the necessities of life difficult. Women told of escorting each other *en masse* out behind the wagon train to stand in a circle facing outward, holding their skirts out to provide a bit of shelter for the one taking a turn.

women, whose numbers throughout the West were often not recorded in the national census. Of the eight hundred thousand women recorded living west of the Mississippi in 1900, approximately 4500 were Chinese, 370 were Japanese, 12,000 were black, and 6,000 were Indians.[1] In those numbers, the Chinese are undoubtedly under-represented, for few women were counted by the census; and Indian women were not registered until late in the 1800s, so their actual number will never be known.

First-hand material from these women is rare—they were often illiterate and seldom encouraged by their cultures to record their thoughts. This is a tragedy, for their insights would have helped all of us—not only humanitarians and historians—to understand what the experience of the women in the West really was. Without these stories, we are left with a curiously one-sided, Anglo-American perspective of the frontier, often gained from the multitudinous collections of Overland Trail journals.

There are literally hundreds of these accounts—some very moving, some as plodding as the oxen that drew the wagons. Those by men were usually filled with surveys, trail descriptions, botanical and geological observations, maps, weather reports, and reports on

Coalville, Utah, 1867.

...nditions contributed heavily to disease ...nd children suffered from dysentery, and ...to travel the necessary fifteen miles a day ...ects. A survivor of the Fourth Mormon ...s how they killed their cattle one by one ...or "those suffering from dysentery, the [beef] did more harm than good. This terrible disease increased rapidly amongst us during these three days and several died from exhaustion. . . ."[5] Although midwives often prescribed dried whortleberries or half a teaspoon of gunpowder for the malady, there seemed little else they could do.

If a woman survived dysentery, there were typhus, cholera, malaria, and childbed fever to contend with, to say nothing of the extreme depression known as melancholia. Little wonder that many popular campfire ballads lamented the early death of young women, and that even in the relatively "safe" territories of Dakota, Nebraska, Utah, and Washington the death rate of women between 1859 and 1860 was 22 percent higher than that of men, including violent deaths.[6] An 1865 study showed the mortality rates in Ohio and Illinois of women between twenty and fifty to be 50 percent higher than men's, while the death rates for men and women in the eastern states remained the same.[7]

Those women who managed to stay healthy could not neglect the sick and dying. For just as common law of the plains demanded hospitality to strangers and those in need, so it was expected that any woman still on her feet would serve as nurse or midwife to those who were not. Without access to pharmaceutical drugs, they dispensed such remedies as turpentine and sugar to prevent worms, or thickened egg whites in vinegar as a cough syrup. These homey combinations of folklore and common sense were in sharp contrast to the prevailing, and often violent, medical practices of the day, such as bleeding, ice water baths, and cathartic drugs.

Many women found themselves surprisingly skilled in their mastery of herbs, bone-setting, and delivering children, and this skill often gained them the title of midwife, a woman whose value to the pioneer community was inestimable. She assisted the sick, delivered infants, cared for new mothers, and buried the dead. Her stock of folk remedies was complete, from determining a baby's sex before birth to advising a young girl in her first use of menstrual rags. (Although it is seldom mentioned in personal accounts of the overland journey, we can only assume that a woman's monthly dependence upon rags which she pinned or tied into place like a diaper, then washed and rinsed as privately as conditions along the trail would allow, must have been the foremost of trials.)

Patty Sessions was a Mormon midwife who accompanied Brigham Young's wagon train from Nauvoo to Salt Lake City. So great was her usefulness and so highly was she esteemed, that when she fell ill along the trail and lapsed into a coma, Young ordered the brethren not to "let go of her body" for fifteen minutes after her death, in hopes that their prayers would revive her.[8] Sessions did recover, and lived to collect the one- and two-dollar debts owed to her by nearly everyone on the train. She was a woman of great personal ambition and, though she herself never went to medical school, she continually urged other women to do so.

The first woman to graduate from medical school was Miss Elizabeth Blackwell, in 1848. By 1879, there were 525 women graduates, but by the time women were graduating from medical school in appreciable numbers, it was too late to provide the kind of medical care the early pioneers needed. They had solved their problems through midwives and the questionable ministrations of such entrepreneurs as Mr. Stokes, who, after amputating her husband's leg, confided to Mary Jones that his career in medicine had been due to chance. Knowing a little about carpentry and a little about surgery but unable to decide what to call himself, he flipped a half dollar and said, "Heads, doctor; tails, carpenter." It was heads.[9]

The westward crossing was an extraordinary undertaking—one that took its toll on the minds and health of women in a variety of ways. For every young girl who saw the crossing as a lark and urged her husband ever forward, there were others who dreaded the endless prairies ahead and the prospect of a future life shut off from civilization. Mary Orrison recalls watching, as a child, the "tired and worn women and children on foot, going to the promised land. . . ."[10] Many became depressed and tried to turn back. There are accounts of women setting fire to their wagons, stealing horses and riding east, even threatening their own children, in an effort to call attention to their distress. Occasionally they drew criticism or rebuke from others on the trail, but in the case of Mrs. Baker, bound for California in 1850 in a wagon train from Iowa, there seemed to be little more to do than tolerate her peculiarities. This "extraordinary neat woman" managed to hold up the train continually. She objected once to crossing the river in a small boat, as it might damage her things. "It was a picnic for the boys to unload her wagon and put the things in a boat," recalled fellow passenger Rebecca Woodson. "Some would call her attention one way, while the others picked up a load and ran with it to the boat. When she looked to see after them, another lot would go. When they got her things on, they caught her and her little step-daughter and put them in the boat. She went screaming. . . ."[11] Mrs. Baker survived, and

Pregnant woman holding down a lot in Guthrie, Okla., ca. 1889.

continued to California, where she and her husband settled and founded the thriving city of Bakersfield.

Living on the frontier—alone or with family—required a special brand of courage. Women wrote repeatedly of the fear they felt when alone at night. They were fearful of Indians, fearful of animals, fearful of anything that rustled or stirred outside. Much of their fear—and that of the men, too—came from their inability to read their environment with any accuracy. They repeatedly misinterpreted Indian behavior, reacting in terror to the sudden appearance of any curious Indian, while casually breaking treaties that Indians held sacred.

Equally frightening were the swarms of vagrant men, either displaced by the Civil War or turned out of work in the mines and fields. Footloose soldiers, out-of-luck miners, ex-slavers, ruffians and outlaws roamed freely throughout the countryside, and women had no way of knowing if the customary "Halloo!" that rang out from the forest belonged to an honest man or not. Mary Orrison recounts the fear she knew as a child when one night two strangers tried to cross the creek and find her family's cabin. "Mother knew there were more than one, and that they were White people, for

Erecting a log cabin in Idaho.

they were talking and swearing about the location of the crossing. She hurried to the house with us, taking two short pitchforks. One she gave to my older brother, the other she kept for herself. She drew the latch string, barricaded the door, and told my brother Arthur if they came and broke the door, to stick the fork in the eyes of one, and she would attack the other."[12]

Fortunately, the men never found the crossing, but they broke into the house of a woman further down the creek and fired into the feather bed under which she and her children were hiding. It turned out they were two drunken men who only wanted a lantern, but like many violent acts on the frontier, this one left its stamp of fear. For some this fear became a continued state of panic leading to melancholia, an extreme depression so common that scholars today have tried to determine if it was due to a fatty diet high in salt pork, fried beef, eggs, milk, and butter, or if trace mercury found in wells dug in the mining areas might have triggered the erratic behavior of many.[13] But whatever its source, countless women like Mrs. Arthur Cowan were unable to withstand its influence. Mrs. Cowan lived, as she recounts, "forty miles from civilization, where nobody lives and dogs bark at strangers."

The wife of a sheep rancher in Woody Island, Montana, she felt her isolation keenly, particularly in the winter—"20 degrees below zero this morning, very cold, lonely weather. How glad I shall be when this cold winter is over." The list goes on:

"Cold day. . . . Sid went to look for poisoned coyotes. Came back nearly froze."
"Cold windy day 24 below zero. Fed the sheep. Very lonesome."
"Dark, dreary day. And the snow is flying. . . ."
"Blustering this morning. Fed the sheep and then took them out on the hills. . . . This is a long lonely winter."
"10 degrees below zero this morning. Have been very down hearted today and had a very bad headache. . . ."
"My heart is very lonely and sad to have no one to sympathize with me. I must bear all my troubles alone."
"Men are working at lambing. Oh I feel so lonely, so sad and discontented."
"The same old routine over again. Running after sheep again all day. This hardly seems like living. . . ."[14]

Her single cheerful entry for the year took place after dining in town with friends, a social occasion seldom enjoyed because of the forty-mile trek to town.

Not all pioneer women were unhappy with their lives, however. To portray only the fatigue, trauma, and failed expectations of some would be to cast an unfair shadow on those whose journals overflow with life and high spirits. In fact, many of these women shared a unique camaraderie within the larger wagon trains. They sewed and gossiped together, sharing recipes, food, and dress patterns around the open fire. Later, when homesteading land that was often miles from the nearest neighbor, they continued to make eager plans to get together. Quilting bees, barn raisings, even communal butcherings of livestock rose spontaneously from the neighborly desire to help out and see one another. Dances, too, were a reflection of this shared excitement, and were a favorite pastime of nearly all women. At the first hint of revelry, out came the hot pokers and rags for hair curling. Mail-order patent shoes appeared

Interior view of a dance in Poker Flat, Sierra Co., Calif.

married couple occupied a wagon for sleeping apartments. The first notice they had of any disturbance was when . . . most of the men and women in the company took hold of the wagon, the men at the tongue pulling, the women at the back pushing, and ran the wagon a half mile out on the prairie. Then the fun began. Such a banging of cans, shooting of cans, shooting of guns and every noise conceivable. . . . The disturbance was kept up till midnight, when the crowd dispersed, leaving the happy couple out on the prairie to rest undisturbed till morning, when they came walking into camp amid cheers and congratulations."[15]

But even without dances and weddings, some women managed to find occasions for joy in their lives, no matter how barren the material circumstances. Such a woman was Frances Clack, of Lytle Creek, Texas. "She loved the outdoors," wrote her daughter Tommie, "and would tell us about trees, the flowers, the rocks, the birds and the animals that lived up and down the creek. . . . At night she would take her astronomy book out into the moonlight and teach us to recognize Ursa Minor and Ursa Major, and how to locate the North Star."[16]

as if by magic, and chapped, wind-burned skin was softened with buttermilk and cornstarch. A thrifty woman usually had a long-hidden bit of ribbon on hand to wrap around her waist, and might bundle up a few roses in a sachet the night before, to scent her clothing. Wrinkle-smoothers and hair tonics were applied liberally—these were concocted from recipes as diverse as tannic acid and elderflower water, or glycerine, alcohol, and rainwater.

In Nebraska, dances broke forth in the soddies and machine sheds, with dozens of kerosene lanterns casting light into the dark shadows and throwing crazy dancing patterns across the dirt floor. The caller would shout out for a quadrille, and sets of four couples would swing and bend to the fiddler's lively "Ole Zip Coon" and "Leather Breeches." Or they would eagerly wait for the fiddle to "pop" on "Pop Goes the Weasel," as the women arched hands and the men ducked under.

Weddings were also grand affairs, with chivarees held afterwards that many a newlywed remembered for years to come. Rebecca Woodson recalled one such occasion on their train en route to California: "Such a Chivaree as they got that night. . . . [The] newly

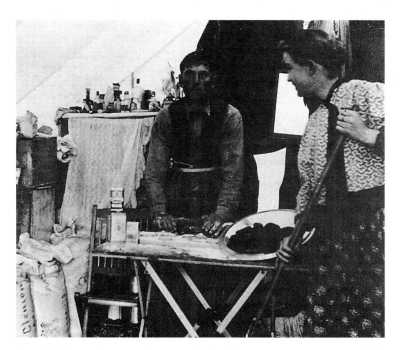

Couple doing chores in tent in Alaska, late 1890's.

This was no defeated woman, overburdened by care and imprisoned by fate. Nor was her sister Mollie, who lived nearby with her husband John. In 1879, as the hot west Texas sun beat on the dry clay hills, she would gather her children around an old plank on which she had painted a keyboard. As each child hit a painted key, Mollie would sing out the corresponding note. They practiced daily until Mollie was able to buy an organ, and then it was her heart's delight to have her children sit down to a real instrument and play.

In the West women experienced an autonomy never before dreamed of, and with this new freedom came the necessity to solve their problems in any way they could. Making do became an art shared by both sexes, and "women's work" soon came to mean whatever had to be done, whether it was herding cattle, checking trap lines, or seeding the rows with corn. Sarah Olds was a Nevada homesteader who, when her son became ill, found it her job to check the trap lines. "On my first trip around the trapline I caught a bobcat," she remembered painfully. "I hadn't expected to catch anything, and now I was faced with the task of killing what I had caught. . . . For a while I stood there and bawled good and loud. . . ."[17] She finally stunned the animal with a tap behind the ear, followed by a death blow to the heart. She also devised her own method of rooting out fleas and lice from hair and clothing. "We all took baths with plenty of sheep dip in the water. . . . I had no disinfectant . . . so I boiled all our clothing in sheep dip and kerosene."[18]

For some, the new egalitarianism brought surprises. Kate Nye Starr recalled interrupting a showdown between her husband and an angry trail hand named Charlie. Charlie had jammed his pistol and Bowie knife into his belt, and, as Kate approached, she noticed that her husband stepped away, "so [Charlie] would have to meet me first."[19]

For others, it brought a welcome opportunity to try new and better-paying occupations. Luzena Wilson started the second hotel in Nevada City by laying two planks together in a tent and setting out a tureen of soup. "From the first day I was well patronized," she wrote, "and I shortly after took my husband into partnership."[20] She lived in the boom-or-bust frenzy of the Mother Lode, where men would not only pay a high price for bread made by a woman, but would also shower her with their unwelcome attentions. Though married women still commanded a Victorian respect from "respectable" men, there were occasional lapses, as when the wife of a Grass Valley, California, minister had to fight off the advances of a drunken miner with a hot poker—he had mistaken her for a prostitute named Fanny.

The women who actively sought these advances, however, were many, for prostitution existed as an art, a social service, and a thriving industry in nearly every major city of the West. It contributed substantially to local revenues, as madams in many cities were obliged to share a portion of each night's take with the local police. It began in earnest in the West during the Gold Rush, when claim-happy prospectors poured into California with high hopes of getting rich. These men had nothing more than the memory of feminine companionship to warm them at night, and were soon joined by the fancy ladies who came by wagon and muleback, by overland coach in the 1880s, and by ship from Europe and South America. In 1860, there were 2,379 men and only 147 women in the Comstock Lode, and, though, statistics are lacking, no doubt many of these women were prostitutes. They set up shop in canvas tents or in saloon backrooms, and before long, according to Mimi Goldman's account, the mining camps rang with laughter and drunken revelry.

A drinking "bee" at White Chapel, Dawson, Alaska.

Prostitute in her bedroom in Alaska, titled by the photographer "One of Dawson's favorites."

By 1870, the Comstock population had grown to twenty thousand, and more and more respectable women had arrived to join their husbands. They were shocked by the decadence they found and banded together to protest the harlots. Their criticism was in no way shared by the miners, who were dazzled by the exotic plumed costumes and elaborate coiffures of the whores. With them they found elegance, companionship, sympathy, and sex—and they often treated even the lowliest saloon girls with affection and respect.

Prostitution was the single largest occupation for women in the Comstock, and it also flourished in the other large cities of the West. At a time when laundry or domestic pay was less than $25 per month, many women turned in desperation to prostitution as a way to pay the bills. Even in Victorian times there were ways to attempt to insure that no children resulted from the occupation. *The Physician and Sexuality in Victorian America* lists numerous contraceptives: condoms like the "French secret," vaginal "tents" often made of eelskin, and vaginal douches made with alum, pearlash, sulphate of zinc, or infusions of white oak bark, red rose leaves, nut galls, or plain water.

There were several levels of prostitution available in the larger cities. First and most profitable were the "class" houses run by businesslike madams. A madam paid her help a regular salary, advised the girls on technique, dress, and deportment, and, in return, expected top performance. Here the girls might encounter only a few men a night, but each was a big spender.

As youth faded, a woman was turned out on the streets to re-establish herself—at best, in a second-class house. Here her expections were lower than before. She worked for a percentage of the profits and turned as many tricks a night as she was able.

The other alternatives were even more degrading: the boarding houses and "cribs." Streetwalkers made their arrangements along the piers and gutters, then led customers back to a rented room in a boarding house. It is an interesting aspect of the times that despite the strictest Victorian protocol throughout society, boarding houses were completely lax about male visitors in rooms. Perhaps, once it was clear that a woman did not belong to a father, husband, or other male relative, she was automatically considered promiscuous, and society lost interest in her activities.

The nadir of a prostitute's career was the "crib," a tiny windowless rented room with a cot and a chair and a door facing the street where she hawked her trade to every passerby for fifty cents to a dollar. This was the fate that all whores dreaded—to end up in a foul room with oilcloth draped across the foot of the bed for customers so hasty they never even shed their boots. Though free of a pimp or a madam, this life was the worst imaginable, and it was here that the old, the sick, and the most hopeless women finished out their days.

The actual number of prostitutes in the West has not been established. In some areas their occupation was listed in the census, as can be noted on the page from the 1870 census of Shoshone County, Idaho. By 1880 H. L. Bancroft in the *History of California* noted that one third of the population in the West was female, but he made no guess as to the number of prostitutes among them. The San Francisco Municipal Report for the years 1884–1885 lists a total population of 30,360 Chinese in Chinatown's twelve square blocks; while the number of women in this figure must have been comparatively slight, it is safe to assume that most were either concubines or whores.

Victorian America was a country bound by intense sexual

Prostitutes in front of cribs in "Lousetown," in the Klondike.

SCHEDULE 1.—Inhabitants in _Hunt Precinct, Mining _____, in the County of _Shoshone_____, State of _Idaho_____, enumerated by me on the ___ day of _14th August_, 1870.

Post Office: _Pierce City_

John Clark, Ass't Marshal.

Page 14, from the Shoshone Co., census of 1870.

repression and fueled by the energy of westward expansion. Both factors encouraged prostitution. According to the tenets of Victorian feminity, women were expected to emphasize their unique differences from men. If men were bold and passionate, women were cold and retiring. They affected pale complexions and wasp waists, as if to emphasize their delicacy. It was not considered proper to discuss intercourse before marriage; refined women commonly thought that contraceptive devices were obscene and that total passivity during sex would prevent conception. Many women believed that celibacy was necessary during nursing, and nursing commonly continued for as long as two years.

Given these obstacles to normal passion, many men viewed prostitutes as a necessity. Besides, prostitutes had enlivened the initial years of the West in ways no respectable woman would have dreamed of. They were an established part of western society, and it was not until 1880 that even the mildest legislation was passed against them. Solicitation became a misdemeanor and minors were barred from saloons and cribs. Prostitution continued unchecked throughout the West until the early twentieth century. After 1905, moral reforms caused the closing of the truly ostentatious parlor houses, and the trade essentially went underground.

From a society in the early 1800s that had been 90 percent agricultural, women emerged by the end of the century to greet the Industrial Revolution with great enthusiasm. For the first time, they had a wide choice of job opportunities, and by 1890, women worked in 216 of the 300 occupations listed by the Federal Office of Opportunity. In some states women could serve on juries, attend college, and receive advanced degrees. Some studied medicine or law, some worked in industry, while still others—often women widowed by the Civil War—found themselves with money to invest. Antiquated laws which gave the husband custody of the wife's person and property were amended; divorces were increasing and homestead enactments made land available to single women for the first time in history.

Homesteading, in fact, proved particularly attractive to young women. When Harriet Strong announced in a Suffragette speech that "it takes brains, not brawn, to make farms pay. We need more women farmers!" she was addressing women who had seen Wyoming pass the first suffrage laws in 1869. Wyoming was followed by Utah in 1870, and by 1914 every state west of the Rockies, had followed suit. By 1910, according to Joan Swallow's *The Women*, 10 percent of all homesteaders were women, and

Woman homesteader receiving the deed to her land.

many states, eager for settlement and stability, encouraged their presence.

It would be impossible in this setting to discuss the complete diversity of women's experiences in the West. The careers, attitudes, hopes, and aspirations were as varied as the women themselves. These were the ordinary people of history, the women who ultimately bore the ravages of their new experience and emerged in whatever way their personal endurance allowed. They beg recognition on the merits of their own lives, not the lives assigned to them by academic historians or curious European travelers. Life on the frontier was not any one way. It was episodic, with bravery, foolishness, satisfaction, and sorrow intertwined throughout. History can make no single judgment of a woman's performance in the West, any more than it can limit the western experience to the white pioneers. For the nineteenth-century woman of the West was more than an overlander. She was Indian or black, Protestant or Jew, Chinese or Catholic. She was homesteader, housewife, mother of many children, sometimes involved in the Suffrage movement, sometimes caught in the grip of Victorian conservatism. She was the teacher, waitress, nurse, dancer, seamstress, and cook. She was the missionary and the maid, the minor actress, the well-dressed city woman who lived in small hotels and enjoyed the theater, restaurants, balls, and bazaars. She was the laundress, the typesetter, the postal clerk, the prostitute. Most importantly, she was part of a time in which women were beginning to discover, little by little, the unexplored realms of their own talents—finding out what they could contribute to the world.

Actresses en route to the Klondike, fording the Dyea River.

Mrs. M.E. Tyler, photographer, in Ashland Oregon, ca. 1892.

"Gurry's Business Block," Deering, Alaska, 1903

Wash day for Mrs. Delaney & son. Pinto Creek Mine, Ariz., 1902.

Tent & restaurant, home & business of Mr. & Mrs. Blankenship, 1903.

Daily Reporter Staff in front of its office, Corinne, Utah, 1869.

Labor Day parade in San Diego, Calif., 1910.

Unidentified family, Humboldt Co., Calif., ca. 1895.

Nez Perce women, members of the David Williams family, Colville Reservation, Washington.

Minority Women

The hardships, customs, and expectations of the white immigrants to the West in the 1800s have been well documented. The women's individual stories were not well known, but they lived, in many cases, strong and dramatic lives, raised their children with courage and direction, and in general did the best they could with what was at hand. But in tracing the path of women throughout the West, it would be impossible to ignore the lives of the Indian women who first laid claim to the spirit, if not the actual acreage, of the West. These were the women who lived in unrecorded numbers throughout the grassy plains, the dry Southwestern canyons, and the verdant forests of the Pacific Slope, roaming freely, gathering what they needed for the oncoming season, living simply upon the land. In light of what eventually happened to this freedom, it is ironic to note that a Shoshone woman, Sacajawea, was instrumental in bringing about the rapid alteration of their way of life. Without her to graciously escort them, Lewis and Clark would probably not have been successful in opening up the Northwest Territory for exploration, and perhaps Great Britain would have clung more tightly to the rich territories of Montana, Oregon, Idaho, and Washington.

As the original inhabitants of the land, the Indians were initially treated with great diplomacy by the federal government. Then, as greater numbers of land-hungry settlers began to push through Indian territory, the diplomatic courtesies were dropped. Indians were viewed as dangerous savages, their lack of Christianity was noted, and it was with less and less hesitation that settlers broke treaties and roughly pushed aside all rights and claims of the western tribes. Tribes that had once called out joyfully, "Our White Brothers have come!"[21] had, by 1850, thrust their spears into herbal poisons and laid siege to whatever straggling wagons they could find.

In 1850, only seventy-six Indians had been killed along the Emigrant Trail, but by the end of 1860, the number had risen to 426. In California, it became an acceptable practice for volunteer military companies or regular Army units to raid and plunder Indian villages—tribes were even attacked as they lived peacefully on their reservations. Bounty hunters were well paid for Indian scalps, and it was clear that the intolerant, volatile, and land-hungry majority of settlers were determined to push the Indians, the so-called "Tartars of the Plains," slowly and systematically from the face of the continent.

Communications between the two groups was limited: of the more than five hundred main tribes, there were seven thousand sub-groups in California alone, and each spoke a separate dialect. There were altercations between the tribes themselves, and the continued encroachment of the settlers multiplied the opportunities for disagreement. When U.S. Army officers gave out land or supplies, the Indians felt cheated; when Indians made promises, the settlers failed to believe them. It was a situation doomed to violence by the ever-increasing need of the immigrants for land, and by the awakening anxiety of the Indians, who were being driven further and further from their traditional lands.

Expansion, not interaction, was the mode of the times, and white expansionists simply did not understand the Indian any more than the Indians could fathom a race whose women dressed in mysterious layers of cotton hose, muslin aprons, calico dresses, petticoats, shawls, and bonnets. Settlers were so busy acquiring land that they failed completely to understand the mind of the Indian, fixing instead upon its vast differences from their own, buoying up incipient racism by seeing Indians only as idlers whose women acted as slaves. It was common for the Overlanders to dwell only on the terrible aspects of those differences. Mary Stuart

Bailey felt she could "almost fly away"[22] from fear of the Indians, while Margaret Hecox noted that they were "just Indians" and doubted if the "savage instinct can ever be eradicated from the wild man's breast."[23] There were frequent accounts of Indians begging along the Emigrant Trail, or tales of their sudden appearance at a homestead where they asked for food or were content just to sit and watch the members of a white family living and working amid the strange paraphernalia of their lives.

Pioneer accounts of Indian life persistently mention the slave-like position of women, but they are not entirely accurate. While some tribes did hold women in very low esteem, other tribes were matrilineal, tracing their ancestry through the mother and bestowing great importance upon women. The women in these tribes were often far more independent than the pioneer women who lived alongside them. White women were still essentially chattels of their husbands, unable to vote, to own their own property or to sign a contract unassisted, while some Indian women went into marriage fully endowed with their own property, which remained their own and could never be touched by male relatives. Very often women held positions of authority and respect within the tribe, and were consulted on all decisions. They shared the responsibility for the tribe's well-being, building by hand the earth lodges and tipis, planting crops, and tanning hides. They raised children and trained them in knowledge and discipline, prepared and stored food, wove baskets and fashioned implements. Their fertility was thought to be analogous to the earth's bounty, and women were respected for their mysterious ability to reproduce.

The Indian women's knowledge of nature's secrets was unsurpassed, and had there been more communication between the two races, it would have greatly benefitted the homesteaders, who often lived near starvation during the long winter months. Indian women knew where to find the wild artichoke, how to survive on strips of bark, how to stalk a gopher's hole to retrieve beans or a fallen nut, how to cure berries and jerky, and how to fashion jerky with tallow into pemmican. They knew how to eat grass and clover for sugar and starch, and raw vegetables in such amounts as to prevent the many diseases caused by poor nutrition which so constantly plagued the settlers. "Eat a raw turnip? We would not have dared!"[24] wrote Tommie Clack of Lytle Creek, Texas, and in her distrust of raw food she spoke for most white women.

Buried amid the tales of fear and misunderstanding between Indians and settlers, there are also tales of compassion—stories that emphasize the basic humanity many Indians felt even toward the white invaders who were taking their land. Lucinda Evans, a settler in Southern Oregon, recalls a friendly Snake Indian warning her father to take his family and flee, as "the Indians are coming here to kill you."[25] In 1852, the Reverend John McGhee was forewarned of the Rogue River War by Chief Sam: "You are a Bible man. I don't want you to be killed. Go away for a little while."[26]

Often these warnings came to favorite settlers, but just as often, a compassionate Indian would spread the alarm throughout an entire community, helping the settlers to escape before a wholesale attack. In return, many settlers tried to protect Indians against acts of bullying or aggression. Mrs. Campbell of Salina, Kansas, recounted how she once hid two Indian boys inside her store while drunken soldiers stood outside, demanding their release. Mrs. Campbell, and many women like her, earned the title of "White Sister," and greatly impressed the Indians with their efforts at justice.[27]

Cheyenne winter camp with cane windbreak around tipis, ca. 1890.

Indians often lent assistance to immigrants. In spite of well-publicized massacres and the near-paranoid fear settlers had of attacks, by 1860 there had been, according to John Unruh, only 362 deaths of whites by Indian attack recorded, while over 250,000 emigrants had traveled westward. Many Overlanders recount how Indians piloted them across treacherous crossings, or forded the rivers in advance of the main party, seeking the best path for them to cross. Indian assistance was invaluable in such dangerous areas as the Humboldt Sink, where a single wrong turn could result in a party's by-passing the last grass and water before the desert. The Truckee River, in fact, is named for Sarah Winnemucca's grandfather, Chief Truckee, who provided the Stevens-Murphy party of 1844 with explicit directions for maneuvering through the Humboldt Sink. Ironically, there are many accounts of Indians who, as they offered friendship and assistance, were instead forcibly detained and made to serve as guides through unfamiliar territory. This occurred in the Jayhawker Party of 1849, and seemed to be a common occurrence among the larger, better-organized wagon trains.

The currents of misunderstanding between the two races were deep and were never altogether successfully bridged. As the years went by and more lands were stolen, feelings of hatred and bitterness increased, traditional cultural ties were loosened, and it is little wonder that "the people" of the plains and mesas began to view their future with dread. For many Indians, assimilation was equal to the betrayal of their tribe, yet continuing in their traditional way of life was impossible. They were caught in an immobilizing dilemma which continues to this day.

Assimilation of the black Americans who came west was also a difficult matter. Their original African culture largely obliterated by slavery, their presence as free men and women continually resented, they found that acceptance by the white community was an unrealistic expectation. The West alone seemed to offer opportunity, so, determined to establish themselves outside the confines of slavery, many blacks began to emigrate west in the 1840s, while even greater numbers came after the Civil War.

Those Northern blacks who came west just before the Civil War had one thing in common: they came by choice. Often young, single, and highly motivated, they were usually prepared to work hard to establish themselves in their new land. Delilah Beasley tells many tales of their success: ". . . the colored people . . . possess property to the amount of $3,000,000 in mining claims, water

The Albert Robinson's restaurant in Julian. In 1887 they built a hotel; it became the oldest continually operated hotel in So. Calif.

rights, ditch stock and some real estate."[28] They also owned farms, ranches, and businesses in Marysville, Grass Valley, Petaluma, and Stockton, California.

Yet the path to financial security was not an easy one, and, despite Beasley's optimistic biographies, was not available to all. White tolerance of the black settlers declined as the number of emigrants increased. As time passed, more and more black women were drawn to the frontier and its opportunities. They came alone or they came to join their husbands, and their coming created economic tension within the levels of occupations they were allowed to pursue. Suddenly there were too many laundresses for the limited jobs available, and since the Chinese worked for less pay, black women often found themselves passed over as domestics. In the mid-1860s, jobs all over the United States were scarce, and black women without established skills or regular incomes found it increasingly difficult to live.

The S.H. Fairfield residence in Topeka, Kansas.

Patience Cooper, sister of noted Abolitionist Jeremiah Sanderson, wrote to her brother describing her stay in debtors' prison: "I am writing and in jail, feeling very bad indeed and awaiting my trial in June. I was taken up on suspicion and it never would have been, if it was not that I owed a small debt. . . . Now I want you to try to send me some money, if it is but ten or twenty dollars. . . . See Mr. E. Wilson Freeman. . . . Tell him to send me some money . . . and to come as quick as he can. Don't neglect me, do all you can for me. . . . My family is all very poor, but together in prison."[29] Her plight illustrated the painful position held by blacks after the Civil War. On the one hand, they were legally free, but on the other, they were not allowed to vote and could not defend themselves in court. This left them vulnerable to injustice, and forced them into a system of patronage whereby a person of wealth or influence was their only legal protection.

Gardener Johnson also found herself in this position. Her owner offered to free her before he and his family moved west, but she declined. "I was afraid to accept my liberty, much as I would have liked to stay [behind]. The word of a Negro was of no value in court. Any bad white man could claim that I had been stolen from him and could swear me into jail. He could buy my services for the time I was sentenced for, and by the time I had served my time for him he could bring up some other false charge and buy my services again, and do whatever he wanted to me, for Negroes were the same as cows or horses and were not supposed to have morals or souls. I was afraid to accept my liberty, so I came to Oregon with my owners."[30]

In 1830, there were thirteen thousand freed slaves in the Territories; by 1870, the number was 44,903. Many were drawn to California with its opportunity-rich gold mines and boom towns. But if black women fared better in California, it was only because local society was still in a state of flux during those years before Reconstruction. After Reconstruction, as displaced Southerners began to move west, blacks—and particularly black women—felt the impact of their bitter prejudice. Neither wealth nor position assured blacks success. Catherine Sanderson, Jeremiah Sanderson's wife, spent her lifetime trying to augment the slender earnings of her well-known husband by taking in wash or by working as a domestic. Sanderson was often away from home, first leaving the family in the East for seven years while he tried his luck in the gold fields, then establishing them in San Francisco while he worked as director of a public school in Sacramento. His talents were well recognized, even by the white community. Yet, because he was black, his earnings each month were less than those of his white employees. Catherine tried to shield him from the full scope of their poverty, but mention of it often crept into her letters: "I have a very large wash this week," she wrote, "about forty-six shirts, and I don't know what I should have done if it had not been for Mrs. Gardner who helped me to iron yesterday and today. . . ."[31]

Unidentified black nursemaid with child.

Here was the usual fate of struggling black women in the West. It was the rare woman who escaped the deadly rounds of poverty and joblessness to establish herself as a middle-class citizen, but a few black women did. In 1872, Charlotte Hay became the first black woman lawyer in the United States when she graduated from Howard University Law School. Biddy Mason also found success, but without the benefit of an education. She was one of the earliest settlers in California, arriving in Los Angeles in 1851 after a grueling journey from Georgia by ox cart. She obtained her freedom papers through the county court and secured work as a confinement nurse for $2.50 per week. With this pay, she managed to save enough money to buy two city lots. These first lots were followed by two more, until she had amassed a fortune in real estate. Because of her charitable nature, Biddy Mason turned her South Spring Street house into a refuge for stranded and needy travelers.

Like Biddy Mason, Aunt Clara Brown was penniless when she arrived in Colorado, but she was determined to make her fortune. She opened a laundry in Central City, charging fifty cents a shirt. By 1866, she had amassed almost ten thousand dollars. She used nearly all of this to form her own wagon train company to transport blacks from the post-Civil War South to safety in the West. Her wagon trains were manned entirely by freed slaves.

Stories about Mammy (Mary Ellen) Pleasant also abound. She possessed a fortune at a time when most black women made less than fifteen dollars a month. Mammy Pleasant was a Georgia slave girl whose quick intelligence and lively tongue had caught her owner's attention. He sent her to Boston to be educated, but instead of returning to the plantation, she met and married a wealthy black Bostonian. After his death, Mammy Pleasant emigrated to San Francisco with fifty thousand dollars in capital and an idea of opening a boarding house.

Homestead of black family, Guthrie, Oklahoma Territory, ca. 1889.

Protected by her wealth and driven by her rambunctious nature, she authored one of the first sparks of black rebellion in San Francisco. The incident occurred as she and two friends decided to take a streetcar home after shopping. Because of their dark skin, Mammy Pleasant and one friend were turned away while the other light-skinned woman was allowed to ride. Mammy Pleasant strode off to find an attorney and returned to file suit against the streetcar company. She managed to collect minimal damages in this, one of the first discrimination cases ever brought by a woman.

This event points out the basic difference in attitude that was held toward men and women of "color" and those who were "black." It was the lightest, wealthiest, and most cautious of blacks who managed to avoid discrimination by embracing white standards of dress, elocution, and deportment. Black women founded charities and clubs similar to those of the white women of society. Members worked at embroidery, pronunciation, and letter writing, and planned bazaars and church functions to raise money for their many causes. One women's club even advertised itself as promoting "better English, good housekeeping, and the social graces, with membership open to ladies with light skin."[32] Light-skinned families often found it advantageous to cross over the color line. They sometimes claimed foreign parentage, adopted a West Indian accent, and abandoned forever their black heritage.

Those who did not cross over carried out their lives in the shadow of the white community, but found in the West greater opportunity than they would have in the South or in the East—and in many cases—greater prosperity. But life was always difficult, whether the blacks tilled land, mended shoes, or tended children. Like the women of other backgrounds who came West, they were challenged by the times and did what they could to survive in spite of the twin burdens of prejudice and discrimination that at times seemed overwhelming.

Jewish women faced discrimination to a lesser degree, but still had to contend with the difficulty of adjusting to life on the frontier, as well as to live in America itself. They came to this country to avoid the racism and economic hardships of Europe and, in particular, the anti-Semitism that had slowly been spreading throughout the newly unified nation of Germany. Some were unprepared for the relative freedom they found, discovering that they could travel, speak, work, and select their mates with unprecedented ease.

In 1850, a poll of Los Angeles residents identified eight Jews, immigrants from Poland and Germany. In 1851, two hundred Jews were living in Sacramento; ten years later there were five hundred. By 1860, there were ten thousand Jews in the West, half of whom lived in San Francisco.[33] As the decade progressed and more Jewish immigrants settled along the West Coast, the roots of a Jewish merchant class were quickly established as their businesses burgeoned into affluence and respectability. John Newmark Levi recalled a childhood of comfort in Los Angeles, where he was provided with piano and violin lessons, tutors, a nurse-governess, and an upstairs maid. On temporary call were a trained nurse, a seamstress, a laundress who came three days a week, and a woman who washed the children's hair. He recollected that the combined salaries of all these workers probably came to a hundred dollars a month.[34]

During the early years of the westward movement, Jewish women were in short supply. Orthodox men who wanted brides had to find them through "dowry marriages," a traditional European practice that spanned the two continents. Prospectors and merchants would send for wives they knew only by recommendation, and "would not begrudge either her fare to America or the costly price of a new outfit."[35] These alliances were evidently popular, for *The American Israelite* stated that "the best husbands and providers are those of the Semetic race . . . not one per cent of our Jewish girls will ally themselves to a Christian who, generally speaking, is improvident and will not go out and peddle, and . . . climb the steep mountains in Indian territories in order to keep his wife and children comfortably." Girls were still hopelessly formal with their suitors, and no well-bred young woman would dream of taking up with a young man who was not known to her family, or to whom she had not been properly introduced.

Regardless of whom she married or how it was arranged, once settled into matrimony, the Jewish wife quickly assumed a prominent role in household organization. If her new home contained such luxuries as a horsehair sofa, black walnut marble-topped table, étagère with closet, or rosewood cabinet piano and lace curtains, it was implicit in her ownership that she would not only care for them wisely, but arrange for the proper social functions whereby they would be enjoyed and shared. She was also active in charities, women's clubs, and sometimes in areas of her husband's business.

If she were called upon to work, she often did so with a skill and daring that netted immediate results for the family. Women such as Rebecca Mayer, who started a number of businesses, often saved the family from dire financial straits.[36]

Of the lives of rural Jewish women we know very little, in part because no letters, diaries, or journals that describe them have been deposited in archives and partly because few Jewish families lived outside the major urban centers. The Western States Jewish Historical Quarterly reports that by 1903, there were only one thousand Jewish farmers west of the Alleghenys and east of the Rockies. One of the reasons that so few Jewish families found themselves on the Great Plains may have been their need to be part of a close religious community.

The manuscripts left to us are by urban women, comfortably middle-class, or well-to-do matrons who noted their daily schedules with great regularity. Their world was one of maintaining the varied and often subtle relationships that were essential to the running of a household, such as dealing with German and Irish kitchen maids, for example, who had little respect for Kosher dietary rules and would knock butter knives against meat platters at will. Or there was a steady stream of vendors who tramped back and forth beneath the backstairs, turning the kitchen into a marketplace. Even relaxation brought its own brand of protocol. If "yacking and card playing"[37] constituted the typical middle-class get-together, as described by John Newmark Levi in his reminiscences, women must have been careful not to love the gaming aspects of card playing too well. *The American Israelite* sharply criticized women's gambling, where "young girls, scarce out of their teens [would] poker away . . . at the same card table with their mothers."[38]

But whether urban or rural, Orthodox or not, Jewish families had a deep concern for family, decorum, and refinement. They clung to a tradition of etiquette that distinguished their homes. Nothing was spared in the homes of the well-to-do, no matter the size of the city they inhabited. "Everyone had servants," wrote Claire Hofer Hewes of her girlhood home in Carson City, Nevada. "We always had from two to three, never less . . . they went right along with the family. . . . It was always a great ceremony for dinner. We must dress and bathe. Everything was served in much decorum. Of course, the meals always had [French] menus. . . . Beautiful candelabra were on the table, and everything was passed by the servants and done the correct way, even to finger bowls. Wine was served. . . . You wouldn't believe it with the little homes there in Carson."[39]

Rebecca Brodek Harris, who came to San Francisco by way of Panama before 1854, with her daughter, granddaughter and great granddaughter.

Yet, whether they lived amid opulence or the more simple comforts, Jewish women still had the matter of their European heritage to contend with. To be a Polish Jew was quite different—in the eyes of the Jewish community—than to be from France or Bavaria. Harriet Levy wrote that "the birthplace of parents determined the social rank . . . birth in the kingdom of Bavaria provided entrance to the favored group, as a circle in Poland denied it."[40] Polish mothers harbored every hope of their daughters crossing over and marrying someone from Bavaria, yet when this did occur, it only served to alienate the mothers of the yet-unmarried daughters, for it meant one less chance at social advancement.

Outside their own community, Jewish women met with varying degrees of social acceptance, depending often on the financial success of their husbands. In some areas they were referred to with respect as "Israelites" or "Hebrews," while in others the term "Jew" was synonymous with acquisitiveness and even dishonesty. In the isolated areas of the West, however, there were many opportunities to put aside religious differences and to respond to each other as human beings would anywhere. The reaction of Flora Speigelberg was neither unusual nor atypical when she wrote: "I always placed my home at the disposal of my Mexican friends to erect their shrine. In fact, I loaned them draperies and cushions for the priests to kneel upon."[41]

By contrast, Chinese women found their lives far removed from those of most women in the West. From the moment a Chinese bride rode forth on a red sedan chair through the alleyways of the local Chinatown, her activities became circumscribed in ways more narrow than the tiny streets she maneuvered. From a girlhood nurtured by a close relationship with both parents, she found herself henceforth totally subjugated to her new husband. If he were a man of means, she would compete with his concubine or his other wives; if he needed money, she would bring from $300 to $2000 on the slave market, regardless of her legitimate position as wife. If he chose to keep her, then her days could be spent cloistered in a dimly lit back room, forbidden to mingle with the commoners on the street or even to leave her dwelling. Most women were expected to contribute to the finances of the household, and often worked from twelve to sixteen hours a day amid piles of shirts to be buttonholed or dresses to be hemmed.

The Lencher family, Golden Gate Park, after the 1906 earthquake.

Chinese woman cooking in San Francisco, 1900-1910.

A slave girl in holiday attire in San Francisco, before 1910.

In 1860, there were only 1784 registered Chinese women in the United States, while there were 33,149 Chinese men. By 1890, the number of Chinese men had jumped to 103,620, while the number of women had increased only to 4522.[42] Most of these women were not respectably married matrons; rather, they were the slave girls or prostitutes who had been sold or stolen by dealers in China, shipped to the port cities of San Francisco or Portland, and then consigned to a life of prostitution in the Chinese ghettos. Here the women would live out their lives as virtual prisoners of their Tong masters, jealously guarded as merchandise, used by dozens of men a night for less than fifty cents apiece. Parlor women in their joss-scented rooms fared a little better and had fewer customers to contend with, as well as more luxurious clothing. Neither group, apparently, wrote letters (or letters extant within the U.S.) or confided to journals, for no first-hand source describing this life has been found.

We do know something of their history, though, through the records of the Christian missionary women who worked among them and through newspaper reports, such as this article in the August 22, 1868 edition of a San Francisco paper, *The Monitor*: "The Pacific Mail steamer *Colorado* had brought a large addition to the Chinese population this week, and we learn by dispatches from Portland that an additional batch of coolies destined, according to Chinese customs, to slavery, formed a portion of the *Colorado*'s passengers, but the vigilance of the police who took charge of them immediately upon the arrival of the vessel and removed them to St. Mary's Hospital may succeed in spoiling the plans of their supposed masters."

By 1875, the slave system was well established on the West Coast. Girls were brought from China as babies after being sold by their parents. They were sometimes raised by the merchants' wives or concubines, but were later sold by the merchants when the men encountered financial difficulties. One such case, obtained from the Presbyterian Women's Board Report, was that of Ah Yung. She was married in China to a wealthy California merchant who obtained her parents' consent to the marriage even though they knew nothing of his background. The couple returned to America in 1902 and lived happily for some months until the husband informed Ah Yung of a business trip that would take him abroad. Would she mind being looked after by a friend? Ah Yung suspected no evil, having been kindly treated thus far.

The friend came to their room, was introduced to the young wife and produced a paper for her to sign, supposedly an agreement to cover room and board. Still trusting, she dipped her finger in the ink and set her seal to her own bill of sale. That evening, as she was conducted to her new residence, a dim sense of the awful truth dawned on her as she was surrounded by solicitous "inmates" of the house, who had come to meet the new arrival.

Donaldina Cameron with girls rescued by the First Presbyterian Mission in San Francisco.

The brothels of the Barbary Coast were not concerned about a woman's marital status or whether she was in this country legally. The brothels flourished unchecked throughout the 1850s and 1860s—a condition that the missionary women were determined to change. Between 1875 and 1916, Maggie Culbertson and later Donaldina Cameron and the many volunteer women of the Presbyterian Women's Home Society rescued Chinese and Japanese slave girls from the vice dens of San Francisco, San Jose, Isleton, and Walnut Grove, California. They did so at a time when anti-Chinese sentiment ran high in the cities; quite often the work of these women was opposed by petty officials and local politicians.

The rescues themselves were planned well in advance. Often the Chinese guards were so nonplussed by the sight of American matrons swarming into their midst that they turned and fled, giving up their chattels to the ministrations of the Presbyterian ladies. If they did rave and threaten or put up a struggle, it was only briefly, for both sides knew that American women were safe in the streets of the Chinese ghettoes. Instead of violence, the Chinese owners sought redress through the courts—hiring attorneys, issuing repeated writs of habeus corpus, and accusing the girls of grand larceny.

One case that awakened great interest—according to the Occidental Board reports—was that of "little Low Ah Fah, the slave of Tong Duck, a depraved old Chinese doctor who keeps an opium room and drug store on Brenham Place. He had four wives until recently when one ran away to China. In last year's report I told of rescuing a little slave girl from this place, but unfortunately we lost her in court. After a time she disappeared, then I was told he had brought another from Sacramento and had made arrangements to sell her to the keeper of a place of sin on Jum Cook Alley. With the help of Detective Reynolds of the Police Department, we rescued Ah Fah just before she was given over to the dreadful life into which the dreadful old doctor was going to sell her. The case was bitterly contested in court, for it meant the loss of $2300 to the owner of this pretty little girl to have her sent to the mission."[43]

Deputies continually knocked on the Mission Home doors with warrants for the slave girls' arrests. If this failed, the angry Chinese would shout up at the windows at the cowering girls, promising that the gods would curse them or their photographs would be placed in the coffin of a dead person, so that the spirit of the deceased would return to make them sick.

There were usually thirty to forty rescues a year. In 1889,

Chinese slave girls' building, Calaveras Co., Calif.

there were thirty-six women freed, including one Japanese girl. In the first thirteen years of the Home's existence, there were two hundred admissions, eighteen letters of guardianship secured for minors, and fifty-five marriages solemnized. Many of the girls returned to China after earning their passage, many stayed on as students or teachers, and some returned voluntarily to their former status.

One missionary woman writing in 1880 noted that in San Francisco's Chinatown women were "fortunate if they have a hole in the roof, or some dim old window, half-boarded up. One woman had never crossed the threshold since her arrival from China seven years before."[44] Another reporter described how a merchant's wife who had lived in San Francisco for six years, begged her carriage driver upon leaving the city to "let me see out. This is the first and last time I shall see the streets of San Francisco."[45]

The energetic missionary women also paid calls upon married Chinese women, seeking converts. Lucy Durham reports on her visit to a Chinese home: "The work is very slow," she wrote. "There are many houses where the visitor is welcomed, but the gospel is received with indifference or barely tolerated."[46] In many cases their visits had the desired effect, however, and the Chinese

Unidentified Chinese family in California.

women did turn to Christianity. After conversion, a steady improvement in the convert's way of life was noted by the missionaries: "Two have a stove to cook by, instead of a few bricks, and another has matting on the floor . . . all steps forward."[47] But there was little effort to incorporate Oriental heritage into their Christian teachings, and the matrons were often quick to point out their dismay at seeing young Chinese women with queues and quilted cotton jackets instead of frills and curls. They were delighted, however, when their Chinese students married in typical Western fashion: "The wedding party entered the parlor to the strains of an organ march, and Mendelssohn's wedding march was played at the conclusion of the ceremony,"[48] says one report.

Lo Kee, Idaho City merchant with his wife & daughter.

The closer Chinese women came to keeping an orderly, Western household with flowers at the window and a freshly washed floor, the more they were accepted by the American women. Ironically, these same women often filled their own overcrowded Victorian homes with carved jade, Tang jars, and the scent of joss—the elements that they tried to discourage in the houses of their Chinese converts.

Why Chinese women did not protest their enslavement, and why that enslavement was so easily accomplished are questions that are difficult to answer. To understand one must try to imagine the position of a Chinese woman, often of peasant background, who was transported to a strange culture, was unable to speak the new language, and was forbidden by her training—if not by her husband—to mingle with outsiders. She was assailed by Americans for clinging to the vestiges of Chinese culture that made her feel most comfortable, yet she could not defy the Confucianist basis of her marriage by showing disrespect for her husband's wishes.

Patrician women were caught in an equally distressing situation. Bearing the mark of their status in their deformed "lily" feet, with toes pulled in and bound to create useless stubs, their very inability to walk was understood by them to be a sign of their own gentility, yet it singled them out for pity and ridicule in the country to which they had been brought.

In addition, it should be remembered that Chinese women were rarely allowed any education. The reply of one Chinese father, when asked if his pretty eleven-year-old daughter could attend the mission school was typical: "No, I not educate my daughter, I educate my son, but not my daughter . . . because it makes a girl so mean to be educated; you let her go to school and learn to read and write, then she get very free, she then not like to stay home and work; she like to go street and see things."[49] Girls were judged for their "white and pretty" faces, their good manners, sweet temper, and ability to manage a home.

Perhaps the answer lies in the feudal society that they left behind. In China, women had few legal rights. Many were peasants who came from rural villages so inbred that every villager bore the same surname. They came to this country already tolerant of unreasonable legal systems: they had lived in provinces that were under the iron rule of a district magistrate, who was under a prefect, who was beneath a governor. The subsequent path of arbitration was so tortuous that Chinese families simply gave up in disgust and fixed upon more subtle methods to gain revenge. This attitude of nonviolence followed them to the U.S. where they faced continued danger and oppression and had little hope of legal redress. One notable exception occurred in Idaho in 1866. In this case, a local Chinese man named George Dyson challenged an Idaho sheriff who was enforcing a law that demanded a $5 per month tax on foreign miners, and then, further claimed that all "Mongolians," whether they were housewives, houseboys, children, or gardeners were min-

Chinese women mourning the death of an unidentified person in California.

ers. Dyson won his suit against the sheriff, but this was an isolated victory, followed by several other suits that failed.

Feeling against the Chinese ran high throughout the country as whites became increasingly resentful of the jobs that they felt the Chinese were taking away from them and as they became increasingly fearful of Orientals in general. *The Working Man's Advocate* of November 20, 1869, reports "that the laundry women of San Francisco hoped to form a Woman's Cooperative Anti-Chinese Laundry." By 1880, there was a treaty calling for the suspension of all immigration from Chinese provinces, and, by 1894, another treaty called for the complete cessation of immigration. For those who had come to America to escape the widespread famine and civil war in China, the door was beginning to close. They had come to earn money in order to return to China and better support the families which they had left behind. In time, however, for those Chinese who had established themselves in the U.S., this dream faded. Those lucky enough to have children continued to teach them their language and culture in the hope that the children would return to the homeland one day. But for the women who slept on rush mats, cooked over a few bricks, and only occasionally glimpsed the colorful spectacle of Chinatown life, the dream of returning home must have been constant. It must have been difficult for those in the cribs and brothels to dream even of that. That they even survived is a testament to the human spirit.

The brothels of the Barbary Coast were indiscriminate and welcomed both Japanese and Chinese women. Numerous Japanese were reported to have been rescued from them, though the 1860 census in San Francisco lists no Japanese while it listed 784 Chinese women. Undoubtedly many of the Japanese women in San Francisco were here illegally, having been smuggled into the port. (Many may have been the wives of well-to-do merchants who traveled back and forth from Japan, which was a common practice.)

By 1880, there were only eighty-six Japanese women registered in the census as living in the U.S., but, by 1900, there were 872, and, by 1910, the number had grown to 6,925. They were greeted initially by a certain ambivalence on the part of the American public. The anti-Chinese campaign had raged for a good thirty years, and—having spent much of its energy—there was a lull before the sentiment against the Japanese arose. Many of the women who came were picture brides—women whose marriages had been arranged by the bride's Japanese family and the prospective groom who was already in America. *Omiai kekkon*—the arranged marriage—was an age-old Japanese tradition, but was particularly popular at the turn of the century because of the prospect of increasing the family fortunes through a wealthy son-in-law in America. In some cases, a wedding in the United States was ar-·ranged to avoid the high cost of a Japanese ceremony.

The women who came as picture brides were often from the educated classes—some were the daughters of Shinto priests, some from well-respected trading and manufacturing families. More often than not they made their lives in rural American communities and were often dismayed at the "vast wilderness" of such places as Livingston, California, or the Yakima Valley in Washington. There they found it necessary to live by the light of a rusty oil lamp when, in Tokyo, they had had electricity.

After their arrival at the tumultuous port cities, the brides went directly to the solitary homes their husbands had established for them. Often they were shocked to find their new homes nothing but a wooden shanty of the poorest material, without flooring, insulation, or stove. Winters were chilly, and dismayed wives wrapped themselves in old futons, papered the cracks with newspapers and sewed woolen shirts and jackets by hand, one pattern circulating from house to house. If there was no heater, they used a flimsy tin stove. They drew water from a well by bucket, then boiled it for cooking or bathing. Unable to bathe daily as they had in Japan, they were often forced to share a tub with a whole community, and to bathe but once a week.

Japanese women working in fruit-processing plant, 1900-1915.

One of the first trials of assimilation was dress. Anxious husbands immediately outfitted their brides in the latest Western fashion, lest the same antagonism that surfaced against the strangely clad Chinese be turned against their own style of dress. "I was immediately outfitted with Western clothing at Hara's Clothing Store," one bride wrote. "Because I had to wear a tight corset around my chest, I could not bend forward. I had to have my husband tie my shoe laces."[50] Some women fainted from the tight corsets, causing their husbands to carry them to privacy where they could undo the corset strings. It is easy to imagine the stunning change from customary dress in a loose cotton kimono to "a large hat, a high-necked blouse, a long skirt, a buckled belt around [the] waist, high-laced shoes, and, of course . . . a brassiere and hip pads."[51] Another bride puzzled over American underwear, comparing it to the Japanese *koshimaki*, the sarong-like undershirt." Wearing western style underwear for the first time," she remembered, "I would forget to take it down when I went to the toilet. I frequently committed the blunder. . . ."[52]

Women who had brought *kotto-butsu*—valuable antiques— with them, were appalled by the rough setting these shacks provided, though they found this Spartan simplicity preferable to the agonizing jumble of Victorian bric-a-brac cluttering the homes of their American neighbors. In these homes Japanese women were often startled to find Oriental vases, fans, and jars placed carelessly about without thought to the religious or social significance of the objects.

The first Japanese immigrants had been quick to buy raw stump land or bottom acreage that no one else cared to farm. For them, no crop was too difficult to nurture, and from Washington to California they carefully tended potatoes, strawberries, cauliflower, and beans. Their farms, if small, were well managed, and those Americans who rented acreage to a Japanese family often counted excess profits from land that they never would have farmed themselves. Women helped their husbands in the fields as well as in all the other daily tasks, and there was no doubt some truth in the 1909 poem of Yone Noguchi:

> "Bits of straw and clay and woman's hair
> So shall be builded my house. . . ."

When Japanese laborers first came in the 1880s, they had been well received. They were seen as being quiet and efficient and it was thought that they served their communities well. Unlike the Chinese who preceded them, they strongly desired assimilation. But as they progressed from being laborers into direct competition as farm owners, antagonism with whites mounted. The Russo-Japanese War of 1904, which the Japanese easily won, put Japanese Americans in an even more feared position. By 1905, citizens began to form virulent hate societies such as the Japanese Exclusion League. One of its tactics was to acquire customer lists of Japanese businesses and to mail long and detailed letters to each customer, exhorting him to discontinue his trade with the "aliens." Because of these discriminatory tactics, Japan, in 1920, ceased issuing passports to the U.S.—at a time when 42.5 percent of the American Japanese male population was still without wives.

The women who returned to Japan after years in America were shocked to find that—even if single or widowed—they still owed allegiance to the oldest male member of the family. He had the right to determine her future, whether this meant the choice of husband or job. The years these women had spent in the United States, though not without struggle and difficulty and great portions of bitterness, had also been laced with uncharacteristic freedom for women from Japan.

Of those women who remained in the U.S., most adjusted to the prejudice and were able to make new lives for themselves. They managed to make light of their hardships, and—like Kazuko Hayashi—even learned to be matter-of-fact about the challenges of this land. When she left Japan to come here, her father-in-law—in anticipation of her possible failure—handed her a well-polished sword, with the advice that "if things don't go well, commit hara-kiri with it."[53]

Mrs. McKinnon with her adopted daughter Mrs. Takaki & children, 1901.

Eighteen men and one woman nearing the summit of Chilkoot Pass, Alaska, 1898.

Women of the West

Mrs. Ben Kelsey, first white woman to cross the Sierra Nevada Mountains.

Mary Richardson Walker

Mary Richardson was born on a farm near West Baldwin, Maine, on April 11, 1811. She possessed a scientific interest and sharp wit that soon singled her out for a sort of local notoriety and caused her, at the age of twenty-two, to begin pouring out her doubts and opinions on paper. For fifty-seven years she continued to keep a journal and became one of America's most prolific diarists.

Her most passionate desire was to serve God on a foreign mission, yet to do so, she had to marry. The same predicament was shared by a gangling young man named Elkanah Walker, and the story of their arranged meeting, brief courtship, marriage, and subsequent journey over the Rocky Mountains forms the content of the following diary excerpts. Though their union was sudden, their temperaments oddly matched and their early years almost intolerably rugged, the two survived to form a loving and permanent relationship in Oregon.

January 12, 1833. If ever I have a husband, may God give me a Christian.

August 7, 1833. I see very few men that are perfect enough to please me.

May 14, 1836. My attention has been called of late to the subject of matrimony. . . . I have had a fair sort of an offer, dont know whether I ought to think of accepting it or not. Did he possess knowledge and piety I should like him. But I fear he lacks a kindred soul. Could I inspire in his bosom the sentiments that expand in my own, but alas, I fear it is impossible. Ought I to bid adieu to all of my cherished hopes and unite my destiny with that of a mere farmer, with little education and no refinement. . . . In a word, shall I to escape the horrors of perpetual celibacy, settle down with the vulgar?

I cannot do it.

September 18, 1836. My mind very much excited, dont know what to do, have always harbored the design of going on a mission. If [I] listen to the proposals of G. [G. was a neighboring farmer who had often proposed to Mary] then farewell to the design.

September 22, 1836. By night and by [day] I scarcely think of any thing but becoming a missionary. I think I feel more engaged in religion than I have ever before. At least I have more freedom in prayer.

In hopes of obtaining a mission somewhere, Mary wrote to the American Board of Commissioners for Foreign Missions in Boston, but was refused because she was unmarried.

Mary met Elkanah Walker through the manipulations of a mutual friend, William W. Thayer, who saw the two as kindred souls to be united in order to realize their shared dream of going on a mission. He wrote to Mary, then urged Elkanah to visit her and see how well they liked one another. In April 1837, Elkanah and Dr. Whitney, a family friend of Mary's, rapped on the door as Mary casually glanced out. She viewed Elkanah as a "tall and rather awkward gentleman," then continued about her work "without hardly stopping to take a second look." Later, after their introduction, she described him further in her diary.

April 22, 1837 . . . His remarks were good. But not delivered in a style the most energetic. . . . After meeting, instead of shaking hands in a kind of free cordial kind of a way as I was anticipating, his attention seemed rather taken up in some other way. . . . I saw nothing particularly interesting or disagreeable in the man, tho I pretty much made up my mind that he was not a missionary, but rather an ordinary kind of unaspiring man who was anxious to be looking up a settlement. . . . [Elkanah presented Mary with a letter which seems to have described his prospects and intentions. After reading the letter Mary wrote:]

The conflict was rather severe. The hand of Providence appeared so plain that I could not but feel that there was something like duty about it, and yet how to go to work to feel satisfied and love him, I hardly know. But concluded the path of duty must prove the path of peace. I could discover a good foundation for true friendship, and altho I almost felt in the morning as if I wanted to throw the bargain off on to some one else, at evening I would not willingly have given up my titles. . . .

Monday, April 24, 1837. Began to feel quite happy about the affair [and] I guess he went to bed rather satisfied with his days work.

Tuesday, April 25, 1837. He seemed a little embarrassed on taking his leave, but finally stepped up and shook hands rather affectionately. He then went into the other room and took leave of the family. Father was at the barn. So he went out there to bid him good bye. He was feeding cattle and knowing full well what [Elkanah's] errand was, he kept him walking round pelican fashion. As soon as [he] was gone I went to bed.

Friday, April 28, 1837. [Elkanah] appears much more interesting than before & I have no more doubt as to being able to love him. I feel he has no rival in my affections. . . .

Sunday, April 29, 1837. That other called. Renewed his professions of attachment. I told him it was no use. Said he, I would rather have seen you pass on a bier than in a chaise with W. I told him I was engaged and satisfied with W. Said he, He does not love you as well as I do. Said I, I love him better than I do you and all I hope is that you will find some one that will suit you as well as he does me. He said that people did not think I was cutting a great cheese.

Saturday, May 27, 1837. His affection for me appears to be becoming very strong & somewhat enthusiastic, & I think I love him full well enough. We sat up for the first time till after 11, that is to say until 1, at the close of our interview he exclaimed: "This is the happiest evening I ever passed. I can be happy anywhere if my Mary is with me. I feel the angels are contemplating our conduct with pleasure."

Mary notes that G. has not stopped his demands for her affection which, to this point, have been unsuccessful. Yet it is difficult for her to overlook G.'s wealth and brilliance as compared to the ardent yet awkward Elkanah.

June 12, 1837. . . .very unhappy all day . . . My mind is perfectly distracted. I feel that my engagements with W. are sacred. They have been made in accordance with a sense of duty & inclination. I have believed that he was the person that Providence designed for me. And can it be that I have been mistaken? . . . I feel that however strong may be my inclination to love G. it would be sinful for me to do so. I feel too, that however little I may feel inclined to love W. [it] is my duty to do so. I have [gone] so far that I cannot go back without forfeiting my Christian character."

As if to remind Mary, once again, of his loving intent even if they are unable to marry immediately, Elkanah writes and tells her that "I love you, therefore I want you. If I could be with you this moment a more heartfelt kiss you never had than I would bestow. To fold you in my arms, hear from your faithful lips that I am still your dearest one would be sweet, sweet indeed."

September 14, 1837. Feel very unhappy. Know not how to feel or act. I feel sad, sad, sad. I fear my courtship with W. will amount to nothing but trouble. Surely I thought my trials in love were over. I feel sick and discouraged. If W. leaves me, what shall I do. I have endeavored to seek relief by prayer.

September 17, 1837. The state of my mind has resembled the weather in time of thunder showers.

October 2, 1837. . . . O Elkanah what a desolate being should I be if you should forsake. It seems to me I could never have the least courage or wish to have any one again.

October 18, 1837. The thought of losing you has made me sensible how firmly the tendrills of my heart had become entwined, & how different from everything I before experienced is my regard for you.

December 17, 1837. Had a letter from Walker last night. The Board wish him to go beyond the Rocky Mountains. The proposal strikes me as favorable. They wish us to be ready to start in April. I hope we shall be able to go. . . . My mind is full of tender thoughts on [bidding] adieu to home. It is indeed trying.

December 18, 1837. A change of clothes is all we want. Buckskin drawers are the best for riding on horseback. Our ladies should also have drawers to prevent being chafted in riding. We should carry no baggage excepting such as we want to wear or use on the journey. . . . all the baggage we carry will cost us one dollar per pound. . . .

January 20, 1838. Recd. a letter from my dear W. It contained such severe criticism as I almost feel as if I could not bear it. It is extremely mortifying for me to meet such reproof. . . . I will, therefore, bear it patiently and determine never to let any one have occasion to notice a repetition of the same. I will however retaliate

a little by just letting him know that I have noticed a thing or two in him as well. . . . I have some distressing fears that Elkanah Walker does not love me or never will. If this be the case, dark & mysterious indeed must be that Providence that brought us where we are.

They were married on March 5, 1838. Elkanah was thirty-three and Mary nearly twenty-seven. The black gown she wore to the ceremony symbolized the grief she felt at parting forever from her family.

March 12, 1838. Nothing gives me such a solitary feeling as to be called Mrs. Walker. It would sound so sweet to have some one now and then call me Mary or by mistake say Miss Richardson. But that one expression, Mrs. W., seems at once to indicate a change unlike all other changes. My father, my mother, my brothers, my sisters all answer to the name Richardson. The name W. seems to me to imply a severed branch. Such I feel to be. . . .

In April of 1838, Mary, one month pregnant, and Elkanah embarked on the overland journey to Oregon with two other couples, the Cushing Eells and the Asa Bowen Smiths. The three couples traveled by horse nearly two thousand miles, from Westport, Missouri, to Waiilatpu, Oregon, spending 129 grueling days on the trail.

April 23, 1838. Left the States about noon. The baggage went ahead. . . . The prairie is spread out before us on every hand.

Tuesday, April 24, 1838. Rested well on my ground bedstead and should feel much better if Mr. W. would only treat me with more cordiality. It is so hard to please him I almost despair of ever being able. If I stir it is forwardness, if I am still, it is inactivity. I keep trying to please but sometimes I feel it is no use. I am almost certain more is expected of me than can be had of one woman. I feel that if I have strength to do anything it must come of God. . . . May God help me to walk discretely, do right and please my husband.

We came to camp about 5, having travelled about 23 miles. Very tired. Feel hardly able to sit up. Never had a poorer appetite.

Wednesday, April 25, 1838. Cold but not rainy. Rode 21 miles without alighting. Had a long bawl. Husband spoke so cross I could scarcely bare it, but he seemed to pity me a little when he found how bad I felt. To-day has been very kind.

Thursday, April 26, 1838. Baked some biscuits. The first cooking I have done since I was married. Mr. Walker remarked that he thought I had done very well [for] one day. . . . Mr. W. impolitely selected the camp grounds.

Friday, April 27, 1838. Some of our horses have strayed. Here we are waiting till the sun is high. Feel anxious. Some of the company feel disposed to murmur against Moses [Gray]. Mr. S. takes it hard if he has to be separated from his wife. I feel that dangers & perils await; that we ought to realize that every day may be our last.

Saturday, April 28, 1838. Came up with the company about ten & the Captains called & were introduced. They sent us some corn & another gentleman sent us a piece of fresh pork. We expect to go in the morning. . . . Would be glad not to have our flight on the sabbath. We cook up a little more than usual & I thought Mr. Smith acted hoggish. . . .

Thursday, May 3, 1838. Rise before sunrise. Our company do nothing but jaw all the time. I never saw such a cross company before.

Sabbath, May 6, 1838. Last night a frost. Ice in the pail. Mr. W. rather sick. Travelled about 24 miles. Not a very pleasant way of keeping the Sabbath. Very cold, almost like winter. Had no idea that we were to experience so much wind & cold. Some of our company expressed regret that they have undertaken the journey. I suspect more from aversion to the toil than real dread of sin. . . .

Monday, May 7, 1838. 13 miles before dinner, 10 after. Cold in the morning, in the p.m. mild & comfortable. Mr. W. took an emetic & some calomel. My own health good. Should feel quite happy if my dear husband were as well & in as good spirits as myself. Our company still have a good deal of unpleasantness among them.

Tuesday, May 8, 1838. Husband sick. In a big worry lest he does not feel as well satisfied with me as he ought.

Wednesday, May 16, 1838. Rose early, kindled the fire, boiled my clothes, finished my washing before breakfast. . . . Rode in the wagon. Mr. Smith short as pie crust. Mr. W. begins to see how things are.

Saturday, May 26, 1838. Passed what is called the fort, chimney & other bluffs, in appearance resembling castles, capitals of cities. . . . Past 7 we encamped. Feel real satisfied with the movements of my husband & cheerfully happy in anticipating our future labours. Mrs. S. tries my patience talking about Gray as she calls [him] all the time. I wish she could see how much like him only worse she acts.

Thursday, May 31, 1838. Washed for myself and Mr. Rogers. Took me most of the forenoon. Almost blistered my arms. Not much fatigued, much less than if I had been riding. To dine with us had Mr. Clark, son of the Clark who accompanied Lewis. He & his brother are travelling in the company through from St. Louis. In the afternoon arranged my trunks.

Friday, June 1, 1838. Ripped & dyed my pongee dress. Made sundry repairs. Recd visit from squaws.

Tuesday, June 5, 1838. A fine day. Frost last night. Rode over hills of a red appearance and passed over what we supposed to be gypsum. . . . Was bled toward night. Came near fainting. Sick some.

Wednesday, June 6, 1838. Considerably out of health. Took a spoonful of wine, went without dinner at night. Felt better. . . . Saw some minerals I wish very much to pick up.

Think what I said to [Mrs. Smith] had a good effect. Arrived at the crossing place. Very tired. Everything almost excites my fears. It would be so bad to be sick in such circumstances. Find it difficult to keep up a cheerful flow of spirits. Think bleeding did me good tho it reduced my strength more than I expected.

Sabbath, June 10, 1838. To-day . . . I have reflected much on the goodness & mercy of God. I think he has given me a good husband & trust he will grant me favor in his eyes. He treats me kindly & I can but believe he loves me. I however, experience some anxiety on this account. But I think I am rather gaining ground. That he feels more confidence in me & sees more plainly the defects of others.

My attachment to him does not in the least abate. I feel as much anxiety as ever to please him. I regard my husband as a special blessing conferred by Heaven & I am determined if possible that my life shall evince my gratitude.

My health at present is rather feeble & I find it difficult to keep up a usual amount of cheerfulness. If I were to yield to inclination I should cry half the time without knowing what for. My circumstances are rather trying. So much danger attends me on every hand. A long journey before me, going I know not whither, without mother or sister to attend me, can I expect to survive it all?

Monday, June 11, 1838. Rainy. The water comes into the tent. I was sick of diarrhea. A little past noon we were summoned to cross the Platte, just at that time the rain ceased. We crossed safely in boats constructed of Buffalo hides & the bottom of two waggons. In the forenoon I cried to think how comfortable father's hogs were. In the afternoon, felt we were dealt with in mercy. The snow-capped Mts. appeared.

Monday, June 18, 1838. Rode some time with husband which I had not done for some time before. I have rode with Dr. & Mrs. Gray and Mr. W. has driven the cattle. So I have been first on the spot and he last. Mrs. S. is a great hand to hurry, but her husband is a real poke and last ready about almost everything. Encamped in a beautiful spot.

June 22, 1838. Busy repairing. Concluding whether we had better cross Popeasia. Mr. & Mrs. S. went out and were gone several hours, so husband came & made me quite a pleasant visit.

June 24, 1838. Mr. S. has gone to living by himself. Query, does not the course he is pursuing cost him some misgivings. It will be pleasant not to hear so much fault-finding. . . . Mr. Walker preached in the A.M. on judgement, sitting in the open air in the shade of our beautiful grove. He had 18 hearers. We enjoyed the meeting much. In the afternoon Mr. Eells preached. Had only our family. . . . Read "Saint's Rest" between & after meetings. Husband seems to like to stay in the tent now. We all put on our Sunday dresses & acted as much like Sabbath at home as we could. I think I am rather happy.

Friday, July 6, 1838. Some of the squaws came to get dresses cut.

We were again saluted by a company on foot. The same musick, scalp, etc. Their faces were painted. White men acted like Indians. It is said that many of the white men in the Mts. try to act as much like Indians as they can & would be glad if they really were so. Several squaws were here who united in the dance. They were warmly clad, [though] the weather was excessively hot. For several nights the noise in the camp has continued nearly all night. Some of the Capts. & I suppose many of the men are drunk nearly all the time.

Sabbath, July 8, 1838. The day has been to us a day of rejoicing. A company of 14 from the Hudson Bay Co. arrived. Among them were Rev. Jason Lee, from the Methodist Mission, on his way to the States & several boys who are going to be educated. They came to Green River, expecting to find the rendezvous there. But on reaching [it] found no signs. The country full of buffalow. But in an old trading house, they found a line, "Come on to the Popeasia; plenty of whiskey & white women." They accordingly came and on the fourth day found us.

Friday, July 13, 1838. Made a camp of 16 miles over hills of red rocks & earth. . . . Poor King having his feet blistered, followed making great adieu. I think I have not felt so weak since I left the States.

Saturday, July 14, 1838. Rode ahead. Could scarcely keep going. I think they drive most too fast. Passed a patch of snow, ate some of it. A good deal of scolding because they drive so fast. Encamped for the last time on the waters [flowing into] the Atlantic.

Sabbath, July 15, 1838. Last night had quite a rain. Felt for the first time the leaping of [the child she carries.] Followed close to the guide. On our right, snow capped mountains. Saw a flock of antelopes. Last night a large band of buffalow passed so near we could hear them pant. Fell in with a company of Snakes [Indians]. Encamped to trade with them on Little Sandy [River.]

Monday, July 16, 1838. In the afternoon we rode 35 miles without stopping. Pretty well tired out, all of us. Stood it pretty well myself. But [when I] came to get off my horse, almost fainted. Laid as still as I could till after tea, then felt revived. Washed my dishes, made my bed & rested well. . . . 45 miles ride in one day is hard.

Friday, July 20, 1838. . . . On reaching the foot of the mountains we passed a beautiful little grove & came at once to an open plain where the tall grass was in a good state to mow. . . . As there were an abundance of roses, I picked rose leaves until my tent was pitched. . . .

Husband came in with the lost heifer before tea, & glad was I to find we were all once more safe in camp. I have suffered considerable from anxiety lest both of us should not live to complete our journey's end. Find it difficult to be reconciled to the idea of separation by death. Find I [am] becoming every day more fondly attached to my husband. Indeed he seems every day to become increasingly kind & I am more & more confident of my ability to please him & make him happy. . . .

Saturday, August 25, 1838. Just as we approached Grand Round, we descended a longer hill than I ever walked down before. Connor's wife was confined. She followed camp about 30 miles. At noon she collected fuel & prepared dinner. Gave birth to a daughter before sunset.

Wednesday, August 29, 1838. Left baggage behind, and hasten on. Rode my pony through the woods & then took Mr. W.'s & then cantered on. Arrived at Dr. Whitman about two p.m. Found Mr. & Mrs. Spalding there. Mr. Gray & wife gone to Walla Walla. We were feasted on melons, pumpkin pies & milk. Capt. Sutor was with us. Just as we were sitting down to eat melons, the house became thronged with Indians & we were obliged to suspend eating & shake hands with some 30, 40, or 50 of them. Towards night we partook of a fine dinner of vegetables, salt salmon, bread, butter, cream, &c. Thus our long toilsome journey at length came to a close.

When the Walker-Eells party reached Waiilatpu, it was to find the only cabin already occupied by the Whitman family. With no time to build their own cabin, they moved in with the Whitmans. Thus nine adults and two children were forced to spend the winter in frustrating proximity, broken only by occasional visits to the nearby Spalding family. Walker and Eells were anxious to establish their own mission, and on September 8 they set out to explore the Spokane area in search of an ideal spot. The result of their search was Tshimakain, or "the place of the spring."

Saturday, September 22, 1838. Mrs. W., E. & myself went to visit the Indians' lodges. Found some eating, some lying down, some dressing skins &c. and some were packing up to move. They, most of the time, seemed busy, especially the women. If they only could have tolerable opportunities, I see not why they would not soon rise to a rank among civilized beings.

Sunday, September 23, 1838, A.M. Morning worship & family prayer meeting. Worship with the Indians. Mrs. W. read from Mr. Spalding's book, prayer in English, singing in Nez [Perce]. In the p.m. sermon by Mr. S. Text "Thy faith hath saved thee." Pretty good for him. Towards evening a marriage. Mrs. W. interpreted for Mr. S. I have read considerable today. But every little while I would find my mind on my husband; it seems a long time already since he left, & longer still before he will return. I can hardly refrain from tears every time I think of him. I know I am foolish but I can't help it. I ought to be more [thankful] than I feel that I have so good a husband & that I have enjoyed his society so much; & not be sad because he is gone a little.

Saturday, September 29, 1838. . . . Got almost out of patience with Mrs. E's habit of snuffing. I wish someone would tell her about it. We were hoping to hear from our husbands by this time. Mrs. E. manifests much solicitude about hers & I would at least like to hear from mine.

Tuesday, October 2, 1838. Washed some & that is about all I have done today that counts. This evening weekly concert, made a prayer. I wish I knew whether my husband likes to have me pray before folks or not. When he comes home I will ask him. Fear when he comes home he will be disappointed to find me no more proficient in the language. Hope I shall soon be able to give more attention to it.

Saturday, October 13, 1838. Stewed pumpkin, baked pies. Mrs. Whitman quite out with Mr. Smith because he was unwilling to let her have Jack help her. Husband & Mr. Eells came about noon. Was glad once more to see my husband & he appears glad to see me & I suppose he really was for he has no faculty of making believe. Could not sleep all night for joy.

Saturday, November 3, 1838. Last night Mr. Pambrun sent us a quarter of beef. He was expecting some Catholic priests to visit him & so he slew the old cream colored cow, which was 23 years old. He also sent the tripe, so that I had the job of cleaning it. Mr. P. also invited the gentlemen to call over and make his guest a visit. They hardly knew what to do about accepting it, but finally concluded it was best. So Dr. W., Mr. W. & Eells have gone. Mr. S. declined saying that it looked too much like countenancing Romanism. Hope our husbands will manage discreetly.

Sunday, November 4, 1838. A long day to me. A day seems a week as it were when my dear husband is absent. Worked too hard. Took cold or something so that I have not felt very well to-day, having felt too irresolute to read much, so have thought & prayed the more. This evening have been reading over my old journals & weeping over fond recollections.

    I love my husband so much that almost the only thing that makes me feel unhappy is the fear that he does not love [me] as much. I find it hard to be reconciled to the thought of ever being separated from him. If he should be taken away, I should be so lonely & disconsolate. I could be more contented to die & leave him, could I know that he would obtain another better than myself. After experiencing so much of the goodness of God shall [I not place] myself, my Husband, my all in his hands? This I will endeavor to do. May God still be merciful to us. . . . May his blessing also rest on the little one which we fondly expect soon to welcome as ours. . . .

Tuesday, November 6, 1838. Slept little last night. Mostly in consequence of something husband said to me. Rather indisposed all day.

Saturday, November 17, 1838. Notwithstanding my resolution not to work so hard, I commenced in the morning & continued till night without ever stopping to warm my feet, which were rather cold. I should think the other ladies might consider me a little more. If I think I will do like the rest, let all go, there are so many suffering about me that I cannot compose myself to sit & not try to make those around me more comfortable. After breakfast Mrs. W. went to her room & there remained through the day without concerning at all how or what was done. I know not, I am sure, what she wishes or thinks. But I think her a strange housekeeper. It is hard to please when one cannot know what would please.

Friday, December 7, 1838. Awoke about five o'clock a.m. As soon as I moved was surprised by a discharge which I supposed indicated approaching confinement. Felt unwilling it should happen in the absence of my husband. I waited a few moments. Soon pains began to come on & I sent Mrs. Smith who lodged with me to call Mrs. Whitman. She came & called her husband. They made what preparations they deemed necessary, left me to attend worship & breakfast. After which at almost nine I became quite sick enough—began to feel discouraged. Felt as if I almost wished I had never been married. But there was no retreating, meet it I must. About eleven I began to be quite discouraged. I had hoped to be delivered ere then. . . . But just as I supposed the worst was at hand, my ears were saluted with the cry of my child. A son was the salutation. Soon I forgot my misery in the joy of possessing a proper child. I truely felt to say with Eve, I have gotten a man from the Lord. With Hannah for this child I prayed. Thanks to a kind Providence for so great & unmerited a blessing. The remainder of the day I [was] comfortable. Husband returned in the evening with a thankful heart, I trust, & plenty of kisses for me & my boy. Mrs. Smith stayed with me thru the night, her husband being gone from home. . . .

Monday, December 10, 1838. Up for the first time. Mrs. Smith took my washing.

Tuesday, December 11, 1838. Nipples very sore. Worry with my babe. Get all tired out.

Wednesday, December 12, 1838. Mrs. Eells takes care of me. Very nervous. Milk so caked in my breasts, have apprehensions of 2 broken breasts. Have it steamed & drawed alternately till it seems better, then cover.

Monday, December 17, 1838. Felt quite out of sorts this morning because they did not bring me plenty to eat. Was very faint for want of food. At breakfast took hold of horse meat with a pretty good relish. Through the day have been well-supplied. Tonight felt had been ungrateful to murmur. My breast still a cause of much suffering. Sat up & tended my babe about half the day. Took a nap. This evening made a cap for my babe, the first time I have sewed any. Fear I have worked too hard today.

Tuesday, December 18, 1838. Very sick all day. Steam pads over my breasts all day. Have taken cold. Experience soreness in all my breasts, relieved by sweating. Take morphine and calomel. Go to bed, sleep some.

Monday, December 31, 1838. Have obtained a [mare's teat]. Hope to succeed in using it. If so I shall rejoice.

Friday, January 4, 1839. Husband went to Walla Walla yesterday, returned tonight. Had a stormy unpleasant ride. Have very little hopes of being able to nurse much. Some times am tempted to murmur. But then when I reflect how many other blessings I enjoy & especially what a "worthy portion" I possess in my Elkanah, I feel that I do not do well to complain of any affliction consequent on my union with him. My mind often turns with strong emotion to the home of my childhood & youth. But I would not return. I some times feel discouraged & fear I shall never do anything to benefit the heathen & might as well have stayed at home. Self must be taken care of & that requires more than all my time & strength. Is it always to be so?

Saturday, January 19, 1839. Babe very worrisome. Mrs. Eells has made my cape, but it has been as much as I could do to take care of my boy. Dr. W. and Mr. Smith in trouble. We do not agree about celebrating the Lords Supper without wine. Mrs. W. busy preparing to go to the Tukanan.

Wednesday, January 20, 1839. Reached the log cabins. Think the location pleasant. Mr. Eells occupies the tent. Mr. Walker his house, find it quite comfortable.

Thursday, January 21, 1839. Have stowed away our baggage so that we have quite a clear spot in the middle. The Indians have covered our house with grass & boughs & chinked it so that we are very comfortable. Little C. is getting better. Weather quite warm.

Sunday, April 21, 1839. Have been reading today the Memoirs of Mrs. L. Huntington. In reading of parting with her husband I have realized how I should feel if called to part with [mine]. I fear I could not be reconciled to such & I dread to think of it. O may it please God to spare his life & that of our dear little son. How frail a thing is an infant. I tremble in view of afflictions because I know I need chastisement. Why I have hitherto received so many mercies I do not know. One thing I know, it is not because I have deserved. I have been so ungrateful I have reason to fear they will all be taken from me.

I have desired to become a missionary & why? Perhaps only to avoid duties at home. If I felt a sincere interest in the salvation of the heathen, should I not be more engaged in acquiring the language that I might be able to instruct them? But instead of engaging with interest in its acquisition, I am more ready to engage in almost anything else, & as I do not like others to excell so I feel a wicked satisfaction in seeing them as little interested as myself. O Lord may I not be left to cherish such feelings. But from this time forth may my attention be directed to the language & may I be willing to forego other studies when they interfere with this. May I realize now the awful responsibility that rests upon me. I have great reason to fear that the object of pursuit with me is not to glorify God but to please myself & my husband. I have at times, yea, frequently the most distressing fears that there is no such thing as experimental religion or if there is that I am a stranger to it. Why is it that I feel so much inclined to shun the [prayer] closet? Is it not because I have not pressing need to be there. O me, the mournful truth is I am not willing to humble my heart before God. I have no adequate sense of his goodness & holiness. I do not have the Savior & I fear he [is] indeed a root out of dry ground to me without form or comeliness.

Tuesday, April 23, 1838. I feel vexed. This is the third morning I have omitted the sweeping when I first got up just to see if Mrs. E. would not take her turn. Sunday morning when I commenced sweeping she remarked she would have done it but supposed I had already. But the floor was so dirty had she looked at it she could not decently avoid sweeping. But some how she managed to get to the tubs & I would not be so impolite as to crowd her away, so while she was washing her clothes I just swept the room. This morning I wished to make haste & iron while babe slept so left an opportunity for her to sweep again. But I left it go till ten o'clock when she took her knitting & walked off after cracking & scattering about nut shells. So I have swept the room with a vengence. I have washed the room every week while we have been here & she not once & I think she shirks more than is decent. Evening, have got plenty words to say.

Thursday, June 27, 1839. Thought husband had got to feeling pleasantly again, but find I am sadly mistaken. He reproached [me] again this morning most severely on account of some ingentilities of which I had indeed been guilty. He almost said had he not supposed me more accomplished, I had not been his wife. I am almost in despair & without hope of his ever being pleased or satisfied with [me]. I do not know what course to pursue. I can never with all my care make myself what he would like me to be. I never intended to be the wife of a man that did not love & respect me from his heart & not from a stern sense of duty & this fear, yes, I have much reason to fear is all that secures me that share of kindness that I receive. I know for the most part I am kindly treated. But I am but too often treated as tho my convenience & wishes were not to be regarded. The thought often occurs, I am glad my friends do not witness & can never know it. This morning as I sat sobbing with my little son in my arms he looked as if he was worrying & I was endeavouring to quiet him, but when he saw me he seemed amazed, sat & looked at me in almost breathless silence till he fell asleep without moving a limb. He had never seen me weeping before & he seemed to say as plainly as looks could utter, Mother what ails you? Has your son been naughty or grieved you . . .? I never witnessed anything [more] interesting in a child.

I am tempted to exclaim, Woe is me that I am a wife. Better to have lived & died a miserable old maid & with none to share & thereby agrivate my misfortune. But it is too late. O may he who in this providence has suffered me to become a wife bless me in that relation & enable me to discharge every duty with Christian discretion & propriety. Yes, God helping me, I will endeavour tho faint & disheartened still to merit the love & esteem of my unfortunate but much loved husband. Perhaps tho I may be an affliction I am given to him in mercy to avert a worse. But reflections like these are but a poor solace to a grieved and disappointed wife. Disappointed, not because he is not as good as I anticipated, but because I have not gained that place in his heart that I fondly expected & which I think a wife ought to possess.

Thursday evening. Tonight told husband how bad I was feeling. He only laughed at me. Said I was mistaken in suspecting he did not love me, for he certainly did. He confessed he had spoken wrong, said he was sorry I had felt so bad. That he had not intended to make me sad. So I think I will try to feel better.

Friday, July 26, 1839.
To Rev. E. Walker,

My Dear Husband I find it in vain to expect my journal will escape your eyes & indeed why should I wish to have it [so]? Certainly my mind knows no sweeter solace than the privilege of unbosoming itself to you. It frequently happens that when I think of much I wish to say to you, you are either so much fatigued, so drowsy or so busy that I find no convenient opportunity till what I would have said is forgotten. I have therefore determined to address my journal to you. I shall at all times address you with the unrestrained freedom of a fond & confiding wife. When therefore you have leisure & inclination to know my heart, you may here find it ready for converse.

Monday, August 5, 1839. Noon. I have just been exercising some boys in adding numbers. I never could make white children understand half as quick. They added the digits to 10 & get it right the second time. . . .

Monday, September 30, 1839. Mr. Eells is building his chimney. I am getting some lazy, shall feel glad when Mrs. E. gets to keeping house again. The Chief has been here today. Is very mad apparently. Son is getting to be a naughty boy, cries to go out doors almost all the time. Strikes when anything does not suit him. As soon as he is put on the bed, he begins to frolic, & I often have to whip him to make him lie still & go to sleep. He is full of mischief as a child can be.

Thursday, November 28, 1839. A sad lonely evening on account of the reproaches of my dear husband. If I deserve them I am sorry, if not, am no less so. I do not know what the most dutiful wife could do for the most deserving husband that I have left undone. I never forget that he is a frail treasure of which I may soon be deprived. I endeavor to discharge my duties faithfully as in the sight of God & when I find my best endeavors fail to receive that confidence & affection I so much prize, it is as tho a mildew had blasted all my hopes. Must my happiness be thus snared always? What can I do that I have not done?

Thursday, February 6, 1840. Plenty of rain last night. Very lonely to day, feel anxious about my husband. . . . Have felt very bad in thinking of our little son. Fear when it comes warm weather he will be out with the Indians all the time. Feel that the responsibility resting on a parent is more than I know how to sustain & shrink at the prospect of renewing the relation.

Monday, March 2, 1840. This morning a part of the wall of our house fell. Husband was in bed in the room when it began to fall. He escaped without being hurt much. Sons little chair was broken to pieces, after he has been sitting in it in the very spot where it fell. Scarcely the least thing besides was injured. The chimney fell with the wall & roof. Just as they fell it was beginning to rain. . . . but it soon ceased & it was determined the roof must be removed. [Having] cleared out the books & some other things & covered the bed with skins, they set about removing the roof. After working a little while, they left to attend a funeral, [and] were detained some time. Just as they returned, there was a shower of rain sufficient to have wet the room pretty thoroughly. . . . They were unable to remove the roof till the shower was over. They succeeded in getting the roof on again & the room in so comfortable a fix we can sleep in it to night. We have much to remind us that here we have no abiding place & that soon our earthly tabernacle will be dissolved. Thus we have great cause of gratitude that no more calamity has befallen us. . . .

Sunday, May 24, 1840. Rested well last night. Awoke about 4 o'clock a.m. Rather restless. Arose at 5. Helped about milking. But by the time I had done that found it necessary to call my husband & soon the Dr. [I had] scarcely time to dress & comb my hair before I was too sick to do it. Before eight was delivered of a fine daughter with far less suffering than on the birth of our son. The morning was pleasant. In the p.m. fine thunder shower. Babe very quiet. Think it weighs not more than eight pounds.

Friday, May 29, 1840. The former part of the night sick & restless. Took assefedita, applied hot rocks to my breast which seem to afford some relief. After midnight got several naps. This morning felt much better & continue to do so through the day. Feed the babe for the most part, mostly with breast milk. . . . I sweat profusely most of the time so that it is almost impossible to avoid taking cold. Do not begin to eat anything yet but gruel, bread, water & milk.

Sunday, June 7, 1840. Feel much rejoiced . . . to find my health so far restored & my little ones doing so well. I feel encouraged to hope that I shall finally succeed in nursing. My babe is very quiet. . . . She does not require to be fed or taken up in the night. Have been reading Mrs. Trollopes Domestic Manual of the Americans the past two weeks, find her disgustingly interesting. We have given the babe the name of Abigail Boutwell.

Saturday, June 20, 1840. Find more & more every day in the character of the Indians to try & perplex me.

Friday, July 10, 1840. Washed, ironed, baked, & what is worse than all, milked. The cows & calves so unmanageable, it takes so long I get all out of patience. Shall be glad to [have] husband home again.

Monday, July 27, 1840. Made a first attempt at teaching. Think I succeeded pretty well as the children seem pleased & are telling over their new ideas, & just now when I asked who would bring my washing water, several answered. I went out to the lodge, took both my children & they were very quiet. I gave them a lesson in geography on an egg shell which I had painted for a globe.

Sunday, August 9, 1840. Last week I went four times to teach the Indians. But it is all I can do to get along, do my work & take care of my children. How I can answer a single letter I do not know.

Sunday, August 23, 1840. Have felt the past week several times as if I could no longer endure certain things that I find in my husband. I find it difficult to gain relief on a subject like this. For I cannot speak of him—nor to him—& if I write I fear he will read. I suspect there is wrong on my part as well as his but I know no way to remedy it. What grieves me most is that the only being on earth with whom I can have much opportunity for intercourse manifests uniformly an unwillingness to engage me in social reading or conversation. I remember it was not always so & that actions & words promised it should never be. But thus it is & every day I feel it more & more & can see no way to remedy it. I would fain render myself more deserving by improving my mind but this I can not do as I am so pressed with care & labor that I can hardly find time to read even my Bible & thus it is that makes me feel much more sensibly the need of social intercourse.

Sunday, November 22, 1840. I have spent some time the past week in fixing our bed room & now live in [it] most of the time. I find it almost as much as I can do to take care of the children, milk, tend my fire, &c from 6 o'clock in the morning till 7 at night. When I find so much that needs to be done, I can spare very little time to sleep. For several weeks I scarcely retired earlier than eleven & frequently sit up till 12 or one. I sometimes feel almost out of patience & discouraged not to say tired. Sarah G. stays in our house most of the day. She helps me some & tires me more. . . .

Monday, January 4, 1841. The annual fast was observed in part. . . . This evening I have been baking but my mind has been very much in contemplation. I have been wishing I were more pious, regretting my coldness & stupidity with little resolution to do better. My husband & children seem to engross my heart & I fear they will be taken from me. I was thinking of the rose bush in Mother's garden when I was a child. I was so impatient to have the roses bloom that I used to pick the buds open, or try to, so that when the flower opened it was but a mangled flower. I have thought that parents often, and perhaps we are of that number, feel the same impatience in watching the opening of the infant's mind. It is certainly better to leave nature uninvaded. I wish not to see a forced maturity in children.

Monday, April 5, 1841. So much troubled, thinking how things have been in this mission, and are likely to be & have been & ought to be, & now so little hope of their going right, that it is with difficulty I can attend to my domestic duties. O that the Lord would show us the right way & incline our hearts to walk therein.

Friday, April 23, 1841. Have been talking all day about going to general meeting. Cast wicks & dipped 19 dozen candles.

Saturday, May 1, 1841. . . . In the p.m. the chimney took fire & continued burning till in the night when we got up & had to throw down a part of it in order to extinguish the fire. Had we neglected to do this our house would in all probability been burnt before morning. . . .

Thursday, May 19, 1841. Feel lifeless as need be today. The weather oppressive. Had boiled corn for dinner. In the evening an express arrived bringing letters from the U.S. One from home. Some of my dear friends are dead but most are living. I am not pleased with the course my brothers are persuing in regard to certain young ladies.

Saturday, August 21, 1841. Baked squash pies & bread & got dinner but had hard work to force myself to do anything. . . .

Sunday, August 22, 1841. Mrs. E's folks commenced eating at home. I have read considerable today but feel miserably sick except when lying down. Am afflicted with nausea & faintness. . . .

Friday, August 27, 1841. More unwell. After dinner rode out. After returning from the ride was quite sick. Took castor oil & calomel.

Monday, Aug. 29, 1841. Felt pretty well when I arose this morning, went & milked, returned tired & sick & have been rather so most of the day. . . .

Tuesday, Aug. 31, 1841. Have felt pretty well today. Made me a new corn broom & washed my floors. . . .

Saturday, Dec. 25, 1841. Made, cut & made two pair drawers for A. & a dress & one pair for Elizabeth. My health good except I can not sit long without my sides aching so I mix in my house work to rest me & sew a great part of the time. Sit up late nights. . . . There is plenty of snow & the weather for a week past has been so cold we have not used our beef because it was frozen too hard to cut any.

Wednesday, March 16, 1842. Rose about 5 o'clock, had an early breakfast, got my house work done up about 9. Baked six more loaves of bread. Made a kettle of mush & have made out to put my clothes away & set my house in order. May the mercy of the Merciful be with me through the expected scene. Nine o'clock p.m. was delivered of a son.

Thursday, March 17, 1842. Rested pretty well last night. The rain disturbed me some. My little boy laid still all night. We call his name Marcus Whitman. Had Kwantepetser help me wash & c. . . .

Wednesday, March 23, 1842. Rose about seven. Got my breakfast, cleared up my room, dressed my babe for the first time. Made a kettle of mush &c, delt out dinners to the family . . . made some pea porridge & washed the children.

Friday, March 25, 1842. A very windy day, took some cold in one breast but with a warm stone succeeded in removing it. This is an Indian medicine & the best I can find. . . .

Saturday, July 16, 1842. Churned a lot of butter, scalded brine, cleaned house. Mrs. McDonald arrived about two p.m. . . . & Gaudies wife & their children, in all 14.

Monday, August 8, 1842. Churned. Some half dozen Indians stood & watched me from the time I put the cream in the churn till the butter was salted.

Friday, September 2, 1842. Reached home in safety about 1 p.m. Found a dinner ready for us. Abigail has the mumps. Wish I knew how to turn these visits to more & better account. It seems to me we do no good & get but little.

Sunday, September 18, 1842. Mr. E. went to the river & Mr. Walker staid at home. I feel depressed. My children, especially Cyrus, is a heaviness to me particularly on the Sabbath day. It is as if he was almost possessed with some demon, he is so noisy. I do not know what to teach him first about his Maker. . . .

Monday, September 19, 1842. Feel lonely, depressed.

Friday, October 14, 1842. I feel constant distress & concern on account of our mission. Sometimes feel that it will be given up. Fear all the time that I may have done wrong in some way myself. If in no other way, I fear I have too often thanked God that I was not like some other missionaries. . . .

Wednesday, November 9, 1842. Cleaned tripe & tried tallow. Have two pails full and a half. Mr. Walker & Eells not done with making the book. Old No-Horn has been lost these last two days, fear she will be quite done giving milk when we find her again. The Indians are about the house the whole time watching me. I scarcely do anything from morn till night without being seen by some of them. Some times I feel out of patience. I [feel] I cannot endure it any longer & then I think if I do not teach them in this way I never shall in any. . . .

Tuesday, November 22, 1842. Washed & think I will not try to wash in the day time again very soon. Cyrus disobeyed in going into Mrs. Eell's house without permission. I tied him to the table leg. He was any how but contented with his situation & at last exclaimed, "I dont want to be tied. I think Indians tie dogs. When I went to the Chief's lodge, I think I saw his dog tied." A while since I kiss[ed] him after washing his face. He asked why I do so, adding "dogs kiss. . . ."

Friday, November 25, 1842. Mr. E. went down to the Chief's encampment & sent off the package [of letters] in order to overtake Ellis. . . . Marcus is as uneasy as a child can be a great part of the time. Seldom sleeps more than half an hour by day light so that among them all they are almost more than I can comfortably manage. I can hardly cook my food & when it [is], I have a hard chance to eat it.

Saturday, November 26, 1842. Killed & dressed some chickens that had frozen their feet. Brought out the big rocking chair & fixed for Marcus a cradle & succeeded in making him sleep several hours, to pay for which I had his company till 8 this evening. .

Tuesday, January 17, 1843. Our ears are pained with hearing how much accord the Indians still pay to their superstitions. . . .

Wednesday, January 18, 1843. Sat up all night to dip candles. Dipped 24 doz. . . .

Tuesday, February 7, 1843. . . . Snow still continues to fall & the poor cattle come home every day almost in search of food. The Indians too begin to think about eating moss. . . .

Monday, February 13, 1843. The poor cattle, I fear, suffer much. They pick their living mostly in the water or along the banks. The horses live by digging. . . .

Monday, March 20, 1843. Washed for Mrs. E. & myself, had two boys to help. Helped wash Mrs. E's floor & cleaned my shelves. Worked harder than usual but did not feel very much fatigued. Think my health improving since weaning my babe, as well as his.

Tuesday, March 21, 1843. Ironed & finished making another suit for Cyrus. The Old Chief came, said he had opened & examined his dead cow, found she died in consequence of eating sticks.

Wednesday, March 22, 1843. The Chief came again & Mr. E. & W. commenced making another book. [*A printing press had arrived at Lapwai in the spring of 1839. Elkanah used it once, in 1842, to produce a primer in the Flathead language. In March of 1843 he was either translating or attempting to print another book.*] I baked 18 loaves of bread. A hard job for our old baker. What a handy thing an oven would be.

Friday, March 24, 1843. . . . I think I never saw a child whose mind was so constantly on the stretch as Cyrus. He is constantly making inquiries in regard to everything he can see or hear of. Wishes every word defined which he hears spoken that he does not understand. Today he stood at the door, halloing a while & then came in, wished to know what it was he heard in the mountain. We did not know at first to what he alluded, but he added, "Cyrus knows. We & the trees & every thing have a shadow & it is like that I think. My voice has a shadow." Seemed to be his idea.

Friday, March 6, 1846. Feel rather dejected. Would give a great deal to see a physician.

Saturday, March 7, 1846. Took a portion of salts before retiring, was restless all night. Somewhat indisposed through the day. About the middle of the afternoon became worse & was delivered of a son about sunset. I think I never felt more gratitude & joy. After a month of solicitude & suspense to find myself so safe & comfortable to see another so fine a son. His father calls his name Jeremiah after his father. . . .

Sunday, March 8, 1846. Mrs. E. staid with me all night. I took no medicine except a little camphor. Rested considerable. Have a tolerably comfortable day. . . .

Monday, March 9, 1846. . . . Plenty of milk for my babe & sound nipples. A comfort I never knew before.

Tuesday, March 31, 1846. About ten o'clock in the morning Cyrus asked for some sugar. I told him to say "please sugar," but he refused but continued to cry, "I want some sugar." I thought best to try the rod which I continued to do with increasing severity till

his father came when I delivered him to him, and he followed the same course till noon when the child became so much exhausted that we concluded to let him sleep but he did not seem to yield at all. He slept till three or four in the afternoon but sighed deeply for a long time. When he awoke seemed refreshed & pleasant. We thought not to allow food or drink till he should say please some, but if he asked for milk & we told him to say "please milk," he would say "I dont want to say please," or "I dont want milk." When night came, we allowed him to rest. In the morning, Apr. 1st, we again tried to compel him to yield but he was still firm. We used the rod till we feared to longer. We tried to tempt him with food & drink but to no effect altho he had taken not a drop of any thing for more than 24 hours. . . . It was affecting to witnes the joy he evinced. We kept him in bed all day & still tried to induce him to say please, but to no purpose.

Wed. April 1, 1846. My birthday, 35 years old. I think I should long remember it.

Thurs. April 2, 1846. We concluded to release our poor little boy. After he was dressed he wanted, he said, to go out & see the bright sun. At breakfast he several times said please when he wanted any thing without being told. I regret the course we pursued tho I do not perceive that he is injured by it except for the time but less severity would I think have been just as well. I often fear being guilty of the very thing for which I punish my child. . . .

Sun. April 26, 1846. The Lord's Supper administered by Mr. Walker, he also preached. Our babe was baptized by Mr. Eells by the name of Jeremiah. I have felt very stupid all day. The cares of my family so engross my mind that I have no room to think of anything else. I feel at times scarce courage enough to try to live, because the prospect is of only an increase in care from year to year for years to come. Still I trust to find strength equal to my day. . . .

Sat. May 2, 1846. Churned & baked. Got along pretty well with my work altho there are so many things that need to be done, I hardly know what to do first. . . .

Monday, Aug. 3, 1846. The Indians who were about us yesterday gave us some trouble & probably pilferred a little . . . I washed & hunted bugs again, found several. . . .

Thursday, August 6, 1846. My health is better this summer than usual. Cyrus is pretty good about work but seldom meddles with a book unless he is compelled to. Abigail does better in some respects, but she hardly knows how to spend time to study her spelling lesson. She is so anxious to be painting or drawing. Marcus learns easy but is so lazy. . . .

Tuesday, August 25, 1846. Mending, mending, day after day, stitch, stitch. Mrs. E. took a vest to make for Mr. Walker. I have so many things that I do not know how to leave undone that I feel almost distracted. . . .

Friday, August 28, 1846. Find nearly every woolen garment in the house covered with nits. Do not know of what but conclude they must be those of flies. . . .

Monday, August 19, 1847. Teacher's daughter had a child born. Her father was enraged & drove her off & threatened to shoot himself.

Thursday, August 5, 1847. Stuffed a sparrow skin & bought a rattlesnake skin ready stuffed except it wanted fixing a little nicer. Mr. W. returned from Colvile, got only one bag of flour. Brought a present of shoes from Mrs. Lewis.

Saturday, August 7, 1847. Had a talk in the morning with Mr. W. Got permission to pursue collecting a few objects in Natural History. Mr. Walker's birthday, 42 years. A quiet day. Went with A. to the creek to bathe, got much fatigued. . . .

Tuesday, August 10, 1847. . . . purchased a few stuffed skins. But think I will wait till I can procure arsenic before I collect more. . . .

Thursday, December 9, 1847. We were hoping to have Dr. Whitman to supper with us tonight. But about sunset Old Solomon arrived bringing the sad intelligence that Dr. & Mrs. Whitman, Mr. Rodgers, John & Francis Sager & others have been murdered by the Indians. Mr. Stanley was apprised of it . . . went to Walla Walla instead of Waiilatpu or he too might have been killed. May God have compassion on those that survive & stay the hand of the ruthless savages. We are safe only under the Divine protection. May we trust only in God.

Sunday, December 12, 1847. We are still the spared monuments of divine protection. And this seems [to be] our only security . . . I wish I felt as anxious in regard to the souls as the bodies of men. We feel very anxious to know what may have been the fate of those who were not murdered—whether they are rescued or are perishing with cold & hunger. We also have fears that we may share the fate of others. I am thankful that we are able to maintain so much composure. I have felt but little concern in regard to my approaching confinement. Feel that all will be well even tho they slay me. I think I can trust in him. But my sense of eternal things seems dull. I do not see why I should expect to be preserved when more faithful servants are cut off. Perhaps in mercy they are taken away from the evil to come.

Friday, December 31, 1847. As soon as Mrs. E. returned home, my illness came on again & I had soon to call her again. Our business went on more tardily than common. However, about breakfast time perhaps 8 in the morning, I was delivered of another son. A fine little boy, weight 9 lbs. Every thing went safely & favorably as could be expected & we feel our cause for gratitude is unbounded. I hope our unprofitable lives may yet be prolonged to look after our children for I hardly know what other good we can hope to do in the world. I fear our labors for the Indians must soon cease or if prolonged will only hasten that certain destruction which ere long seems to await [them.] The hope of our seeing them much better than they now are, fondly as I would wish to cherish [it,] is all hope against hope.

Mary and Elkanah Walker left Tshimakain shortly after the Whitman massacre. She returned only once, in 1888. They settled in the Willamette Valley and, in January of 1853, the American Board closed its operations in Oregon. The Walkers resigned themselves to living simply in Forest Grove, raising their eight children as best they could. Unlike so many emigrants who never returned home, they once traveled back to Maine by railroad.

Elkanah Walker died in 1877, and entries in Mary's journal at that time reveal her loneliness without him. "It seemed as though I can't live without my husband," she wrote on December 18 of that year. "I feel so lonely," she later wrote. "[I] think of so many things I want to tell Mr. Walker. I realize more and more how much more I loved him than any one else."

Mary Walker died on December 5, 1897. She left five sons, one daughter, twenty-five grandchildren, and six great-grandchildren. She had survived her husband by twenty years.

Mary Richardson Walker at age 60, taken in 1871.

A thorough housecleaning, Green Lake, Seattle, Washington.

A family camped out during the land rush in Oklahoma.

A pioneer home on the Niobara River, Knox Co., Nebraska.

Miriam Davis Colt

Miriam Davis was born December 18, 1817, the twelfth child of seventeen in the household of a poor New York City tanner. From the beginning she was bright and eager for education, but a realistic look at her family's circumstances convinced her that her father would never provide her with an education.

"What I crave must be gained by my own effort," she wrote, and from the age of fifteen she took upon herself the double burden of bringing money into her parent's home, as well as paying for her own tutors and brief sessions at the district school. She kept house for neighborhood matrons, often earning less than a dollar a week. She taught the poor in "Hell's Kitchen," worked part time in a hotel, sewed and quilted for hire, and continually strove to dress as well as her income allowed.

After eight years of daily toil and nightly scholarship she finally won her teaching certificate, which was followed by a teaching post at the Old Academy in Parishville, N.Y. It was here that she met a fellow teacher, William H. Colt, whose background was in marked contrast to her own. He was descended from an English peer, Sir John Colt, and has spent a leisurely youth on the family farm near Parishville. He was noted as a scholar, and at the time of their meeting was bound for Montreal to start his own academy.

The two were married in the spring of 1845, and the following seven years in Montreal were a time of great joy for her. She delighted in her work and in the city itself—particularly pleasing was her ready acceptance into "polite" society, which was far removed from the poverty of her youth. Here, too, her children Willie and Mema were born. So when her husband one day announced his need for "more of Heaven's pure air" she was dismayed, but wrote that she was "willing to comply with his decision, but, long after, I vainly hoped, and even prayed that some favorable turn in fortune would give me back a home in Montreal."

His need for a change led them to join an experimental vegetarian settlement colony in Kansas. Each member of the colony was entitled to a 160-acre tract purchased from the government at a minimum price of $1.25 per acre. Since William Colt's parents and his sister, Lydia Colt, were going also, the Colt family's combined 720 acres would have been worth a fortune had the colony prospered. But only eight members of the 100 had previous farming experience, and there was nothing in their backgrounds to prepare them for the hardships that lay ahead.

January 5th, 1856. We are going to Kansas. The Vegetarian Company that has been forming for many months, has finally organized, formed its constitution, elected its directors, and is making all necessary preparations for the spring settlement. . . . We can have, I think, good faith to believe, that our directors will fulfill on their part; and we, as settlers of a new country, by going in a company will escape the hardships attendant on families going in singly, and at once find ourselves surrounded by improving society in a young and flourishing city. It will be better for ourselves pecuniarily, and better in the future for our children.

My husband has long been a practical vegetarian, and we expect much from living in such a genial clime, where fruit is so quickly grown, and with people whose tastes and habits will coincide with our own.

January 15th. We are making every necessary preparation for our journey, and our home in Kansas. My husband has sold his farm, purchased shares in the company, sent his money as directed by H.S. Clubb. . . . I am very busy in repairing all of our clothing, looking over bags of pieces, tearing off and reducing down, bringing everything into as small a compass as possible, so that we shall have no unnecessary baggage.

April 15th. Have been here in West Stockholm, at my brother's, since Friday last. Have visited Mother very hard, for, in all probability, it is the last visit we shall have until we meet where parting never comes—believe we have said everything we can think of to say.

April 16th. Antwerp, N.Y. Bade our friends good bye, in Potsdam, this morning, at the early hour of two o'clock.

April 22d. Have been on the cars again since yesterday morning. Last night was a lovely moonlit night, a night of thought, as we sped almost with lightning speed, along in the moonlight, past the rail fences.

Found ourselves in this miserable hotel before we knew it. Miserable fare—herring boiled with cabbage—miserable, dirty beds, and an odor pervading the house that is not at all agreeable. Mistress gone.

April 23d. On board steamer "Cataract," bound for Kansas City.

April 24th. A hot summer day. The men of our company are out in the city, purchasing wagons and farming implements, to take along on the steamer up to Kansas City.

April 28th. The steamer struck a "snag" last night; gave us a terrible jar; tore off a part of the kitchen; ladies much frightened. Willie is not very well; the water is bad; it affects all strangers.

April 30th. Here we are, at Kansas City, all safely again on terra firma. Hasten to the hotel—find it very much crowded. Go up, up, up, and upstairs to our lodging rooms.

May 1st. Take a walk out on to the levee—view the city, and see that it takes but a few buildings in this western world to make a city. The houses and shops stand along on the levee, extending back into the hillsides. The narrow street is literally filled with huge merchandise wagons bound for Santa Fe. The power attached to these wagons is seven or eight and sometimes nine pair of long-eared mules, or as many pair of oxen, with a Mexican driver who wields a whip long enough to reach the foremost pair, and who does not hesitate to use it with severity, and a noise, too.

Large droves of cattle are driven into town to be sold to emigrants, who, like us, are going into the Territory. Our husbands are all out to-day buying oxen, provisions and cooking utensils for our ox-wagon journey into the Territory.

This is the anniversary of my wedding-day, and as I review the past pleasant years as they have passed, one after another, until they now number eleven, a shadow comes over me, as I try to look away into the future and ask, "What is my destiny?"

Ah! away with all these shadowings. We shall be very busy this year in making our home comfortable, so that no time can be spared for that dreaded disease, "home-sickness," to take hold of us, and we mean to obey physical laws, [*Since members of the community were vegetarians and subscribers to the temperance code, we may assume that the "physical laws" would be those set forth in their by-laws, which were: ". . . to abstain from intoxicating liquors and the flesh of animals; to reap the rewards . . . of industry and not [suffer] loss by the indolence or indifference of members . . . to assemble together frequently . . . for the discussion of agricultural, physiological . . . and other sciences [to avoid] the dullness and monotony of country life."*] thereby securing to ourselves strength of body and vigor of mind.

May 2d. A lovely day. Our husbands are loading the ox-wagons. . . . Women and children walk along up the hill out of this "Great City," wait under a tree—what a beautiful country is spread out before us! Will our Kansas scenery equal this . . .?

One mile from the city, and Dr. Thorn has broke his wagon tongue; it must be sent back to Kansas City to be mended. Fires kindled—women cooking—supper eaten sitting round on logs, stones and wagon tongues. This I am sure is a "pic-nic." We expect "pic-nic" now all the time. We are shaded by the horse-chestnut, sweet walnut, and spreading oak; flowers blooming at our feet, and grasshoppers in profusion hopping in every direction. This is summer time.

May 3d. The women and children, who slept in their wagons last night, got a good drenching from the heavy shower. It was fortunate for mother, sister, myself, and children, that lodgings were found for us in a house. My husband said not a rain drop found him; he had the whole wagon to himself, besides all of our Indian blankets. Father, it seems, fell back a little and found a place to camp in a tavern (not a hotel), where he fell in with the scores of Georgians who loaded a steamer and came up the river the same time that we did. He said he had to be very shrewd indeed not to have them find out that he was a "Free States" man. [*Kansas in 1858 was still undeclared as to whether it was a slave or free state. If it chose to welcome escaped slaves from neighboring Missouri, this would threaten the nearby Southern slave economy. Thus bands of "border ruffians" frequently patrolled the Kansas borders, hoping to terrorize abolitionist settlers into leaving.*] These Bandits have been sent in here, and will commit all sorts of depredations on the Free State settlers, and no doubt commit many a bloody murder.

Have passed Westport, the foothold for Border-Ruffianism. The town looks new, but the hue is dingy. Our drivers used their goads to hurry up the oxen's heavy tread, for we felt somewhat afraid, for we learned the Georgians had centered here. Here, too, came in the Santa Fe and Indian trade—so here may be seen the huge Mexican wagon, stubborn mule, swarthy driver with his goad-like whip, and the red man of the prairie on his fleet Indian pony, laden with dried meat, furs, and buffalo robes.

"What! fast in the mud, and with our wagon tongue broke?" "Why yes, to be sure." So a long time is spent before my husband and Dr. House can put our vehicle in moving order again. Meanwhile, we women folks and children must sit quietly in the wagon to keep out of the rain—lunch on soda biscuit, look at the deep, black mud in which our wagon is set, and inhale the sweet odor that comes from the blossoms of the crab-apple trees that are blooming in sheets of whiteness along the roadside. . . .

May 6th. Dined on the prairie, and gathered flowers, while our tired beasts filled themselves with the fresh, green grass. . . . Have driven 18 miles to-day . . . so here we are, all huddled into this little house 12 by 16—cook supper over the fire . . . fill the one bed lengthwise and crosswise; the family of the house take to the trundle-bed, while the floor is covered . . . with men, women and children, rolled in Indian blankets like silk worms in cocoons.

May 11th. "Made" but a few miles yesterday. Forded the Little Osage; the last river, they say, we have to ford . . . our "noble lords" complained of the great weight of the wagons. . . . That our wagon is heavily loaded, have only to make a minute of what we have stowed away in it—eight trunks, one valise, three carpet bags, a box of soda crackers, 200 lbs. flour, 100 lbs. corn meal, a few lbs. of sugar, rice, dried apple, one washtub of little trees, utensils for cooking, and two provision boxes—say nothing of mother, a good fat sister, self, and two children, who ride through the rivers. . . .

At nightfall came to a log-cabin at the edge of a wood, and inquired of the "Lord of the Castle" if some of the women and children could take shelter under his roof for the night; the masculine number and whichever of the women that chose, couching in the wagons and under them. He said we could. His lady, who was away, presently came, with bare feet, and a white sack twisted up and thrown over her shoulder, with a few quarts of corn meal in the end that hung down her back. I said to myself—"Is that what I have got to come to?" She seemed pleased to have company—allowed us the first chance of the broad, Dutch-backed fireplace with its earthy hearth, and without pot hooks or trammels, to make ready our simple evening repast. . . .

Are now [May 11th] crossing the 20 mile prairie, no roads—Think Mrs. Voorhees will get walking enough crossing this prairie. She is quite a pedestrian, surely, for she has walked every bit of the way in, so far, from Kansas City, almost 100 miles.

Arrive at Elm Creek—no house to lodge in tonight—campfire kindled—supper cooked, and partaken of with a keen relish, sitting in family groups around the "great big" fire. Some will sleep in wagons, others under the canopy of the blue vault of Heaven.

The young men have built some shady little bowers of the green boughs; they are looking very cosily under them, wrapped in their white Indian blankets.

We ladies, or rather, "emigrant women," are having a chat around the camp-fire—the bright stars are looking down upon us—we wonder if we shall be neighbors to each other in the great "Octagon City. . . ."

May 12th. Full of hope, as we leave the smoking embers of our camp-fire this morning. Expect tonight to arrive at our new home.

It begins to rain, rain, rain, like a shower; we move slowly on, from high prairie, around the deep ravine—are in sight of the timber that skirts the Neosho river. Have sent three men in advance to announce our coming; are looking for our Secretary, (Henry S. Clubb) with an escort to welcome us into the embryo city. If the booming of cannon is not heard at our approach, shall expect a salute from the firing of Sharp's rifles, certainly.

No escort is seen! no salute is heard! We move slowly and drippingly into town just at nightfall—feeling not a little nonplused on learning that our worthy, or unworthy Secretary was out walking in the rain with his *dear* wife. We leave our wagons and make our way to the large camp-fire. It is surrounded by men and women cooking their suppers—while others are busy close by, grinding their hominy in hand mills.

Look around, and see the grounds all around the camp-fire are covered with tents, in which the families are staying. Not a house is to be seen. In the large tent here is a cook stove—they have supper prepared for us; it consists of hominy, soft Johnny cake (or corn bread, as it is called here), stewed apple, and tea. We eat what is set before us, "asking no questions for conscience' sake."

The ladies tell us they are sorry to see us come to this place; which shows us that all is not right. Are too weary to question, but with hope depressed go to our lodgings, which we find around in the tents, and in our wagons.

May 13th. Can any one imagine our disappointment this morning, on learning from this and that member, that no mills have been built; that the directors, after receiving our money to build mills, have not fulfilled the trust reposed in them, and that in consequence, some families have already left the settlement. . . ?

As it is, we find the families, some living in tents of cloth, some of cloth and green bark just peeled from the trees, and some wholly of green barn, stuck up on the damp ground, without floors or fires. Only two stoves in the company. . . .

We see that the city grounds, which have been surveyed . . . contain only one log cabin, 16 by 16, mudded between the logs on the inside, instead of on the outside; neither door nor window; the roof covered with "shakes" (western shingles), split out of oak I should think, 3½ feet in length, and about as wide as a sheet of fools cap paper.

May 14th. Some improvements are being made in the "centre octagon" to-day. [*The octagon plan designated sixteen farms around a communal eight-sided building.*] My husband has put up some shelves on one side, by boring holes into the logs, putting in long and strong wooden pins, and laying on some of the "shakes" for shelves.

May 15th. A cold, drizzling rain. The prairie winds come whizzing in. Have hung up an Indian blanket at the door, but by putting trunks and even stones on to the end that drags, can hardly make it answer the purpose of a door. It is dark, gloomy, cheerless, uncomfortable and cold inside.

Have a fire out of doors to cook by; two crotches driven into the ground, with a round pole laid thereon, on which to hang our kettles and camp pails, stones laid up at the ends and back to make it as much as it can be in the form of a fireplace, so as to keep our fire, ashes and all, from blowing high and dry, when these fierce prairie winds blow. It is not very agreeable work, cooking out of doors in this windy, rainy weather, or when the scorching sun shines.

The bottoms of our dresses are burnt full of holes now, and they will soon be burnt off. If we stay here we must needs don the Bloomer costume. Our bill of fare is limited—hominy, Johnny cake, Graham pudding, some white bread, now and then stewed apple, a little rice, and tea occasionally for the old people. . . .

Father has got a broom stick, and is peeling a broom. He says, "I intend you shall keep this stone floor swept up clean."

May 16th. Still rainy, damp and cold. My husband has brought in the two side-boards that fill the vacancy between the "wagon bed" and the white cover, has laid them side by side in the loft above, and says, "Miriam, you may make your bed on the smooth surface of these two boards."

I say to him, "No, as you have to work hard, you shall have the boards and with one pillow and your blankets you will have an even bed, though it is hard. I will take the other pillow, the comfortable and blankets, and with the children will couch close by, endeavoring to suit myself to the warpings, rough edges and lappings of our 'shaky' floor.

A few feet from me and the children, Mr. and Mrs. V. have their quilt and blankets spread, while a foot or two from their heads can be seen Dr. House and Mr. Sober, mummies in their Indian blankets. So every part of the "centre octagon" is appropriated. . . .

May 17th. The greater number of the company that came in with us, and others that were here, left this morning for Kansas City; and from there they know not where they will go! They feel so much disappointed, they care not to go home again, and indeed some have not the means. It is saddening to think about.

May 19th. Mrs. V., Sister L. and self, have been to the creek and done up our last month's washing. Had the inconveniences of hard water, a scanty supply of soap, and only a one-pail full camp-pail to boil in. Expected our Secretary, who was to purchase necessary articles for the settlers, would not neglect to have a supply of one of the most necessary articles, *soap*. Starching and ironing will be dispensed with, for the want of what we have been in the habit of calling indispensible, flat-irons. A rub through the hand is all my own and the children's clothes can have, and the same will be done to their papa's linen, though that is to be exchanged for the striped blue wear.

May 20th. Have been busy all day in my kitchen. . . . Have raised salt yeast by keeping it covered tightly in a kettle of warm water, to exclude the ashes and flying dirt—raised the bread and baked in a Dutch oven. The oven is small, could only bake one loaf at a time. The wind has blown so hard, that I was obliged to lay up stones all around the oven to keep the coals under it; made a fire on the top of chips, laying stones on to the chips, to keep them confined so as to serve my use. Have really labored hard all day, and have baked only two small loaves of bread, while, in a family of seven like ours, one can be dispatched at each meal.

May 22d. Members of the company . . . can claim and hold, by the preemption right, 240 acres of land—160 timber, and 80 prairie.

My husband, his father, and sister L. are each claimants; they have accordingly located their claims side by side, making 720 acres of land belonging to our family. It is two miles east from the "centre octagon," and joining the Osage Indian lands. My husband says, the timber on our claim is fine; there are different kinds of walnut and oak . . . and that for several rods on the river is the prettiest bed of pebbles he ever saw, nice for walks. We intend, some time, to have walks made of them.

May 26th. Have been washing to-day, and dried our clothes right out in the burning hot sun. We dare not leave them out in the dewy nights, for fear of the Indians, who come thieving round—slying about—taking everything they can lay their hands on. . . . They are soon going two or three hundred miles west on their buffalo hunt, where they go twice a year, staying three months at a time. . . .

These [*Osage*] Indians are said to be friendly, but I cannot look at their painted visages without a shudder; and when they come around our cabin, I sit down and take Willie on my lap, and have Mema stand by my side, with my arm around her, for fear they may steal my children from me. They point to my boy and make signs that he is pretty. "Chintu-chinka," they call boy, and "che-me chinka," girl.

The whole Indian population of Kansas, at the present time, is probably twenty-five thousand, scattered over a territory of eighty-one millions of acres. Four thousand Osages just across the Neosho from us, living in their city of wigwams. They take life easy, depending upon their hunting tours and their annuities from the government for support.

Some of these Indians dress, others dress but little except a breech cloth, moccasins, deer-skin leggings, to keep off the snakes, and their blankets. They come into our cabin, and sit down—while sitting, their blankets slide from their shoulders, revealing their large, dark, brown, and nearly nude forms, to the shudder of the unaccustomed beholder.

I have seen some Indians wear little bells, strung on a strip of deer skin, and fastened around their legs just below the knee, making a noise for them every time they stirred. The squaws wear their long black hair hanging down their backs. They dress in calico loose-gowns and "brief" skirts; ornamented with beads and jewels, but not so heavily as the [men.]

May 28th. Took my children into our white-topped wagon, and

went with my husband two miles, to his claim, to plant corn. A bright and lovely day came in with the rising sun, not a cloud in the heavens above. . . . Not a stump, fence, stone or log, to mar the beautiful picture. . . . We sat in the wagon, while my hopeful husband planted corn and garden seeds. After the ploughing, the planting is done by just cutting through the sod with an axe, and dropping in the seeds—no hoeing the first year; nothing more is to be done until the full yellow ears are gathered in the autumn time. . . .

After we had eaten our dinner in the wagon, we went and selected a site for our log cabin, a little way from the clear, stony-bottomed creek that flows through our claim. . . . My husband says we shall have an elegant building spot, and that he will build a neat little log cabin; that he will get the large flat stones from the creek that will cleave apart, for walks to the creek and around our cabin. . . . I do not like to hear the voice which whispers, "This never will be;" but still it will whisper.

May 30th. Am wearing the Bloomer dresses now; find they are well suited to a wild life like mine. Can bound over the prairies like an antelope, and am not in so much danger of setting my clothes on fire while cooking when these prairie winds blow. Have had Mrs. Herriman's baby here for a few days, she is so very sick. Mr. H. wanted to plant his corn and garden seeds; he could leave his sick wife with the little two-year-old boy, but could not leave the little one to cry when its mother could not stir to take care of it.

Have been over to see Mrs. H; she is some better. Picked another bouquet of very rich flowers on my way, and placed them for her to look at; there were Japan lilies, large beautiful snake's head, larkspurs of many colors, and much larger than those we cultivate at home . . . wild peas and beans are scattered broadcast over these green fields; their blossoms are very pretty; they are eaten by the Indians—are said to make good coffee, and when green they are sometimes pickled. Beds and beds of onions are growing here and there, with the little onions all clustered in on the top, not larger than kernels of wheat.

June 3d. A most terrific thunder-storm came up last night; the thunder tumbled from the sky, crash upon crash . . . the rain came in torrents, and the wind blew almost tornadoes. . . . When we heard the storm approaching, we dressed ourselves, wrapping Indian blankets about us, and made ready to protect our children from the rain that was then dripping through the roof. We put all our bedding around them and all we could see to get by the glare of the lightning, (could not keep a candle lit), spread our umbrellas, (five in number), placed about, and held over them. We all got wet, and were obliged to lie in our wet beds till morning. This morning all was calm; the bright sun ascended up into a cloudless sky, as majestically as though there had been no war in the elements through the night. But the rain had dissolved our mud chinking, and the wind had strewed it all over and in our beds, on our clothes, over our dishes, and into every corner of the house. Have had all our sheets to wash, beds and blankets to dry in the sun and rub up, our log walls to sweep down, our shelves and dishes to clean, and our *own selves* to brush up. "Such is prairie life," so they say.

June 5th. Our young and very much respected Mr. Sober, has left the settlement, and gone back to his home in Michigan. . . . Disappointment has darkened every brow. . . . We are 100 miles from a grist-mill, and 50 from a post office. Mr. Clubb has petitioned to have the mail come here.

The Indians have gone away now on their hunt; it seems quiet and good, to have our fear removed for a time. The people say we have had our hardest time here, but it does not seem so to me. I often ask myself, "Why do I have so many presentiments of coming sorrow?" . . . I am so impressed some nights with this feeling, that I sit up in bed for hours, and fairly cringe from some unknown terror. I tell my husband, "We are a doomed ship; unless we go away, some great calamity will come upon us; and it is on me that the storm will burst with all its dark fury."

June 7th. My husband is up at his claim planting corn. Hopeful man. . . ! The one plough is broken. Father started off this morning to go twenty five miles, down to the Catholic Mission, where is the nearest blacksmith, to get it mended. . . .

I have cooked so much out in the hot sun and smoke that I hardly know who I am, and when I look in the little looking glass I ask, "Can this be me?" Put a blanket over my head, and I would pass well for an Osage squaw. My hands are the color of a smoked ham, and get so burnt that the skin peels off one after another. I should feel happy if we were going along with Mr. Herriman, as he wants us to.

June 10th. Mr. Clubb has returned from Fort Scott, and the goods, groceries, seeds, and some provisions belonging to the company have arrived. They were bought with the company's money, still we are charged a very high price for them. Potatoes, four dollars per bushel; can't afford to have even one meal of them—have cooked one for mother. . . . I hear that Mrs. Clubb felt greatly annoyed while her husband was away, by an intruder at her feet in the night time; in the morning found that a large rattlesnake had been occupying the bed with herself. They are fond of a comfortable place to coil up.

June 16th. What are we to look for, and what fear next? The mosquitoes have come upon us all of a sudden. They troubled us very much at the creek to-day while washing. . . . Our bed being short, in the night they have a good chance to nibble away at our protruding extremities. I lie awake. . . . I try to keep my children covered, so they wont eat them all up before morning. As for myself, I get so infuriated that I get up, descend the ladder, make my way out into the wet grass upon the run, not minding what reptiles may be under my bare feet; I then return from my dewy bath, lie down and try to sleep, but it is almost in vain.

June 17th. The soil of rich layers of vegetable mould is throwing up the rows of dark green blades of corn. Our cornfield of six acres looks promising, as do all cornfields around. Pumpkins, squashes, melons, cucumbers, beans, peas, potatoes, and tomatoes are thriving finely. The next work our settlers will find to do, will be fencing cornfields, splitting rails, cutting poles, and drawing them from the bottom lands to do it with. . . .

June 21st. Baking day, and hominy pudding day come here every day, so that a great share of my time is spent in the large kitchen. I tended the boiling hominy, and baked a good Johnny-cake this forenoon. Now one of my white loaves is out of the Dutch oven, and the other is baking; it will soon be done. The old people think the fare here is hard, and so it is, for them—they don't want to eat anything made of corn; and where we shall get the next flour, I know not; it will be very high, wherever we can find it.

I live entirely on food made of corn-hominy and milk and Johnny-cake and milk—and try to persuade the children to, leaving the wheat bread for grandma and grandpa. To-day, at dinner, I told Willie, Mamma had got some good Johnny-cake, and asked him to have some in his milk. He said, "Willie rather have white bread;"

and the little fellow will eat it clear, and relish it much better than children with pampered appetites do their round of goodies.

June 26th. Several members of our company have suddenly been taken with the chills and [*malarial*] fever; and here in our own cabin it has fallen upon Mr. V. and wife, mother, sister L. and Mema. It is sorrowful to see what a change comes over them in one day. Mr. V. thinks this is too much for him to stand—will leave cornfield, and all the prospects of this beautiful country, and hasten to the North again. . . .

June 29th. A lovely Sunday. I, too, have fallen victim to the dreaded disease. Mr. & Mrs. V., Mema and myself, have occupied the loft today. Dishes of water have been set near our heads, so that we could help ourselves to drink when it seemed as though we should burn up with fever. My head has ached dreadfully; am glad to crawl down the ladder, with weakened limbs get out door here, sit down on a stone, lean my dizzy head against the logs of the cabin, breathe a little fresh air, see the sun go down, and ask, "Can this be the same sun that shines [on] our Northern friends, who are enjoying blessings and comforts they know not how to appreciate?"

June 30th. Mr. V. has spoken for a passage in an ox-wagon, for himself and wife, to Kansas City; my husband thinks we had better make preparations to leave the Territory with him, and not wait till he and father get sick; so he has done the washing to-day himself, and packed our trunks. And now, since our paroxysms of chills and fever went off for the day, sister L. has packed their trunks, and I have been trying to help my husband cook a little to take on our journey Northward. I have mixed up some bread, using baking powder for risings, for I could not tend to rising yeast. I find myself very weak—was obliged to sit down twice while mixing my bread. When I began to feel faint and dizzy, I would sit down on a stone, and when the dizziness passed off, go on with my mixing.

My husband is now baking the bread in the Dutch oven. This is the first lesson he has taken in baking in my big kitchen, and it troubles him to keep the coals on the oven. I believe we shall be ready to start any time now, when the command is given. . . .

July 1st. The water is fast drying up; the spring that was cleaned out and dug deeper, in the gulch below our cabin, is almost dry; the water is not fit to drink.

Disappointment is on the approach again! Am afraid father is going to upset all of our calculations about getting away. He declares, out and out, that he will not go. Mother and sister L. have been very anxious to leave the country; have tried to persuade father that it was best to go—so has my husband; but his indomitable will is not thus to be turned. . . .

July 2d. "A doomed ship!" thought I, this morning, as father unceremoniously yoked the oxen, put them before the wagon, placed in mother's bed, their trunks, some provisions and cooking utensils, told mother and Lydia to get in, and said, "I am going to the old Indian house, where I can get some water to drink. . . !" The difficult question comes up now to be answered; "What shall we do?" To leave the Territory is impossible; and to me it seems like going into utter darkness to go up to that old Indian house. There we shall be four miles from neighbors, and on the Indian lands, too. If they should return from their hunt and find us there, they would think we were intruding almost too much, and I know not what our fate would be. We cannot stay here without water, neither can we leave the old people four miles away, alone, to do without milk, (for it is all we have to make our food palatable). We conclude that we must submit to the dominion of paternity, and take the result.

July 4th. To-day the sun comes pouring down his floods of heat again. I can't step outside the cabin door without burning my feet. The prairie grass makes such wear and tear upon our shoe leather, that I am trying to save my own calf-skin shoes, for I see that they are being worn badly now, and I shall want them more when cold weather comes; so I go barefoot inside, and slip my feet into my rubbers when I go from the cabin.

July 6th. A hard thunder-storm was upon us this morning, which kept us in bed, in our damp bed, until about ten o-clock—that being the dryest place we could find. Everything was drenched with water; our fireplace was one complete mortar bed. I chanced to have a few chips up one side of our cabin that were dry; of these I made a fire in an old tin pan, strung a tea kettle on to the broom handle making one end fast between the logs of the cabin, while my husband held the other, and over that fire in the pan I made Graham pudding for our breakfast.

Mr. Adams came, milked the cow, fed the calf, and brought some water from the creek.

My husband feels cold and sick. I have been to Mr. Adams' for some ginger; my strength almost failed me on the way there and back, but he has got the ginger tea; hope he will feel better.

July 7th. Found no improvement in health this morning. Neighbor Adams came, loaded our trunks, bed, and few cooking utensils into our wagon, tied our cow behind, leaving the calf to frolic at its pleasure; we then seated ourselves inside and started for the Indian house. . . .

Father unloaded the wagon, I made up our bed on the floor in the east room. . . . A fire place in each room, no glass in the windows, but doors opening on to a piazza on the north side. This old dilapidated house, as rude as it is, is a palace to the rude cabin we have left.

I see by the dish of boiled greens on the rough, bench-like table in one corner, that father has been to the purslane beds at the wigwam ruins.

July 16th. . . . I have been writing to friends, sitting on the floor, with my portfolio on a cracker box for a writing desk. My husband is lying on our bed of prairie grass, on the floor; his fever is passing off. Willie lies on an Indian blanket near the door, calling for water. Mother lies on her bed in the other room; seems very sick. Father on a blanket, on the floor; his fever is raging. Lydia has got up and is sitting on her trunk; looks weak and sad. Mema's fever is off; she is out beside the house, amusing herself by picking up Indian beads that are washed up from the dirt, with the drippings from the eaves when it rains. Just three months to-day since we left home; mark the contrast!

Sickness, the loss of their oxen, and threats from the Indians convinced Miriam and William Colt that their stay in Kansas should end. William tried unsuccessfully to get part of their money back; when they left on September 2, they were nearly penniless. William's parents and his sister remained at the settlement and it was not until months later when Miriam finally reached New York that she received news of their deaths.

When the Colts left, they joined Mr. Wheeler, Mrs. Wells, and the teamster Henley for the long trip to St. Louis. From the beginning they were besieged with problems. Outside the Cherokee Indian lands in Missouri, Miriam noted: "The water is very bad here; a green scum covers the top of it; have made tea of it, and cooked rice in it; my husband and Mr. Wheeler drank the tea, and my darling children are so thirsty they must drink this water, that is so full of disease."

Henley began to drink and his behavior turned violent. One night he abandoned them, forcing Miriam to seek food at a nearby house where the family was just sitting down to supper: "I could hardly realize," she wrote, "that I was gazing upon the home comforts of chairs, tables, good beds . . . and plenty of good food. The good lady was just taking a loaf of wheat bread from a Dutch oven . . . the largest loaf of bread that I ever saw."

Miriam was concerned with her family's survival but the townspeople noticed only her mode of dress: "I should think that the good people of this little town never saw a woman dressed in the short dress before; I seem to attract much notice when I go for water; I have heard words from a shop near by . . . saying, 'O, God, look at her! Look at her!'" She had adopted the bloomer because, as she said, "[Fashion] and show hold so small a place in my mind, now that to please a few . . . [I would not submit myself to] wearing long dresses, when I can go so nimbly around in my short, loose, and easy dress, to bring water, pick up chips, bring in wood, milk . . . cook in the kitchen, wait upon the sick. . . ."

Their criticism soon turned to sympathy: Willie was violently ill with ague and diarrhea and, after crying out for "white bread, big apples and white corn," he died on September 24. William Colt died on October 3, leaving Miriam stranded. She sold her remaining possessions for gravestones and auctioned their trunks for traveling money. Sympathetic citizens helped her apply for the nearly two thousand dollars in insurance that her husband had left and helped arrange for her return to New York with Mema.

Miriam then purchased a five-acre tract of land but she lost it through foreclosure in 1861. In an effort to earn money to support herself and her daughter, she wrote Went to Kansas, *which was published in 1862.*

Miriam Colt later heard that emigration to Kansas "was coming in very fast" but today all that remains of that ill-fated settlement is the name Vegetarian given to a small creek that flows past the spot where the colony once lay.

A mother & her children, Oak Creek Canyon, Arizona, 1897.

The Harvey Andrews family at the grave of their nineteen-month-old-son Willie.

Woman bringing lunch to gold diggers in Auburn Ravine, Calif., 1852.

P. Britt,   Photographer,   Jacksonville, Oregon.

Sister Victor with Mollie Britt.

Sister Mary Catherine Cabareaux

Mary Catherine Cabareaux was born in Nimes, France, on September 6, 1813. Her family was religious, but her destiny was shaped by a monk who lived some years with the family after his monastery had been destroyed in the Revolution. He recognized Mary Catherine's early interest in the church, and read her scripture and Bible stories. She grew up with a craving for a life of prayer—which her parents first ignored, later tried to prevent, and ultimately conceded to.

In her early teens she had a vision of the Blessed Virgin, and also saw the face of the Reverend Mother St. Joseph, head of the Religious Order of the Sisters of Notre Dame de Namur. Catherine's great hope was to become a nun.

At nineteen she finally overcame her parent's objections and became a novice. Four years later, in 1839, the sisters decided to comply with repeated requests by Father Peter DeSmet that they travel to Oregon and establish a Catholic mission there. Mother Constantine selected seven nuns to sail to the mouth of the Columbia: Sisters Aloysia, Loyola, Albine, Cornelia, Norbertine, Reine, and Catherine—because she "stormed heaven" with her earnest request. Of the seven, only Sister Reine failed to complete the mission. She asked to be put ashore after the ship had remained in port for thirty days waiting for wind; the sailors' foul language was too much for her to bear. But the remaining six braved lack of food, rats so avaricious that they nearly devoured the hull of the ship and the taunts of the sailors as they finally made their way to the treacherous bar that guarded the mouth of the Columbia River.

We embarked on the 12th of December, the feast of our Lady of Guadalupe, patroness of Mexico, under whose government California then was. Our dear Mother Constantine accompanied us to the *Infatigable* and made a minute personal examination of our surroundings. This good mother urged us to keep united to God, who would always come to our help, if we had recourse to Him with confidence. These words seemed to take all fear from our timid hearts. We felt that our good Mother Constantine had sent us to labor for the conversion of the Indians, and not to become the food of worms.

After giving us a farewell blessing, our beloved mother entered a skiff and returned to the shore. We watched her as long as a speck of skiff could be seen, then realized we were with God alone.

Five priests and one lay-brother were our fellow passengers on *L'Infatigable*. Sister Mary Aloysia arranged the piano for an altar. When the weather permitted, we had five Masses daily. After breakfast we spent our time on deck, as we needed fresh air.

We studied English under the direction of Reverend Father DeSmet. I frequently brought them little delicacies with which our Good Mother Constantine had abundantly provided us. This obtained for me the name "Sister Providence." This office caused me much pain and anxiety, when my efforts to benefit the [priests and nuns who were ill] were not successful, I often begged God to prolong their lives until we reached Oregon.

Our sleeping accommodations and food coincided with the sea sickness. As for me, while going to table I said interiorly,

"Courage my soul, let us mortify Brother Ass, who loves his ease so much." Yet for a mortified soul my meal would have been a delicious banquet. There was not room to place two chairs in our cabins. Four Sisters slept in two beds. One was so narrow, I went out quickly in order to relieve my companions. I took a mattress and slept on the floor. It was then that another kind of mortification [*a form of penance resulting from discomfort or abstinence*] had to be undergone. Big rats made a procession over my body, from head to foot. To prevent their injuring me I wrapped myself up in blankets, and when I felt them on my body, I began to move so as to scare them. Our two Sisters Superior Mary Loyola and Mary Cornelia laughed more than once at this comedy. . . .

When we embarked on the vessel Father DeSmet purchased a goat to furnish milk for our coffee. It took two to milk her: one to hold the horns, the other to milk. I went every day to help Sister Norbertine to accomplish this feat.

As we approached the desired port our zeal was increased and we doubled our prayers to obtain from Heaven the assistance that could not be obtained from navigation. An unfavorable wind blew us backward, instead of onward. Finally the Captain, who was in the last stages of consumption, told his anxiety to Father DeSmet, who shared the Captain's fears without communicating them to us, [and] urged us to pray fervently for a successful crossing of the Bar.

The failing health of our Captain, together with his sordid look of anxiety made us realize that we were in a perilous position. What could we do but [beg] "Mercy! Mercy!"

During the first days of July a ray of hope dawned upon us; the coast of California came in sight and we knew the mouth of the Columbia could not be far distant. . . . During the night a contrary wind blew us in an opposite direction from the much desired port. We were discouraged in soul and body. . . . The Captain became discouraged, he could not sleep, so remained seated, then it was one of the sailors dared to tell him that he was too good to risk his entire crew for a few _____ [*Sister Mary Catherine chose not to share this word*]. "If I were in your place I'd drop them all in the ocean, then go direct to Manila."

Someone who heard the conversation went immediately to inform the Fathers, [and] this only increased their anxiety. . . . After dinner, fresh trouble arose, and the Captain proposed leaving us in California. This did not suit us at all . . . we prayed again.

The Mate then proposed taking a skiff and examining the terrible bar to find a safe way of entering. The Captain consented to this, and five sailors started on an exploring trip. Next morning the sailors returned, saying the entrance to the river was not so dangerous as first imagined. The truth was, they dared not go as far as the Bar, owing to the dangerous reefs which would have sunk their little skiff.

The manner that the sailors performed their work made us realize that the solemn moment was at hand . . . we heard the sailors who were sounding the Bar shout:

"Three fathoms of water only." And the hull of our vessel had only four feet of water, Oh! we are in great danger!

Then our courage was renewed on hearing the cry of, "Eighteen feet!" This was followed by the announcement made in a frightened tone:

"Only two and a half fathoms!"

When they uttered this depressing announcement we were resigned to the worst. The joyful cry "five fathoms!" reanimated the crew. The vessel had passed the most dangerous place; we were then on the Columbia River.

"Te Deum" came from the voice of Sister Superior. "Te Deum."

Then the Indians surrounded our vessel, anxious to get sight of us. I looked at them with compassion, their miserable appearance only enabled me to value all the more their souls. I felt happy in being able to contribute to their salvation. As our vessel ascended the river, crowds of them came on board. Owing to their unfamiliar language, we kept silence, but tried to conciliate their favor by giving them pictures and what remained of the delicacies sent up while in Antwerp by our dear Mother Constantine. . . .

When we arrived at Oregon City, we were obliged to cross the falls between forty and eighty feet high. We were obliged to get out of the skiff and walk along the mountains, while our boatman dragged the skiff across the sandy shore, and replaced it in the river when the falls no longer impeded its progress. While awaiting the skiff I enjoyed myself contemplating the immensity of these falls. The rocks which formed them are apparently indestructable. . . .

[In Oregon City] we were invited to visit the church. The badly constructed altar was covered with very clean linen. . . . We scrubbed the floor before we adorned the sanctuary, then placed in it a statue of the Blessed Virgin which we ornamented with flowers gathered from the woods.

It was very encouraging to see how the good people appreciated all this. They could not find words to express all their gratitude, they spoke by signs, as we did not understand Chinouk. When we returned, we began preparing mattresses for the night, but what dirt and vermin! We intended scrubbing the room the next day; that night no one could sleep. As for myself, I felt so happy that emotion kept me awake more than the visits of these insects. The next day the floor was scrubbed. This was most fortunate, as the doctor was called to visit two sisters who were ill. We had only one apartment for our use.

Father Blanchet had already announced to the parishioners that the sisters would teach catechism and prepare the women and children for their first communion, so we had to begin work at once. Sister Mary Cornelia and myself were the first to make the effort. The half Canadians were my portion. About twenty understood French, [which] I spoke simply to them. Nearly all were married and brought their babes with them.

Sister Mary Cornelia had the best portion, which consisted of about a dozen old Indian women who did not know a word of French, yet were requested to know their prayers in that language. Imagine, then, what a painful task for pupils as well as teachers!

Meanwhile, we received the remainder of our baggage. We found among them all the soiled clothes that had been used since leaving Valparaiso. I was the only one to do the washing. The clothes were black with dirt and I had never washed. What was I to do?

As we had brought a boiler with us, I asked an Indian on the place to heat the water for me, he placed it against a fallen tree and so filled it. I was obliged to go down into a ravine and fill two buckets at a time. . . . I summoned up all my courage and commenced by putting the clothes to soak while I gave instructions to my good women. Then I began to wash, trying my best to restore the clothes to their original whiteness, but I failed, and being somewhat discouraged, I went to our good Sister Norbertine, who although quite ill, gave me directions how to succeed.

When I told her I put soap on the same articles five times without success, she answered, that I could have made the clothes white without soap. This did not help me any, besides, I was very tired and somewhat discouraged at the sight of the pile of soiled clothes still to be washed.

But my prayers had not been in vain. After my instructions to my young women, several . . . followed me to my tubs and helped me with all their hearts until dinner hour, and wanted to continue working until the washing was finished.

The hardest for my poor nature was the want of water, and the distance to procure sufficient water to restore the primitive whiteness of our clothes. When all was nearly finished, Rev. Father Blanchet, who came to give the women instructions in Chinouk, saw . . . the boiler with the fire under, and he asked who was washing. The women hastened to answer in compassionate tones that it was Sister Mary. He turned to me, saying "Oh! my poor Sister, have you come so far to do this kind of work!"

During the evenings when we were together, we ironed the clothes and mended those belonging to the Rev. Fathers as well as our own. Our two sisters . . . soon recovered, and we were able to move into the house being built for us . . .

Sister Mary Aloysia began painting, and I placed the panes of glass in their place in the frames. Then as I was the most robust of the sisters, I took the saw and hammer to open our numerous boxes which contained all our clothes, library and kitchen utensils. . . .

Exteriorly our convent had the appearance of a grand residence, but was nevertheless a mere shed, consisting of several rafters supported by beams covered with boards between which were open spaces.

The roof was covered with shingles, a number of them were split before being placed so that from the dormitories the stars could be seen and the rain saturated our [students] during the night. In order to remove this inconvenience we went into the forest to gather moss to stop up these openings. The planks in the floor were not nailed and at every step taken, the boards would move under our feet. A partition was placed in the dormitory to make a private apartment for the Sisters, but the planks were so poor everything could be seen from one room to another.

The cold weather was very severe on us as we had no chimney. We had only one stove to heat the whole house; it was placed between the school rooms and the refectory. The pipe went through the top of the building. A kind of shed had been built at the corner of the house which served as a kitchen. It was ten feet square, the door faced the Sisters' Refectory, and during the intense cold we went there to warm our benumbed hands.

The house was situated in the middle of thirty to forty barren acres. The wind, rain and cold supplied us with matter for mortification. A well was dug not far from the kitchen. When we washed there was no place to warm water. A boy, a half negro, placed the boiler on four supports in the middle of the yard. I made a fire under it, but the wind blew so violently that the flames went in every direction but the right one and the water remained cold.

I shivered in this severe temperature.

In December we began receiving boarders, but their destitution was perfect. A few rags in a box, a mat of rushes, a small pillow of moss, a pair of woolen blankets, formed their trousseau.

The first time Sister Mary Aloysia and myself conducted them to the dormitory, we assigned the places to put the beds. They remained standing, not knowing what to do. After saying night prayers, they fixed their mats and pillows, wrapped themselves in their blankets and stretched themselves full length upon the floor. "Oh" exclaimed Sister Aloysia, looking at them: "This resembles a graveyard!"

She left me in surveillance, saying as she left, "What a beautiful subject for the meditation on death!"

On the first story of the house were three comfortable, spacious rooms, sufficient for the number of sisters and pupils. A smaller room was used for a parlor, and one of the same size served as our refectory. Partitions were made of brick and dried in the sun. Clay was placed between them.

It was curious to see the number of open spaces in that kind of a wall. It was not necessary to have a door to see in the adjoining room, and cold and wind always found a free passage. During the first two years we employed one of the rooms as a chapel, having only rough and inconvenient benches, but as the Divine Master was to dwell in it, His presence made us enjoy ineffable sweetness.

During Holy Week [Father de Vos] was our confessor, and directed the first retreat in our poor Chapel. I could not keep my mind fixed on any subject, I was not mistress of my heart. As soon as I had placed myself in the presence of God, I felt so absorbed and penetrated with such sentiments of affection, that the hour of meditation seemed too short for me to enjoy them, so I could not follow the conditions described by St. Ignatius [*which were a prescribed series of prayers used by the Sisters of Notre Dame de Namur*].

When I recited my rosary I was lost in contemplating the mysteries, that is to say, it was difficult for me to vocalize my Ave Marias. I did not know what to say to make myself understood. My heart seemed swimming in consolation, that was all I could say.

My worthy Superior, seeing my numerous infidelities to grace in my intercourse with the sisters and pupils, became alarmed, I think, and told me that I must follow the ordinary exercise prescribed for the spirit . . . that I was still so green and so novice in the practice of virtue, that perhaps the evil one had a hand in it, that the safest way for me was to follow the most ordinary way.

I made attempts to comply with her desires, but after making efforts to follow the subject of meditation . . . the entire hour was spent in conflict with my poor soul.

We had been in our house without making a retreat, and as Rev. Father De Smet had come from the mountains, he complied with the request and heard our confession.

His manner of giving the exercises inspired us with confidence, so I resolved to make known my difficulties to him, regarding my meditation and the advice given me. This charitable Father consoled me a great deal, through the wise reflections he made, recommending me at the same time to be submissive to the decisions of my Superior, to prepare carefully for meditation, then to abandon myself in perfect simplicity to the movements of grace my Divine Master bestows upon me, and allow Him to govern my heart.

All this greatly encouraged me, and put my conscience at ease. I made efforts to better resist myself, fearing that I had not obeyed my Superior though I had tried my best to do so.

I imagined my Superior watched me very closely. Being only six sisters, it was very easy for her to do so, particularly in our little Chapel, where we knelt on the planks, having only ordinary benches made with an axe and without support. . . .

I was exceedingly careful to carry out, as far as possible, the intentions of my Superior. I must say the truth, and acknowledge that it was very painful for me to spend the time of my meditation in combatting, as it were, instead of allowing my soul to be absorbed in the presence of my well-beloved Master.

During the day, I had continual struggles with so many distractions, occasioned by the various dispositions of these children, without principles, lazy to the extreme, only seeking to gratify nature, always ready to play, eat and sleep. Nevertheless, good Christians must be made of them and it was not without labor.

When I wanted to obtain anything from them I was obliged to promise as a reward either something to eat, or some amusement, so that I was always plunged into material matter.

The great drawback in the beginning was our ignorance of their dialect, for I frequently remarked that a word accompanied by signs was sufficient to communicate in my presence what they would not dare say, if they thought I could understand. In such cases, I had recourse to the Divine Master, begging of Him to remedy this evil I could not prevent. In a short time I was able to prevent the snares laid across the path of these poor children.

By degrees they were forbidden to speak Chinouk. They could read French and study the catechism so that they learned how to correct their perverse inclinations. While our dear Sister Superior directed the outside work, Sister Mary Aloysia directed the entire painting, etc. It was pleasant to meet her with hammer and chisel in hand. As to the saw, that instrument was reserved for me, for I had more strength. Besides, I loved to use the saw in preparing wood for our French stove which we had brought from Namur, also for the stoves used in the school rooms, which we made red hot in order to warm our poor children so badly clad and shod. The want of shoes and stockings brought on chillblains, which caused the poor children much suffering. . . .

The children's dormitory was confided to my care. The children slept on mats wrapped in blankets. I had something which resembled their beds; it consisted of four planks nailed to four posts, two poor planks on which our mattress rested. There were curtains, but . . . a feast of mortifications was not wanting.

After the children had risen in the morning, we began to hunt vermin. These children had long, coarse hair, and very thick, so that it was impossible for the sister to make the comb reach the scalp of the head. The consequence was that these poor children were devoured by vermin, and the constant scratching produced sores. Sister Mary Albine and myself were obliged to take them aside during the day and extricate vermin from these disgusting sores. I armed myself with courage and a long needle and more than once I was obliged to take off my bandeau and relieve my poor head of these intruders.

In the course of time a kitchen was added and two cellars were made. The kitchen and bakery were under the same roof, a boiler had been placed against the oven of the bakery, and was so convenient to heat water on wash days that I felt amply repaid for all my previous trouble.

We had to make our own bread, and Sister Superior gave me the charge, explaining how to make it as well as she could. I prepared the yeast and did my best to make it succeed, but having no idea of the required proportions, the bread was very heavy. Ah! how sorry I was that the poor Sisters had no other bread to eat for three days. At last a friend told Sister Superior how to make the bread light; one of the ways was to work the dough during half an hour.

Sister Mary Albine and I got up at 4 o'clock in order to perform this exercise, we were so animated over it, that we were heard at a great distance. We did this hoping to succeed, but with what result? The dough had become so cold, it could not rise, and after two hours work it became sour and the oven cold, when the time came to draw it from the oven, oh! horrors! the dough was rather brick than bread. My consolation was that I knew nothing of household work. I had acted on the advice my Superior had given me. I hoped God had not been affected by my awkwardness.

Among our children one needed the severist punishment that could be inflicted, which was the rod. Sister Superior ordered me to perform this act, for the benefit of the child. I took her into a small room where there were several chairs, taking a very serious tone, I reproached her with obliging me to perform a duty that was so painful to my heart. Then I gave her a few strokes on the back and hands and a few harder on her dress, then many harder on the chairs and wall. She was very much frightened to see herself thus flagellated by one who had always taken so much interest in her on all occasions.

Our kitchen being very small, and the [water] closets being very close to it, we were obliged to remove them, particularly so as the odor was becoming very disagreeable. Sister Superior asked a man, whose child she had taken through charity as a boarder, to empty the sink [latrine] for us; he began to do so, then came to me asking for a little whiskey as he was sick and unable to continue the job. Sister Superior told him we had no liquor in the house, but thanked him for what he had done, telling him that he could go home. But what were we to do? The place could not be left exposed in that manner.

Sister Norbertine had fortunately taken the precaution to dig ditches along the vegetables in the garden, so she said if I would assist her, she could manage to hitch the horse to our little wagon, on which we could place two barrels, and empty in them the buckets I would fill from the sink. On representing our plan to Sister Superior, she approved it.

But this operation could only be accomplished during the night. We were only six sisters and it was necessary that one at least should remain in surveillance with the children, since the intended operation was to be performed during the night by moonlight.

The following plan was then carried out. Sister Superior remained in the kitchen to prepare coffee for us. Sister Mary Cornelia watched the children in the dormitory, while the rest of us clothed ourselves with all we had that could be burnt. Afterwards Sister Mary Albine stood near the hole and by means of a utensil with a long handle dipped its contents into a bucket which Sister Mary Aloysia brought to the wagon upon which stood Sister Norbertine by a barrel.

I emptied the bucket into the barrel, while doing so, I spilt it all over me. Our dear old Sister, laughing, said "Cologne water!" Long after, Sister Mary Cornelia and Mary Aloysia repeated in song, "Heaven will be the reward. . . ." Finally, when the barrels were filled, I led our blind horse to the ditches. Sister Norbertine stood between the two barrels, which she carefully covered to avoid losing any of the precious "Cologne water."

It was nearly two o'clock when we finished emptying the hole. We then went to the well and made use of as much water as possible to get rid of an odor so disagreeable even to "Madame Nature." We threw away our rags and resumed our night clothes. The perfume had reached the brain, so it required time and patience to get rid of it.

The poor horse did nothing but sneeze.

The Sisters who were not of the party could hardly remain near us in the Chapel and Refectory. . . . Well, for us the affair was ended, and our good Sister Norbertine took three of our strongest pupils to help her cover all that we had emptied during the night. . . .

The necessities of the first years had obliged us to learn the use of the scythe. Urgent necessity inspired our intrepid Sister Superior to propose our gathering in the harvest ourselves. We accepted the proposal!

Another inconvenience we had to suffer from was want of wood for our kitchen. We were obliged to gather up all the stumps, and chips around the neighborhood. But to make these stumps and sticks fit in our stoves we were compelled to use the saw. During my walks with the children in the forest, I noticed broken branches of trees, which I thought would make excellent firewood. I asked Sister Superior's permission to take our horse and wagon to lay in a supply of wood. She smilingly granted my request.

Taking two strong children . . . I started, not remembering there was only a path, and that a wagon going through would tempt providence as it would either upset or get broken. I paid no attention to all these obstacles, all I wanted was to fill my wagon with these stumps, but after doing so, thought we could never leave the forest. I told the children to invoke the holy angels instead of crying "Wah! Wah!"

Finally we got out of the forest. Proud of the success of our expedition, we unloaded our wagon near the kitchen.

Sister Norbertine was our cook, besides which she had charge of the poultry yard, the garden, the orchard and the making of the butter and cheese from the milk of eight cows. The poor sister had so much to do with all this that she frequently forgot about dinner. A number of times the half past eleven bell would ring, and the good sister, surprised at its being so late, would hurry to put the potatoes on the fire.

She always had salt meat cooked two or three days ahead, our soup was a bowl of milk and our dessert, a piece of home made cheese. When Sister Superior saw this repeated too often, she took upon herself the chore of cooking. This was very painful to us. I proposed to Sister Mary Cornelia and Mary Aloysia to take the little girls, and I would relieve our good Sister Superior from the kitchen, so that she would be free to perform her legitimate charge. . . .

Donning a large apron, I was ready for my new office. This made the Sisters laugh. I applied to Sister Superior for information regarding the proportions of salt, pepper and butter required. With great patience and charity she complied with my request. Having no idea how to season anything, I made many mistakes, and caused many a mortification to my sisters.

Not having the little ones to distract me from my interior recollection, I closed the door of the kitchen, and entertained myself with my good Master. Although my heart had suffered from the obligation of resisting these loving impulses, all at once my soul became absorbed and inundated in consolation. My tears flowed and I felt all inflamed with love. At the moment I least expected it, Sister Superior entered the kitchen, seeing my face very red, she asked what was the matter. I quickly answered, "Nothing. Sister Superior, the butterflies are flying around!" and I began to laugh.

Sister Superior, assuming a very serious tone, said "Oh! at your grimaces again!"

We had a very laborious life, but in 1847 the hope of assistance sustained the courage of every one. It was then that my poor Sister Superior said to me frequently, "Oh, how glad I shall be to have you replaced!" I imagined then that I would have considerable more time for my spiritual exercises which I had been so often obliged to sacrifice.

Finally, seven Sisters came to us on the feast of the Holy Heart of Mary. What thanksgiving was ours! The first charge that Sister Superior gave was that of cook, so Sister Norbertine and myself were permanently discharged from that office. This came most a propos, as our garden needed great care.

In order to economize on the coffee we had brought from Europe, Sister Superior had chicory planted. This plant would thrive near any weeds, so we were obliged to spend hours with our pupils, pulling up these weeds. When ripe, we had to dry it, then grind it in the coffee mill. . . . What time spent to save three bales of coffee, which were snatched from us in one hour by fire on January 29th. This chicory cost us many a sacrifice, particularly to Sister Mary Cornelia, who felt that her pupils stood more in need of their schooling than weeding.

Besides this, I commenced to make paths around the grounds. With Sister Aldegondis' assistance we cut six hundred feet of shrub, two feet wide, all with spade and hoe. Such exercise was very painful to those who had never used these kinds of instruments.

I forgot to mention that we were so annoyed with bed bugs.

We made a mixture of potassium and soap, and with a great quantity of water we succeeded in destroying millions of eggs, but not all the insects. You should have seen us after this operation!

The Sisters obtained weaving frames, leather, linen, tools, and other supplies from Europe in their efforts to improve their Mission. They continued to recruit boarders for the school, but a fire in 1849 destroyed the buildings and the nuns lost everything. That disaster, coupled with the loss of many of their male parishioners who joined the rush to California after gold, ultimately defeated them in their efforts to reconstruct their Mission.

In 1850, an epidemic killed eleven of their children and left the nuns, including Mary Catherine, feverish and weak. After her convalescence she experienced a vision of a "little chain of mountains" lying next to a fertile valley. When she later accompanied Sister Loyola to San Francisco to greet an entourage of Belgian nuns, they were persuaded by Bishop Alemany to visit the countryside, where he hoped they would establish a Mission. Near San Jose, which was then a village of eight hundred people, Sister Mary Catherine was startled to observe a chain of small mountains like those in her vision. The Sisters set about obtaining contributions from the farmers, most of whom were lapsed Catholics, in the hope that they would be persuaded to send their children to the nuns' future school. They decided to close the houses in Oregon and in 1853 the Oregon Mission of the Sisters of Notre Dame de Namur was closed forever.

Sister Mary Catherine worked for the order in San Jose as chief bookkeeper, a position that she held even after undergoing surgery for cataracts. The remaining chapters of her journal—written after the move to San Jose—reveal that she paid greater attention to her duties at the Mission and less to her revelatory prayer experience.

She died on November 17, 1903, after serving the order for seventy-one years. As she said in her journal: "I devoted myself to everything that presented itself, either in the garden or housework, having always been a bouche-trous [jack of all trades], I continued in this capacity with all my heart!"

Havasupai pupils in Arizona, 1903.

Hoopa Indian Reservation, ca. 1896.

Indians on Colville Reservation, Washington.

Unidentified Indians, probably in the Dakotas.

Two Presbyterian missionaires visiting an aged Apache woman, Andarko, Oklahoma Territory.

Sarah Winnemucca

Sarah Winnemucca was born in 1844, the grandaughter of Chief Truckee and member of a nomadic tribe of Paiutes who roamed the deserts of northern Nevada. She lived to see nearly half her family die while her tribe was herded from one reservation to another—first to the Pyramid Lake Agency, then to the Malheur Indian Reservation in Oregon, and finally to Yakima. Because she had lived briefly with a trader's family, her command of English was good and she became a translator for the U.S. Army.

Her work for the Army eventually brought her much recognition. She was called a heroine for her part in bringing about the end of the Bannock Uprising, and her lectures were well attended and well publicized by Eastern liberals, who were eager to hear of the injustices done to her tribe. Despite her popularity with whites, she never lived long apart from her tribe. If they suffered, she suffered. When they went hungry, she did also.

Her life was given over to helping her people. One result of this effort is her book, Life Among the Piutes. *[The name of the Paiute tribe was spelled "Piute" during Sarah's time.] She was given editorial help on the book by a staunch supporter and friend, Mrs. Horace Mann. It is from this work that the following pages are taken.*

I was born somewhere near 1844, but am not sure of the precise time. I was a very small child when the first white people came into our country. They came like a lion, yes, like a roaring lion, and have continued so ever since, and I have never forgotten their first coming.

My people were scattered at that time over nearly all the territory now known as Nevada. My grandfather was chief of the entire Piute nation, and was camped near Humboldt Lake, with a small portion of his tribe, when a party travelling eastward from California was seen coming. When the news was brought to my grandfather, he asked what they looked like? When told that they had hair on their faces, and were white, he jumped up and clasped his hands together, and cried aloud:

"My white brothers—my long-looked-for white brothers have come at last. . . !"

The next year came a great [pioneer] emigration, and camped near Humboldt Lake. . . . During their stay my grandfather and some of his people called upon them, and they all shook hands, and when our white brothers were going away they gave my grandfather a white tin plate—it was so bright. They say that after they left, my grandfather called for all his people to come together, and he then showed them the beautiful gift which he had received from his white brothers. Everybody was so pleased; nothing like it was ever seen in our country before. My grandfather thought so much of it that he bored holes in it and fastened it on his head, and wore it as a hat. He held it in as much admiration as my white sisters hold their diamond rings or a sealskin jacket. . . .

The third year more emigrants came, and that summer Captain Fremont (who is not General Frémont) . . . gave my grandfather the name of Captain Truckee, and he also called the river after him. Truckee is an Indian word; it means "all right," or "very well." A party of twelve of my people went to California with Captain Fremont. I do not know just how long they were gone. . . .

That same fall, very late, the emigrants kept coming. It was this time that our white brothers first came amongst us. They could not get over the mountains, so they had to live with us. It was on Carson River, where the great Carson City now stands. You call my people bloodseeking. My people did not seek to kill them, nor did they steal their horses—no, no, far from it. During the winter my people helped them. They gave them such as they had to eat. They did not hold out their hands and say: "You can't have anything to eat unless you pay me." No—no such word was used by us savages at that time. . . .

The following spring, before my grandfather returned home, there was a great excitement among my people on account of fearful news coming from different tribes . . . there was a fearful story they told us children. Our mothers told us that the whites were killing everybody and eating them. So we were all afraid of them. Every dust that we could see blowing in the valleys we would say it was the white people. In the late fall my father told his people to go to the rivers and fish, and we all went to Humboldt River, and the women went to work gathering wild seed, which they grind between the rocks. The stones are round, big enough to hold in the hands. The women did this when they got back, and when they had gathered all they could they put it in one place and covered it with grass, and then over the grass, mud. After it is covered it looks like an Indian wigwam.

What a fright we all got one morning to hear some white people were coming. Every one ran as best they could. . . . My aunt overtook us, and she said to my mother: "Let us bury our girls, or we shall all be killed and eaten up." So they went to work and buried us, and told us if we heard any noise not to cry out, for if we did they would surely kill us and eat us. So our mothers buried me and my cousin, planted sage bushes over our faces to keep the sun from burning them, and there we were left all day.

Can any one imagine my feelings buried alive, thinking every minute that I was to be unburied and eaten up by the people that my grandfather loved so much? With my heart throbbing, and not daring to breathe, we lay there all day. It seemed that the night would never come. . . . At last we heard some whispering. We did not dare to whisper to each other, so we lay still. I could hear their footsteps coming nearer and nearer. I thought my heart was coming right out of my mouth. Then I heard my mother say, "T'is right here!" Oh, can any one in this world ever imagine what were my feelings when I was dug up by my poor mother and father . . . ?

Well, while we were in the mountains hiding, the people that my grandfather called our white brothers came along to where our winter supplies were. They set everything we had left on fire. It was a fearful sight. It was all we had for the winter, and it was all burnt during that night. My father took some of his men during the night to try and save some of it, but they could not; it had burnt down before they got there.

Those were the last white men that came along that fall. My people talked fearfully that winter about those they called our white brothers. . . . This whole band of white people [undoubtedly the Donner Party] perished in the mountains, for it was too late to cross them. We could have saved them, only my people were afraid of them. We never knew who they were, or where they came from. So, poor things, they must have suffered fearfully, for they all starved there. The snow was too deep. . . .

We remained there all winter; the next spring emigrants came as usual, and my father and grandfather and uncles, and many more went down the Humboldt River on fishing excursions. While they were thus fishing, their white brothers came upon them and fired on them, and killed one of my uncles, and wounded another. Nine more were wounded, and five died afterwards. My other uncle got well again, and is living yet. Oh, that was a fearful thing, indeed. . . . The widow of my uncle who was killed, and my mother and father all had long hair. They cut off their hair, and also cut long gashes in their arms and legs, and they were all bleeding as if they would die with the loss of blood. This continued for several days, for this is the way we mourn for our dead. When the woman's husband dies, she is first to cut off her hair, and then she braids it and puts it across her breast; then his mother and sisters, his fathers and brothers and all his kinfolk cut their hair. The widow is to remain unmarried until her hair is the same length as before, and her face is not to be washed all that time, and she is to use no kind of paint, nor to make any merriment with other women until the day is set for her to do so by her father-in-law and by her mother-in-law, and then she is at liberty to go where she pleases. The widower is at liberty when his wife dies; but he mourns for her in the same way, by cutting his hair off. . . .

Our children are very carefully taught to be good. Their parents tell them stories, traditions of old times, even of the first mother of the human race; and love stories, stories of giants, and fables; and when they ask if these last stories are true, they answer, "Oh, it is only coyote," which means that they are make-believe stories. Coyote is the name of a mean, crafty little animal, half wolf, half dog, and stands for everything low. It is the greatest term of reproach one Indian has for another. Indians do not swear—they have no words for swearing till they learn them of white men. The worst they call each other is "bad" or "coyote," but they are very sincere with one another, and if they think each other in the wrong, they say so.

We are taught to love everybody. We don't need to be taught to love our fathers and mothers. We love them without being told to. Our tenth cousin is as near to us as our first cousin, and we don't marry into our relations. Our young women are not allowed to talk to any young man that is not their cousin, except at the festive dances, when both are dressed in their best clothes, adorned with beads, feathers or shells, and stand alternately in the ring and take hold of hands. These are very pleasant occasions to all the young people. . . .

My people have been so unhappy for a long time they wish now to disincrease, instead of multiply. The mothers are afraid to have more children, for fear they shall have daughters, who are not safe even in their mother's presence.

The grandmothers have the special care of the daughters just before and after they come to womanhood. The girls are not allowed to get married until they have come to womanhood; and that period is recognized as a very sacred thing, and is the subject of a festival, and has peculiar customs. The young woman is set apart under the care of two of her friends, somewhat older, and a little wigwam, called a teepee, just big enough for the three, is made for them, to which they retire. She goes through certain labors which are thought to be strengthening, and these last twenty-five days.

Every day, three times a day, she must gather, and pile up as high as she can, five stacks of wood. This makes fifteen stacks a day. At the end of every five days the attendants take her to a river to bathe. She fasts from all flesh-meat during these twenty-five days, and continues to do this for five days in every month all her life. At the end of twenty-five days she returns to the family lodge, and gives all her clothing to her attendants in payment for their care. Sometimes the wardrobe is quite extensive.

It is thus publicly known that there is another marriageable woman, and any young man interested in her, or wishing to form an alliance, comes forward. But the courting is very different from the courting of the white people. He never speaks to her, or visits the family, but endeavors to attract her attention by showing his horsemanship, etc. As he knows that she sleeps next to her grandmother, in the lodge, he enters in full dress after the family has retired for the night, and seats himself at her feet. If she is not awake, the grandmother wakes her. He does not speak to either young woman or grandmother, but when the young woman wishes him to go away, she rises and goes and lies down by the side of her mother. He then leaves as silently as he came in.

This goes on sometimes for a year or longer, if the young woman has not made up her mind. She is never forced by her parents to marry against her wishes. When she knows her own mind, she makes a confidant of her grandmother, and then the young man is summoned by the father of the girl, who asks him in her presence, if he really loves his daughter, and reminds him, if he says he does, of all the duties of a husband. He then asks his daughter the same question, and sets before her minutely all her duties. And these duties are not slight.

She is to dress the game, prepare the food, clean the buckskins, make his moccasins, dress his hair, bring all the wood—in short, do all the household work. She promises to "be himself," and she fulfills her promise. . . . [*This meant that the women promised their fathers to make their husbands "themselves."*] They faithfully keep with them in all the dangers they can share. They not only take care of the children together, but they do everything together; and when they grow blind, which, I am sorry to say is very common, for the smoke they live in destroys their eyes at last, they take sweet care of one another. Marriage is a sweet thing when people love each other.

At the wedding feast, all the food is prepared in baskets. The young woman sits by the young man, and hands him the basket of food prepared for him with her own hands. He does not take it with his right hand; but seizes her wrist, and takes it with the left hand. This constitutes the marriage ceremony, and the father pronounces them man and wife. They go to a wigwam of their own, where they live till the first child is born. This event also is celebrated. Both father and mother fast from all flesh, and the father goes through the labor of piling the wood for twenty-five days, and assumes all his wife's household work during that time.

If he does not do his part in the care of the child, he is considered an outcast. Every five days his child's basket is changed for a new one, and the five are all carefully put away at the end of the days, the last one containing the navel-string, carefully wrapped up, and all are put up into a tree, and the child put into a new and ornamented basket. All this respect shown to the mother and child makes the parents feel their responsibility, and makes the tie between parents and children very strong.

The young mothers often get together and exchange their experiences about the attentions of their husbands; and inquire of each other if the fathers did their duty to their children, and were careful of their wives' health. When they are married they give away all the clothing they have . . . and dress themselves anew. . . .

My people teach their children never to make fun of anyone, no matter how they look. If you see your brother or sister doing something wrong, look away, or go away from them. If you make fun of bad persons, you make yourself beneath them. Be kind to all, both poor and rich, and feed all that come to your wigwam, and your name can be spoken of by every one far and near. In this way you will make many friends for yourself. Be kind both to bad and good, for you don't know your own heart. This is the way my people teach their children. It was handed down from father to son for many generations. I never in my life saw our children rude as I have seen white children and grown people in the streets. . . .

My people capture antelopes by charming them, but only some of the people are charmers. My father was one of them, and once I went with him on an antelope hunt.

The antelopes move in herds in the winter, and as late in the spring as April. My father . . . chose two men, who he said were to be his messengers to the antelopes. They were to have two large torches made of sage-brush bark, and after he had found a place for his camp, he marked out a circle around which the wigwams were to be placed, putting his own in the middle of the western side, and leaving an opening [in] the eastern side, which was towards the antelopes. . . .

The women and boys and old men who were in the camp, and who were working on the mounds, were told to be very careful not to drop anything and not to stumble over a sage-brush root, or a stone, or anything and not to have any accident, but to do everything perfectly and to keep thinking about the antelopes all the time, and not to let their thoughts go away to anything else. It took five days to charm the antelopes, and if anybody had an accident he must tell of it.

Every morning early . . . the people sat around the opening to the circle, with my father sitting in the middle of the opening, and my father lighted his pipe and passed it to his right, and the pipe went round the circle five times. And at night they did the same thing.

After they had smoked the pipe, my father took a kind of drum, which is used in this charming, and made music with it. This is the only kind of musical instrument which my people have, and it is only used for antelope charming. It is made of a hide of some large animal, stuffed with grass, so as to make it sound hollow. [Then] the two men who were messengers went out to see the antelopes. They carried their torches in their right hands, and one of them carried a pipe in his left hand. . . . This was done every day for five days, and after the first day all the men and women and boys followed the messengers, and went around the circle they were to enter. On the fifth day the antelopes were charmed, and the whole herd followed the tracks of my people and entered the circle where the mounds were, coming in at the entrance, bowing and tossing their heads, and looking sleepy under a powerful spell. They ran round and round inside the circle just as if there was a fence all around it and they could not get out, and they stayed there until my people had killed every one. But if anybody had dropped anything, or had stumbled and had not told about it, then when the antelopes came to the place where he had done that, they threw off the spell and rushed wildly out of the circle at that place.

When Captain Truckee, Sarah's grandfather, died, his last request was that his grandchildren, three little girls and two boys, be sent to the mission school in San Jose which was established by Mary Catherine and the other Sisters of Notre Dame de Namur. They arrived in the spring of 1860, only to depart several weeks later after many complaints from outraged white parents. These Spanish Californians had gone to much trouble to separate their children from the Indians who lived near the San Jose mission, and had no desire to board their children with five Indians from Nevada.

In that same year Pyramid Lake Reservation was given to the Paiutes, with the stipulation that they would regularly receive government "issue"—supplies, such as clothes, dry goods, and farm implements. Sarah wrote that "though there were thirteen agents there in the course of twenty-three years, I never knew of any issue after that first year."

The reservation, in her memory, was at first "sixty miles long and fifteen wide. The line is where the railroad now crosses the river, and it takes in two beautiful lakes, one called Pyramid Lake, and the one on the eastern side, Muddy Lake. We Piutes have always lived there on the river, because of those two lakes we caught beautiful mountain trout, weighing from two to twenty-five pounds each, which would give us a good income if we had it all, as at first. Since the railroad ran through in 1867, the white people have taken all the best parts of the reservation from us, and one of the lakes, also."

The first work that my people did on the reservation was to dig a ditch, to put up a grist-mill and a saw-mill. . . . They dug about a mile; but the saw-mill and the grist-mill were never seen or heard of by my people, though the printed report in the United States Statutes, which my husband found lately in the Boston Athenaeum, says twenty-five thousand dollars was appropriated to build them. Where did it go? The report says these mills were sold for the benefit of the Indians who were to be paid in lumber for houses, but no stick of lumber have they ever received. My people do not own any timber land now. The white people are using the ditch which my people made to irrigate their land. This is the way we are treated by our white brothers. Is it that the government is cheated by its own agents who make these reports?

In 1864–65 there . . . were no whites living on the reservation . . . and there was not any agent as yet. My people were living there and fishing, as they had always done. In 1865 we had . . . trouble with our white brothers. It was early in the Spring, and we were then living at Dayton, Nevada, when a company of soldiers came through the place and stopped and spoke to some of my people, and said, "You have been stealing cattle from the white people at Harney Lake." They said also that they would kill every-

thing that came in their way, men, women and children. . . . The days after they left were very sad hours, indeed. . . . These soldiers had gone only sixty miles away to Muddy Lake, where my people were then living and fishing, and doing nothing to anyone. The soldiers rode up to their encampment and fired into it, and killed almost all the people that were there. Oh, it is a fearful thing to tell, but it must be told. . . . I had one baby brother killed there. . . . Yet my people kept peaceful. . . .

During this time my poor mother and sister died, and . . . I came down from Virginia City to live with my brother Natchez, while there were some white men living on the agency. The agent was living there, and had a store of dry goods which he sold to my people. I stayed with my brother all winter, and got along very poorly, for we had nothing to eat half of the time. Sometimes we would go to the agent's house and he would get my sister-in-law to wash some clothes, and then he would give us some flour to take home.

In the month of May the agent sold an Indian man some powder. He crossed the river, when [the Indian] was met by one of the agent's men, who shot him dead on the spot, because he had the powder. . . . All our people were wild with excitement. . . . Our people said they would go and kill him.

As soon as we got to our home, my brother got all his people together, and told them to get ten young men and go and watch the crossing of the river, and if [any Indian] tried to cross, to catch him; "If there is more than one, kill them if you can; by so doing we will save ourselves, for you know if we allowed our people to kill the white men we should all be killed here. It is better that we should kill some of our own men than to be all killed here. . . .

Just then someone was seen coming. . . . He said, "Oh, somebody has killed a white man and another is almost dead. . . ." Very late that evening two of our men came as before. They brought me a letter; these were the words:

Miss Sarah Winnemucca—Your agent tells us very bad things about your people's killing two of our men. I want you and your brother Natchez to meet me at your place to-night. I want to talk to you and your brother.
Signed,
Captain Jerome—Company M, 8th Cavalry

It took me some time to read it, as I was very poor, indeed, at reading and writing; and I assure you . . . I am not much better now. After reading it four or more times, I knew what it said. I did not know what to do, as my brother had not returned. I had no ink to write with. My people all gathered around me waiting for me to tell them something. I did not say anything. They could not wait any longer. They asked me what the paper said. I said, "The soldiers are coming. The officer wants me and my brother to see them at our place." At that time, my brother and I had a place on the reservation.

They said, "Oh, it is too bad that he went off this morning; you and he might be the means of saving us. Can you speak to them on paper?"

I said, "I have nothing to write with. I have no ink. I have no pen."

They said, "Oh, take a stick—take anything. Until you talk on that paper we will not believe you can talk on paper."

I said, "Make me a stick with a sharp point, and bring me some fish's blood." They did as I told them, and then I wrote, saying:

Hon. Sir—My brother is not here. I am looking for him every minute. We will go as soon as he comes in. If he comes to-night, we will come some time during the night.
Yours,
S.W.

Many of our people did not sleep that night. Brother called all his people together at one place. He told them the soldiers were their friends, and not to be afraid of them. . . . So we watched for their coming the next morning. At last they came, and camped alongside of brother's camp. The first thing he did was to tell us not to be afraid. . . . He asked us what we had to eat. . . . Two days afterward a soldier came in and told brother that the captain had three wagons of provisions for him and his people. Oh, how glad we were, for we were very poorly off for want of something to eat. That was the first provision I had ever seen issued to my people . . . !

Five days after, five soldiers came down from the Fort with a letter for the captain. After he read the letter, he called brother and me to him, and said: "You are to go with me to Camp McDermitt, and you can get your father and all your people to come into the army post, where you can be fed. Now, if you will go, we will start by the first of July. . . ."

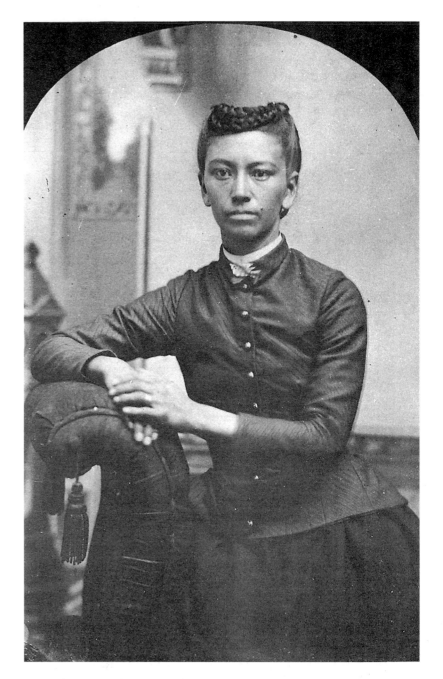

Jane Silcot, a guide in the Pierce Expedition.

I went into council with my people. My brother, Lee, who was there, and I sat up all night talking with them, and telling them what we wished them to do. We Indians never try to rule our people without explaining everything to them. When they understand and consent, we have no more trouble.

Some of the interpreters are very ignorant, and don't understand English enough to know all that is said. This often makes trouble. Then I am sorry to say these Indian interpreters, who are often half-breeds, easily get corrupted, and can be hired by the agents to do or say anything. I know this, for some of them are my relatives. My people are very reasonable and want to understand everything, and be sure that there is fair play. . . .

There were now nine hundred in all at Camp McDermitt. Every head of a family was furnished with a good tent of the requisite size for his family, such tents as are used by the soldiers and every morning, at five o' clock, rations for the day were issued. . . . I remained at Camp McDermitt after Col. McElroy's death. . . .

In 1875 I was in Camp Harney, Oregon, to see my father. It was in May. I had not been there but a little while when my brother Lee came from the Malheur Agency, bringing me a letter from the agent, Mr. Parrish, inviting me to come to Malheur Agency, and act as his interpreter to my people. . . . So we got ready very early one morning, for we wished to make it in one day. Mr. Parrish was very glad to see us. He gave me a very nice little room to live in, and said he would pay me forty dollars per month to talk for him. I took that offer, for I had no other way of making a living for myself. The army had no more prisoners, and therefore they could not give me a place to interpret for them, so I went to work.

This reservation in Oregon was set apart for my people in 1867. . . . [On] the first day of May, 1876, our school-house was done, and my people were told that it was ready, and for the little children to come to school. . . . Mrs. Parrish was to be teacher, and I was to help her, and get the same pay for teaching the children English. I had given up my position as interpreter to my cousin Jarry, because he was almost blind. I asked Mr. Parrish to give it to him, because he had a wife and daughter, and no way of making a living for them. So Mr. Parrish sent for him to come and take my place.

On the first of May, Mrs. Parrish and I opened the school. She had her organ at the school-house, and played and sang songs, which my people liked very much. The school-house was full, and the windows were thrown open, so that the women could hear too.

All the white people were there to sing for them. I was told to tell the children to sing. All of them started to sing as well as they could. Oh, how happy we were! We had three hundred and five boys, twenty-three young men, sixty-nine girls, and nineteen young women. They learned very fast, and were glad to come to school. Oh, I cannot tell or express how happy we were! Mrs. Parrish, the dear, lovely lady, was very kind to the children. We all called her our white lily mother.

We had not been teaching but about three weeks when very bad news came. Our white father, Parrish, told me to tell all the people to come to the school-house. They all came with sad faces. . . . Then he told us that he had received a letter from our Big Father in Washington, saying another man was to come in his place—a man better than he. "I am sorry to leave you," he said, "because I know I can make a good home for you. The man who is coming here to take care of you all is a good man. . . . You must do just as he wants you to do. . . ."

Father said, "I don't want anything from you, because it will make me feel so badly after you are gone." It is the way we Indians do. We never keep anything belonging to our dearest friends, because it makes us feel so badly, and when any of our family die, everything belonging to them is buried, and their horses are killed. . . .

On the twenty-eighth of June, 1876, our new agent, Major Reinhard, arrived. . . . "Now Sarah," he said, "tell your people that the Big Father in Washington has sent me here. He told me how I must make you all good people. This land which you are living on is government land. If you do well and are willing to work for government, government will give you work. Yes, government will do more than that. It will pay you one dollar per day; both men and women will get the same. . . .

All the time he was talking, my people hung their heads. Not one looked at him while he talked. . . . Then Egan got up and said, "Our father, we cannot read; we don't understand anything; we don't want the Big Father in Washington to fool with us. He sends one man to say one thing and another to say something else. The man who just left us told us the land was ours, and what we do on it was ours, and you come and say it is government land and not ours. You may be all right. We love money as well as you. It is a great deal of money to pay; there are a great many of us, and when we work we all work."

Then the agent said, "When I tell you to do anything I don't want any of you to dictate to me, but to go and do it."

Mary Masislaw, date unknown.

The Indians worked for a week but when they went to be paid, the agent charged them for the supplies they had been issued and refused to pay them in cash for their labors. The Indians were outraged. They knew that the government provided the supplies for their use without charge.

In 1878 a few of the Paiutes joined the Bannock tribe on the warpath, and the Army paid Sarah $500 to persuade the Bannocks to give up. Upon reaching the perimeter of the Bannock encampment of about "three hundred and twenty-seven lodges . . . four-hundred-and-fifty warriors," she discovered that the Paiutes were actually prisoners. Her brother, Lee Winnemucca, urged her quickly to "take off your hat and your dress and unbraid your hair, and put this blanket around you, so if they should come down, they would not know who it is. Here is some paint, paint your face quick."

Sarah explained that the Army was en route to attack the Bannocks, and that they, the Paiute captives, must flee in order not to be a part of that attack. That night her father and the remaining Paiutes left the camp after dark, and were followed by the Bannocks. Sarah realized that their only hope was for the tribe to hide, while she and her sister Mattie rode to the troops to get help. "That was the hardest work I ever did for the government in all my life," she remembers. "The whole round trip, from 10 o'clock June 13 up to June 15, arriving back at 5:30 p.m., having been in the saddle night and day; distance, about two hundred and twenty three miles. . . . I, only an Indian woman, went and saved my father and his people."

But her efforts were not over. She was asked to return with the Army as interpreter and guide for the duration of the Bannock war. Her bravery throughout the rest of the campaign brought her much public attention, but the outcome for her tribe was not favorable. Though they had been innocent of the Bannock's insurrection, the bedraggled tribe of half-starved Paiutes were sent first to Camp Harney, then informed they must march, in the dead of winter, to a prisoner camp in Yakima, Washington Territory.

The resulting march to Yakima through the snow in a staggering convoy of old men and women, children and invalids was a nightmare for Sarah. Along the way many were lost, but the remainder finally did arrive at the Yakima reservation, weak, frostbitten, and completely bewildered by the turn of events. The Christian Indians showed them lodgings in a livestock shed without heat or food. Later, the Paiutes were turned out to work in the fields, clearing sixty acres of land for wheat, all the while having to defend their property from the reservation Indians, who stole from them.

Sarah's sister Mattie died in May. Sarah continued working for the government as an interpreter, but received only minimal pay. Her disgust with the government continued to grow, and in 1880 she met with Secretary of the Interior Carl Schurz. He made her many promises which were not kept, and the Paiutes sometimes blamed Sarah for the government's deception. After her marriage in 1882 to a white man named Hopkins, she nonetheless continued to lecture and travel in behalf of her people, decrying the injustices they could not escape.

In 1884 a bill passed Congress granting the Paiutes land, but it was never implemented. Sarah finally retreated from public life to establish an Indian school near Lovelock, Nevada. It closed before her death in Montana, on October 16, 1891.

Sarah Winnemucca, date unknown.

"Day's End" on paint horse.

Unidentified woman on burro in the Southwest.

Sybil Harber, a midwife in Lakeview, Oregon. She was also the mother of cowboy Bert Harber.

Pauline Lyons Williamson

Pauline Lyons Williamson, whose letters follow, was from a middle-class black family, was doubtlessly educated, and possessed some skills as a nurse. When she emigrated to California, she was a widow with a young son to support. She planned to board with her Aunt and Uncle Thomas, find a school for her son, and work in a hospital training program. Since Aunt Thomas was ill Pauline would provide care for the older woman, who would, in turn, watch out for the boy Harry while Pauline was at work.

Yet the ensuing letters, written chiefly to her sister May between 1880 and 1892, trace an inexorable path of mistakes, lies, illness, and prejudice that eventually lead to the defeat of Pauline Williamson's hopes. Much credit for this failure is given to her aunt—who conceived a scheme to marry Pauline off without telling her a word about it—and her uncle, who became increasingly insensitive to Pauline's financial woes.

A clipping from an unnamed newspaper, 1885.
Mrs. Pauline Williamson and her little son, arrived in Oakland on the overland train last Friday, from Plainfield, N.J. She is stopping at the residence of Mrs. W. Thomas, 917 Union Street, Oakland. She expresses herself as having had a pleasant trip across the continent, and was shown every courtesy by the conductors and others. Mrs. Williamson is the youngest daughter of Mr. and Mrs. Ambro Lyons of Plainfield, and has come to California to make it her future home.

[No date]
Dear May,

[Your letter] came safely, and gave me a great deal of pleasure. I do so love to hear from home. . . .

I have got my suit case and am waiting every day now for a summons. It will be some work getting myself educated, but my greatest drawback will be Harry. You see, while Ms. Thomas is not a confirmed invalaid, still she is very much like mother, and there are a great many days when she is ailing and she is easily worried, and very nervous, yet like mother, she wont give up till she has fallen.

You well know Harry's disposition, and although he has really tried . . . to be good, when I am gone away to work he will be troublesome.

Aunt Susan is too old to take any care of him, and he needs a good deal of looking after and keeping out of mischief. . . . You well know what the care of child of that age is, then he will not always mind as readily as he should. . . .

Now, what do you think? [Should] I try to send him away to a good school and let him stay there until he gets older. He really needs the guidance of a man. If Uncle was here, that is if he was home all the time, it would make a great difference, but with only three old women, I dont see how it will work. He is doing nicely in school and has a reward for every week since he has been there. I would like to stay out this way, but I must do the best, now what advice can you give me. . . ?

Now I will tell you about myself. I have been miserable off and on ever since I came, I suffered a great deal with my head, and I have had something growing in my mouth. It commenced to grow last winter when I was sick, but I paid no attention to it. It is a lump of flesh growing on the inside of my cheek, and it has kept growing so large that about two weeks ago it got so I could not shut my teeth.

I went to a doctor and he said it would have to come out. He tried to burn it out with caustic, but finally I had to have a piece cut off. I can now shut my mouth, but it is very sore, and I think another piece will have to be cut. I will have to go again on Tuesday so as to let him see it.

Now my sister, not a word of any thing I said must be written home. Ms. Thomas has been laid up with a very bad eye and we have been a sorry pair.

Write soon to your sister,
Pauline

Oakland, Nov. 10th, 1885.

My dear May,

Now my dear . . . it seems that before I came to California a friend of Mrs. Thomas'—a gentleman, saw my picture and being desireous of getting a wife questioned Ms. T. concerning me, the gentleman being a West Indian by birth is very wealthy, but has refrained from marrying because he could not meet any lady who came up to his ideas of what a wife ought to be.

The gentleman, who was a perfect stranger to me but a friend of Ms. T agreed with Ms. T. that I was the one suited to be a good wife. The name of the West Indian gentleman I do not know so I will call him Mr. H. Ms. T's accomplice in the business I shall call Mr. B. Mrs. T & Mr. B put their heads together to make me marry Mr. H, they both saw Mr. H, [and] set forth my charms, and they agreed that it would be all right as soon as I came, so Mr. H. said he would marry me.

Ms. T told him the only obstacle in the way [was] the child but he promised her that he would fix that all right, he would send the child away to boarding school, so it was settled. Ms. T was to receive a diamond ring for her trouble and Mr. B was to receive a diamond scarf for his trouble from Mr. H as soon as the marriage took place.

October was the time fixed for it so as to give him time to arrange for his going into business for himself. He opened a perfumery store in Panama during the holiday week, [and] we were to sail immediately for Panama which was to be my future home.

Behold the sequel: neither party told me anything of what was going on [when] I came. Mr. B was the first one to broach the subject to me, then he did not tell me about Mr. H, but simply hoped I would like California and he knew I would become so much attached that I never would want to leave, and finally, I would marry some one here.

I told him I did not care to marry, but he assured me I would marry out here, [since] every one that came to make a living ended by marrying, and in a few days he would show me some thing that would bind me forever to California. But still I did not suspect anything because I thought he was only showing off. But he kept it up so much that I finally told [him] I did not see why people worried so about my getting married. I came to earn a living and not to hunt a husband, and I intended to remain single. [Still] not a word about Mr. H did [my aunt] say.

So one day in talking I told [her] I had a friend in New York that I thought I would marry if he did what I wanted him to do, [which] was to come out to California. And if he came I would marry him.

So whenever the California gentlemen were mentioned I would bring up New York gentlemen, and in fun on my part lauded them up to the skies, my own in particular being lord over all.

Now in the mean time Uncle comes home, and we are invited to take tea at Mr. B's. That was the time fixed for me to meet Mr. H for the first time, but before the day arrived Uncle, Mr. B, Ms. T and myself were in Frisco and it seems Mr. H passed us on the street, and she steps up to him and tells him the game is all up, I am engaged to be married. He says he is very sorry, and thanks her kindly for the interest she has shown, and refuses to be introduced to me, as he does not wish to place himself in any ones way and unless he can have the lady to himself, he will not even call on her or be introduced.

I remember that she stopped in the street and spoke to some one, but as I was ignorant of all this, I did not pay any attention to what went on, but walked along with Mr. B. . . .

Mr. H would not come to the party as he felt much disappointed at the way the affair had turned out. Mr. B has told me since that if I had only said I would marry that he would have gone right after Mr. H and in ten minutes time it would have been all fixed.

A little while after I received a letter from my friend in New York saying he had changed his mind and would [not come] to California, so I told [Ms. T]. Well, then the storm broke over my head, and she was furious. For it seems she had been around telling people that I was engaged to be married, [and] that the gentleman was a coming out from New York. Then she up and told me about Mr. H, and what she had planned for me, but that since I would have my own way she was done with me. And she did not care what happened, and a whole lot of stuff.

She had even gone so far as to make out who she intended to send cake [to]. She intended to make New York and Brooklyn jealous of my good fortune, and all was to be done at her expense—cake and all. Then as soon as I was safely in Panama, she was going to arrange her affairs and come to Panama and pay me a visit, but sure as I prefered a New York nigger I was served just right.

She would love to set my ass in a butter firkin and I would have had servants to wait on me and plenty of money, but I would not, so then she thought I had better go home, that I was not happy, and she didn't want any one around that was not contented.

I was always fretting because I was not at work, and she did not see why I was in such a hurry to work. Then I said, I missed father and mother so much, I had better go back to them. When Uncle came home he would pay my fare back home, that is why she wrote to you as she did, for she was dreadfully put out on account of my not fulfilling her wishes, when she had bragged and boasted of me to him.

Well, I can't repeat all that was said, but finally I told her if Mr. H would come and see me I would accept his attentions, so she said she would see Mr. B and see what could be done.

Mr. B came to see us and the matter was talked over, he said he was afraid it was too late now to do anything as Mr. H had gone to Panama, so he wrote to him, and two weeks ago he received an answer saying that Mr. H would think the matter over and would let him know in a short time what he would do.

So there the matter rests. There will be a steamer in from Panama about the 1st of this month, and then I suppose he will send his answers. He is a Roman Catholic but I dont think he will come back as he is very high tone.

You may rest assured I will never consent to have my boy sent away from me for any man, and I think the whole transaction was crazy to go so far and without my knowledge.

My dear sister, Ms. T is a very uncertain person. What pleases her one day tries her the next. [To her] sometimes Harry is a perfect devil and sometime he is an angel, just as the notion takes her. You see, she does not enjoy good health, and about every other day is very miserable. She has a nervous neuralgia in the head, and it is very irritating. . . .

By the way, those letters she sends she does not write herself, as she can not read as well as Harry does. I think some white person writes them for her, that much I have found out. She can not read a newspaper correctly. She told me one day that Harry was a little devil, that he wanted to destroy everything in the house, that she did not love him at all, then she told Uncle that Harry was such a good child, [and] was so respectful to her, and she really loved him and liked to have him about. . . .

You see, Uncle does not know anything about the match she had on hand, and she dont want him to know either.

[She also] said she wanted me to go to work in the Palace hotel as a chambermaid, but he said the idea of such a thing, that if he had come home and found me in the Palace he would walk me right out of it. She made him think I wanted to go there, when it was her own proposition, and after he went away, she told me that I was very foolish to mind what he said, that he had no right to control me, and that if she was me, she would go to the Palace any way.

You see, she is a good woman in her way, but she is old and cranky. I try to steer clear of all the unpleasant things I can, because I know she means well, and she thinks she never says or does any thing wrong, and she will fight all the children in the neighborhood for Harry. . . . I would never have written all this stuff, but you have asked for an explanation and of course I had to give it to you. But use your own judgement about telling father and mother.

I made up my mind when I came to . . . write only the pleasant things home. I shall never leave the field until I am thoroughly convinced that I cant get a living here.

As for my plans, I got along nicely with my case and got $20 for the two weeks, but I have found that the one great obstacle is, I have no certificate to prove I am a trained nurse and [without one] I shall have a hard time to get established. People and Doctors both require some proof of ones proficiency, so I have been trying to get into the only training school that there is in Frisco. I can not enter now, but I have a promise from the board of directors that in the spring they will admit me on probation, and if the term is passed satisfactorily, that they will give me [permission] to take the [course].

They were willing to take me this month, but the nurses, of whom there are eight, would not work with a colored person. As their accommodations are small, they could not . . . accommodate me under the existing unpleasantness of the nurses. But in the spring, their new building will be complete, and there will be other changes made which will [be] to my advantage. . . .

Hope my explanation is satisfactory. I shall let you know if Mr. H comes in time, but I shall not be sorry if he does not.

Love,
Pauline

San Francisco, Jan. 8th, 1886
Dear Mother,

You can see by this that at last I have got a job and am now in the City. I am with a lady who is paralyzed. It is very hard work for she can not help herself much and has to be lifted and turned and it is very hard on my back.

I have many things to learn before I can become a good nurse. . . .

Harry is a great comfort to me, and if I can only take good care of him until he is able to help himself, I shall not mind the hard work.

Love to All From
Pauline

[*No date*]
Dear May,

. . . I want you to send me by return mail Mr. Thomas' address here in Frisco . . . on his arrival he will get [the letter] before he goes home which is what I want him to do. So you send me the address as I do not want to ask the Madam for it. . . .

Dr. Brown will be here Saturday, February 27, so I will hear what she has to propose, and say then I will decide what to do. I think myself that if I am more independent, the Madam will like it better, but she has always opposed my doing any thing. She even took my sign down, saying that she did it because some one told her it did not pay to have a sign, [and] I would do better without it than

with it. . . . Will let you know what Dr. B. says,

Yours,
Paul

January 18, 1886
Dear May,

. . . I went to Oakland on Saturday and quietly set myself down and had a talk with the madam [her aunt, Mrs. Thomas] and she says she does not object to keep the child if he was contented, but when I am a way he frets about me, and most every night cries himself to sleep and it worries and frets her, too. . . .

I talked to Uncle William, [and] . . . he feels as I do, that Auntie is not a suitable person in disposition to train a child of Harry's disposition. . . . He is fond of Harry, and I now firmly believe that he intends to do some thing for his welfare, so I shall let it rest until he tells me what to do . . . he knows that the Madam will and does spoil Harry a great deal quicker than I do. . . .

Last Friday morning I went with young Dr. Blake to see an operation performed. There were present two doctors, a nurse and myself. It took two hours to do it. The patient was a lady and her womb was taken down [and] a piece of flesh cut off and parts that had been injured during child birth were sewed up. I tell you I enjoyed it. Everything was so scientifically done, and so neatly. One doctor gave the ether and the other performed the operation. The nurse and myself assisted the doctors by holding the vagina open with the speculum and washing sponges. We took turns, [but] the ether made me deathly sick and I did not get over it for several days. . . .

I wish you would get together all the books . . . on chemistry. I think some of them are in the next to the top drawer in the bureau in my room. . . . I think a glorious future is before me if I can only get the training I want. . . .

I guess I am pretty safe about the lifting business, you should see the sister I handle daily. I find it is not so much the main force one uses, but it is the knowing just how to handle them. . . . I am learning to give the galvanic battery. I give the lovely sister a shock every day in the arm and leg. Just think, I have been away seven months. . . . wonder when, where and under what circumstances we will meet again?

With love,
Paul

Unidentified black family in California, date unknown.

San Francisco, Jan. 21st, 1886
Dear May,

... I had a message from Doctor Brown saying that [they] would make room for me to enter the hospital immediately.... I wrote to Uncle, asking him what I should do with the child. This is his answer:

"Now it is impossible to pay Harry's board and clothes both, off of ten dollars a month." [That] is all I would get in the Hospital the first year, so what had I better do?

The lowest board I can get for the boy is $8.00 per month for one year ... if I get $10.00 in the hospital it only leaves two for clothes and other expenses per month. [Maybe] I had better throw up the whole thing and try to get us both back to New York. [Or I could] give up going into the hospital, go into service, pay board for the child, save what I can and in the course of a year or two try to open a little store. I could earn $20.00 or $25.00 at services. I now feel that the sooner I make myself independent, the better. I did think that he ... would have offered to help me with the child's board ... if he had only offered me $5.00 per month for the child's board it would have been a great help.

So here I am ... I am so tired of being dependent. I did so hope that my coming here would be the means of giving me a chance to live independently. I hate to give it up, for I know full well I can not always have father and mother and you to fall back on, and I aim to help myself all I can, but it seems I am one of those unfortunate ones, every thing I try seems to fail. ...

I will leave this place where I am first of March. I would not stay here longer, as I am not willing to do so much work as they want one person to do. I take care of four rooms and bath to get three meals a day. And take the entire care of the lady who is paralyzed. I have to do every thing for her, give her the galvanic battery every day, medicine three and four times a day, wash [her] sometimes twice a day and it is very hard for she is a large woman and it strains me much to lift her.

From a little after six in the morning until nine at night I am on the go and nothing must be forgotten, I can tell you. And they are very close on the food. ...

With Love,
Paul

San Francisco, January 1st, 1887
Dear May,

What is the matter with you that you do not write to me, never since I have been home has so long a time passed until now that you have not written to me. I told you I would try to get a long until spring and I have done so. I was much surprised when reading Father's letter to learn that Mr. Thomas was willing to help me to get home, for he told me he was not willing to do so, he says one thing to me and writes another to Father.

Had I known he would have passed me on to Om'aha I would have risked the weather and come, for I am not able to get along out here. I have not the health to do the hard work necessary to get along, and now I am all most discouraged. I think and feel that I don't much care what becomes of me. I hope in the spring some way will be opened for me to return home. . . .

I do not know when Mr. Freeman will come to New York, but when he does you will hear from him. Now, May, please do write me soon and tell me about Father.

Love,
Pauline

March 1st, 1887
Dear Mother,

Harry is now getting well very slowly, and it will be some time yet before he is himself again. The sores heal very slow, and the scabs do not drop off easily. He has now twenty-five places on his head besides other parts of his body that have yet to heal up. He is at present in no condition to travel. . . . Harry has had a close escape from death, had not the disease broken out all over him as it has done, he would have died from blood poisoning. [*It is not known what this disease was.*]

Now mother, from what you wrote I think you seem to feel as though I willfully left Mrs. Thomas without cause . . . had you been in my place, I think you would have done just as I did, and come to the same conclusion that I did—that Mrs. Thomas is a fraud. It is all well enough to do that which makes a good show and talk, but a good deed in sickness is not in her line. . . .

It is all very well for [Mr. Thomas] to write beautiful letters, and smooth things over, but it dont amount to the [unintelligible] with me. The only thing I am sorry for is to have been the cause of any feeling between you and them.

Mr. T has not supported either myself or Harry since we came out here. On our arrival . . . he [gave] the child ten dollars, but that has not supported him nor bought his medicines. The burden has been on me. . . .

I can not make up my mind yet about coming back. Harry is not well enough yet. I think you have no idea how he has been, and his face run all the time and I have to be be so careful to that I did not get the matter on to me for fear I might get poisoned by it. . . .

I hope before many days to be able to write you a letter. . . .

Paul

March 6, 1887
Dear Mother & Father

. . . Harry is in a fair way to get well, he has improved wonderfully in the last week past. . . . I have not seen Mr. Thomas yet. I sent to him, asking him when I could see him, and he sent word that he was so busy that he did not know when he could see me.

If I do not hear from him in a few days, I will go to him, and if he will arrange matters for me, I will return to Plainfield. . . .

Today has been a beautiful, clear sunny day . . . God has indeed made the climate of San Francisco all that man can desire, and I for one shall leave it with great regret. . . .

I am feeling better the last three or four days than I have felt for two months. Write soon with much love from

Harry and Paul

May 21, 1887
Dear May,

. . . I hope the time is drawing near when we shall meet. I presume you have by this time got my last, in which I spoke of a desire to have all things in readiness, so as to lose no time after Mr. T comes. I shall have to give him a date for starting, without which he will not be able to do anything. . . .

I have not earned $10 since the first of January, and I am not at work, and at present there does not seem any chance to get any. And I have not money to pay Harry's board any more, and . . . $4.50 is every cent I have in this world and how I am to raise this months board, the Lord only knows.

I have to pay eight dollars a month for Harry, without his washing. I tell you this not to complain, but to let you see how necessary it is to try to bring the thing to an end this month. So I want every thing in readiness by the 25th, then if he says he will give me the ticket, it is a perfect waste of time to write and tell you, when if every thing is ready and I have the money I can take him right up . . . for if we stay half a month [later] I must pay the whole. You see what a lot of time I will lose by having to write back and forth so many times.

You need not be afraid to send the money, I shall not use it for any other purpose and if he refuses to get the ticket why, I will return the money. [*It appears that Pauline's family sent her an amount of money for incidental expenses, while Mr. Thomas was being asked to pay for the actual passage.*]

Harry will need a pair of shoes, and as it is not warm weather I can make his old over coat do, and I had some clothes given me which I have cut over for him. I want a hat and a pair of gloves, and I am now trying to fix one of my old dresses over to wear in the cars, and my cloak wants some new fringes, and I can make that do, and I want some flannel to wear.

If I can manage those things I can get a bag. Of course if he refuses to get the ticket, I might be obliged to wait, but I don't want to ask any favors of him, more than is really necessary.

We had an earthquake this morning about seven and we are now having shockwave.

Love,
P.W.

P.S. I think that $10.00 would fix us both up to travel. . . .

May 22, 1887
Dear Mother and Father,

The money came all safe and I have it carefully set aside. The steamer came in yesterday—she was some what behind time, so I am now waiting to hear from Mr. Thomas. He will take his own time and you and father must not feel disappointed if he fails to do his part, for I am sure he will back out of it if he possibly can.

I feel much worried at the state of affairs in Plainfield, and about Father's health. I think the church treats him shamefully, for he has been faithful to them, but I am not surprised, for this one thing I have well learned: the minute one can not serve a white man's ends he is ready to kick one out. No matter how much suffering it may cause. . . .

Harry seems to be quite well this last week. He is at times languid and drooping, and the confinement of school seems to disagree with him. He has been out of school for a week, and I do not think he will go back again until after vacation, but he is not running wild, [but] working, and I think the change for a while will do him good. He goes to work at six o clock in the morning and gets home a little after eight at night. He has been doing it for nearly a week, he is keeping a place for a little boy who is sick, so he is doing the work while the boy gets well. . . . in a private family boarding house as bell boy, he gets three dollars a week, one day he made 25 cents and yesterday he made 45 cents. He went of his own free will, he is perfectly crazy about earning some money. Had he been perfectly well I should not have let him come out of school, but I think when he gets a good taste of what work is he will be contented to go back to school and remain there until he is more able to work.

Dear mother, should I not come home and you have to move, do the best with my things that you can, if you can keep them, do so; if not what you cant keep give them [away].

I should let you know as soon as I hear from Mr. L. but in my mind I feel he will not keep his promises. Mother, the doctor says that Harry is passing through a critical change in life, and he says it will be more than likely he will not live over the age of 15, and if that disease breaks out again it will go very hard with him, the disease being [unintelligible] it will now either leave him for good and in good health, or it will carry him off at an early age. We know you do not forget us. . . .

Yours,
Pauline

Although nothing more is known about Pauline Williamson's life, it is painfully evident that in the late 1800s the task of supporting her young son while trying to educate herself proved impossible for her. Her reluctance to be a domestic servant made her task more difficult. Her continued desire to be independent, despite the many obstacles, singles Pauline Williamson out as an unusual woman.

Family dragging its belongings into the Yukon, 1898.

A halt during a journey through the Navaho country.

Covered wagons on Main Street in Ottawa, Kansas, 1866.

MEMORANDUM OF AGREEMENT,

Between Joseph Dana & Co., and *E. Butler*   Witnesseth —

Said Dana & Co. agree to take   *E. Butler*   to Council Bluffs on the Missouri River, in cabin of steamboat, and from thence will provide good strong wagons, and at least three yoke of oxen to each wagon, to go over the Plains to Sacramento City, in the State of California ; and will furnish provisions for the journey, to consist of Bacon, Flour, Meal, Sea Biscuit, Hommony, Beans, Sugar, Coffee, Pepper, Salt, &c., so that each man can have at least three pounds of provisions per day. The Company will be required to select a Committee of five men from the Company before leaving Council Bluffs, to examine the quantity and quality of provisions provided, and their decision shall be conclusive as to sufficiency. Said Dana & Co. shall have the privilege to direct the train or teams in regard to stopping or starting. The teams will be required to keep together, and rest as often as one day in each week, unless otherwise directed by said Dana & Co. Any one of the Company may be expelled by a vote of the majority of the company, and in case he is expelled, shall have a proportionate quantity of provisions set off to him, and shall not again be taken into said Company without the concurrence of the whole Company. Each member, in consideration here mentioned, agree to pay said Dana & Co., one hundred and fifty dollars, as follows: One hundred dollars upon signing this contract, and fifty dollars when landed at Council Bluffs, and will furnish for themselves, a gun, ammunition, knife, and two blankets. The Company will form themselves into messes of five, and will cook for themselves, and stand sentry by turns. Each man will procure a sack for his clothes, and will be entitled to take only twenty-five pounds of baggage, exclusive of blankets and gun. Dana & Co, also agree to furnish one tent and cooking utensils to each mess, and such other articles as the proprietors think necessary to facilitate the journey. Any man of this Company taking his family will be provided with a light spring wagon and will be charged two hundred dollars for each one of the family and the man will perform same duties as other members of the Company. All the members of this Company will be in readiness to leave Cincinnati about the 1st of April next.

CINCINNATI, *March 2* 1852.

Joseph Dana
L. D. Dana } Proprietors.

Agreement between Joseph Dana & Co. and E. Butler, "to go over the Plains to Sacramento City in the State of California," 1852.

Unidentified family and others being ferried with cow across river in the West.

Keturah Penton Belknap

Keturah Penton Belknap began her journal at the age of fifteen. She undoubtedly wrote as she spoke and, while she was very bright, she had little opportunity for formal education. We have tried to preserve the spontaneity of her journal entries; punctuation and spellings have been changed only where confusion might arise.

These journals draw together the two major waves of migration that swept the United States between 1815 and 1900: the expansion into the Northwest Territories in the early decades of the nineteenth century; and the move on to the West Coast after 1840. Mobility marked both Keturah's life and that of her parents, who moved twice after crossing the Alleghany Mountains in 1818. Keturah and her husband moved four times during their own married life.

Keturah Belknap was a hard-working, religious woman whose faith sustained her throughout her life. She is remembered fondly by scores of descendents throughout the West who own copies of her manuscript—"Keturah's Chronicles"—and who refer to her simply as "Aunt Kit."

My father Johon G. Penton was born in the State of New Jersey January the 26 1783.   his Father came from England and was killed in the revolutionary war at the Battle of Brandweine. [*The Battle of Brandywine was in 1777, so the date of her father's birth is evidently a mistake.*]

My Mothers father came from Sweden and her Mother from Holland. (I forgot to say my Fathers Mother came from Ireland).

My Mother was Born January the 1, 1784   they wer Maried in 1804.

Mothers Maiden name was Magdalena Burden.

they Emegrated to the State of Ohio in 1818   Crossed the Alegany mountains with a waggon and a three horse team (what you would call a spike team)   there was three familys 17 souls in all at Pitsburg   they put the familys on board A flat boat and they rowed themselves to Cincinnatti and my father took the team and waggon and went by land and met them at Cincinnati on the bank of the Ohio.

They sold their boat and loaded their early possessions in the waggon   the Smallest children rode and the rest went on foot   the women took turns riding as one had to stay in the waggon to keep the Children Strait.

the next thing was to find a place to winter. Cincinnatti was but A vilage then   they traveled out 16 miles in Hamilton Co on the little Miamic and their father bought a farm of 40 acres, and gave one of his Horses and his waggon and fifty dollars for it. it is now worth a hundred dollars an acre. their was ten acres cleared and fenced. the rest was all heavy timber.   no buildings of any kind on it.   but he soon put up a log Cabin of round logs I think it was 14 x 16 feet with A Huge fireplace and chimney of Sticks and clay. the flore was Split from the larg Hickory trees that grew near by. the Hearth [was] made of large flat stones that was abundent along the little Brook that ran near by and was very nice and as timber was plenty and handy to get other buildings soon followed.

and the next thing was to find work to get some thing for his family to eat.

he found plenty of work near home. their was two old setlers near by that had two crops of wheat to thrash so he got all he could do. he thrashed with a flail and cleaned it up in the wind and got the tenth bushel   he could get corn for twelve and a half cents per bushel. and could get 50 cts a day for gathering corn out of the feild so they had plenty to eat   got a good cow for 10 dollars. then father went a round and helped butcher and got his meet. Mother and my oldest sister worked all winter at any thing that came to hand and took flax to work up on the shares and they would spin evenings till ten or eleven oclock so by spring they had a long piece of linen ready to get wove to cloath the family for summer.

then Mary (that was next to the oldest girl) went and worked for a woman to get it wove and the rest made Sugar so we had our own sweeting and lots of lasses to put on our corn bread for that was their bread most of the time   wheat coffee with sasifras tea for a change was the drink for breakfast.

Then in the summer they took the wool right from the sheeps back and washed it and carded and spun it for half, to make cloaths for the next winter so they got through the first year finely as I have often heard father say. and had a home of their own. Something they never could have had in Jersey.

I, the fifth child of my Parents was Born on the 15 of August 1820 and that log cabin was my home till I was six years old. about this time my Father experienced releigeon and his house became a home for the Preachers and we often had preaching their and Prayrmetings as the familys wer so far apart the Prayr and Class metings wer passed round from house to house,   the first time I remember going from home to meeting my Father carried me before him on Horseback and that was the first text that I ever remembered, the words wer: is their no Balm in Gilead is their no Physian their?—Jeremiah 8:22.

about 1826 I think it was father thought his farm too small to support his increasing family so he sold out for four hundred dollars and let the money out on intrest and went near Cincinnati and rented a small farm and raised a garden and I think about ten acres of corn—the rest was put in garden truck of all kinds.

It was their my first work commenced when not shaking with [fever]—I was kept busy weeding onions or picking the bugs off the cucumber and melon vines for that had to be done evry day till the vines began to run (and this is the way we done it—the whole family would go out in the morning early while the bugs was stupid and search evry hill and catch the bugs and pinch their heads off—they was a small long shaped striped bug with wings yellow and black but could not fly while it was cool in the morning)—then in the evening their always seemed to be more to come, and if left all night they would just riddle the leaves and almost spoil the vines—we had to get ahead of them some way: for we could not see them so we would take some straw or old paper (papers was not so plenty then as they are now) so we would take some fine straw and make little bunches betwene about evry fourth row then one would go a long with a little toarch on fire and touch to the straw and the rest of the family would take a little limber bush and brush the vines and the bugs would fly to the lite and get singed   then we could go to bed and have a little nap then up and at it again, and after that was all done and we had a bite of breakfast then we all worked in the truck patch, father and Mother and Jimey (that was my oldest brother) would hoe and the younger ones would pull the weeds out of the hills.

so we all had to learn to work. then when it came time to go to market that was worst of all. we had to gather the vegatabels in the after noon and load them up in the evening and then get up a bout three oclock and drive six miles into town and back up to the side walk on market Street and take out the hind end gate and get their truck in Sight   they had large splint bushel baskets to take out their things.   cucumbers and sweet potatoes and eggs and Butter and Melons and a little of evry thing to tedious to mention.

Mother or one of the children always went a long as it took two to measure and count out the marketing. the rest of the family staid at home to get diner and tend to the House so all would be ready to gather another load for the next day and so it went every day in the week.

Sundays we had Prayr meeting and class with ocasionly a sermon from some good old Local Preacher   so as one week went all was about the same till fall then the marketing changed and it was Chickens and Ducks and geese and turkys both dreased and live and cornmeal and Apples and fall vegatables of all kinds. and then oh how we did begin to shake with the ague [malarial fever] some times the whole family would be in bed at once and father come home from town shaking so he could hardly unhitch his team: but then we did not go to town but but about twice a week:

We lived in an old log house that was built while the Indians were troublesome in that country   it was made of large round logs with the bark on and but one window   that was in the end and up so high that if the Indians shot through it it would be so high it would not hit any one in the House.

the dores wer made of heavy boards split out of the large black Walnut treas that grew in abundance on the creek near by, hung on large woden hinges fastened on with inch Hickry pins instead of nails   the door had fastened with a strong woden boalt and a bar clear across it to drop down in a notch in the log of the wall, but now it had a large woden latch with a leather string to raise it up with. when the folks would leave us children at home over night they would tell us to pull in the string when we went to bed and then we thought we was perfectly safe.

the chimney was made of roughf stone inside of the house with a fireplace that would take in a back log four foot long and it seems to me it was about six feet in front with a nice smooth hearth of large stones.

then there was a pole (we called it the lug pole) that went across the chimney and their was a place for the ends of the pole to catch on each side to hold it their. it was aimed to have it high enoughf from the fire so it would not catch and burn off, and on this pole their was some peices of chane with hooks in the links to hang the pots on   the hooks was in the shape of a letter S and it could be raised or lowered to suit the fire by a chaing in the links of the chain. Their we hung the diner pot and the tea kittle and the mush pot. and on washing days their was a ten galon Iron kettle swung on in place of a wash boyler:

we had two large Dutch ovens to bake bread in   [we] would set one in each corner and put coals on the lids and at the bottom and as they died out put on more fresh coals and turn it a round with a bail So all sides would take   then we had two Skilets with long handles one to take our short cake in and the other to fry meat in and the griddle for the Buck wheat Pancakes.

We had no soda in those days [so we] mixed the dough with sweet milk and shorting, roled it in a thin cake as large as the bottom of the Skilet then put it on some coals and had the lid hot and put on coals of fire and gave it a quick bake   then [we] Split it and buttered it while hot. when we got enoughf Say three or four (according to the size of the family) cut them in three cornered peices like pie. and with a little maple sirup they was good I tell you.

Those wer the days that tryed mens souls and bodys too, and womans constitutions   they worked the mussle on and it was their to stay.

we lived on that place four years doing the same thing over evry year   evry thing was sent to market that would bring a copper   evry child had something to do   we would gather nuts to Send to town and the money was layed up we never thought of buying candy   thought it enoughf to have a lump of homemade Sugar once in awhile or a piece of Mothers made of gingerbread evry thing was saved to help get us a home   we had two suits of home made cloaths they was washed and Ironed nicely and put on us clean for Sunday and we thought we was nice.

Mother and ann (that was my oldest Sister) made hats for Father and the boys for summer out of Rye straw braided and sewed them and [they] would make some to sell every summer   got a half dolar apiece for them. the rye was cut and bound, then in the winter, thrashed, we would get the largest bundles and cut the heads on the barn flore to thrash and cut the straw of at the first Joint below the head and see who could get the bigest bunch   then in the winter the big girls would braid evenings when they had nothing else to do.

about this time Father began to think as the market business increased so did the price of land and he began to look for a home.

so he went back on the Miamic near where he first settled and bought a place   80 acres this time but the title was not good. it was called Ministerial land   it was land that Goverment gave to the old Prysbyterian Church when the country was first settled to help them to build churches and support Ministers   the taxes was paid to the church   the land was valued and taxed according to its worth and the title ran (thus) subject to revaluation evry five years, so if A man improved his land his taxes went up.

and now the family was eight in number four girls and two boys and the girls was all able to support themselves   about this time I got the first calico dress I every had   it was Blue calico twelve and a half cts per yard. and about this time a new [care] commenced in my life.

this summer I am ten years old and began to think about earning my own liveing. went to schol in the winters and worked round in the summer when not needed at home in the corn field. my work was to tend babys and wash dishes for which I got a dollar and a half a month but some of the time only 25 cents a week but I cloathed my self. we made our own flanel for winter ware and Father always bought A side of upper leather and one of sole leather and had a shoe maker come to the house with his [bench] and tools and shoe the family and that was all we expected till another

The Neely family, making music and popping corn, in the Florence area, Oregon.

winter   some times we had them patched a little and a half sole put on but they had to do for Sunday and all we children took turns washing and greesing the shoes evry Saturday night so as to have them nice for Sunday. then with our clean shoes laced up with a good leather string and a flanel dress and a clean calico apron and a small round cape to match we was ready for meeting, for we did not go to church in them days   meetings was always at our house or some neighbors or perhaps at a School house.

as soon as we got settled the Methodist Itenerate found us, and our house became a preaching place again. we had preaching at our house on week days, most of the time on tuesdays [every other week]. Had two Preachers on the circuit and they Preach at Cincinnatti three times on Sunday then Monday was a restday, then out to our house was 15 miles   preached there at three oclock on tuesday and all ways staid all night.

we had but one Room down stairs that was finished fit to live in so that was Meeting House and dining room and siting room and the Preachers bed was in it also   their was another large room that had a fire place in but it was too open for winter time so we had to all keep still and tend to our kniting when the Preacher was studing but about eight oclock in the evening the Books wer laid by and then we would have a fine time for an Hour or two.

the Preacher would join with us and tell us Bible Storys and then explain them to us while we all cracked Nuts and Poped corn. then when we began to tire they always had a fund of aneckdotes to tell and they would draw us out till we would ask some questions. then he would turn the conversation and ask the older ones some question and then would pass it around to all the children and before we knew it we would answer questions in the catechism, so we learned to love and reverence the preacher and we children all thought it was a happy day when Preaching day came for we all expected a good time and a chicken dinner.

once I remember A lady came that had A little baby . . . it had the cholic and cried . . . and she was fixing to go out dores with it and the preacher said dont go out Dear sister the child will soon get quiet, and he asked the congregation to give him their Prayerful attention while the sisters took care of the dear little child, and by that time Mother had some water boiling in a tin cup on the coals (for we had a fire place) and her root of Calamas and had some warm tea. so she took the baby from its young excited mother and gave it a few spoonsfull of the tea then made it comfortable and turned it on its Stumach with its feet to the fire and in a few minutes it was asleep and this was all done right in meeting, and nobody thought it any thing out of the way. then when meting was out the babe was still sleeping and my Mother would not have it waked so the woman Stayed to tea and we girls went part way Home with her and we thought it a great treat to get to carry the baby.

this year all my Fathers children Joined the church and his joy knew no bounds   he would cry and laughf and shout all at the same time

this year [1831] my Father went back to the State of New Jersey to see his Mother and sister that was all the near relitives he had, their was no railroads then   he went with A Waggon and two Horses, Started in September and got back in January, and while he was gone when he wrote home we would be looking for A letter. some of us children would take A quarter of A dolar and walk to the Post office four miles   if we did not get a letter oh we could get so tired going home but if we got one we could Just skip home   it took a letter about four weeks to come from N.J. to Ohio and twenty five cents to get it out of the office. so we did not get Many letters in them days.

we staid on that place about six years and they was all about the same—raise corn in the summer and go to school in the winter, come home at night and eat supper and that did not take long (for we always had mush and Milk or corn bread or thickened milk for a change)   then the girls would spin flax or knit till bed time. that was Generaly about ten oclock. we would [have] spin races and knit races to see who could do the most.

Father and the boys would shell corn for we had a greal deal of the corn ground and sold the meal   I believe the meal brought 50 cents per bushel   it was always measured in the half bushel. we never sold things by weight in them days.

and now [1835] they are beginning to talk about building a church and we are talking of going to a new country [in the fall]. they are laying the foundation for A Brick church about a half mile from our house, and it was finished the next summer, but this fall Father started out to find a new country where he could get land at government prices. this is one dolar and fifty cents per acre.

he went out in the north part of the State of Ohio in Alen Co. on the Auglaze River. in the Beach woods all heavy timber and the under brush (as we cald it) was so thick a Bird could hardly fly through it so it all had to be first grubed out. then the trees cut down and cut up and roaled together and burned. so you see it ment some thing to make a farm under them circumstances.

but the first thing was to get logs together to build a House   that Father proceded to do before he came home . . . he took a team and waggon when he went to look for land and two of the neighbors went with him. they went to work and got logs together and cleared a spot so as to be out of the trees falling on the house, and put up two cabbins [and] helped each other and the setlers that was their all ready was so glad to have neighbors that they turned out and helped them.

they put up the House of round logs   then scored and Hued is with the broad ax inside. Had it five logs above the Joist: that made it high enoughf for a good room upstairs   then they split oak boards to make a Roof and flore upstairs and chinked the cracks and daubed them with clay mortar, then nailed some Puncheons for the flore, split out thick and Hued nice on the upper side. and you may believe it was ice hard and as white as a bone when it was scrubed   the chimney was made of clay and sticks with back wall and Jams of damp dirt pounded in solid between timbers   then when it got solid take out the inside boards and it would last for years.

the hearth was made in the same way   Split timber and Sharpen the ends and drive them down round the edge of the flore to hold the dirt   then fill up the fire place and hearth with damp clay dirt and pound it down well,   then make a stiff morter and cover the dirt three or four inches and pat it down well and lay some boards on to keep it from cracking while it dryes   then hue out a piece of hard timber and put on the edge to cover the ends of the timbers you drove down to hold the dirt from spreading out under the flore and you have a fire place complete,   their was no stones or bricks in all that country, though we was on the banks of the Auglaze river. the country was very flat and the streams run on the ground, or did not run but Just moved a long.

well the House is done now, all but the dore. the logs are cut out the proper width for a dore and some pieces split out and Smoothed a little and Stood up for the caseings, and then pin them on with hickory pins   then their was one of the old setlers came and told Father he had some sawed boards if he would come over and stay all night with him he would give him a board to make a door so he went and got a beach board and the next day made his door and was ready to start home, but then it was too late in the fall to move and as the feed was mostly on hand for the Stock they thought it best to not move till toward spring   their was no railroads then.

So the 10 of February of 1836 we left our old Home to try a new country. it was only one hundred and twenty five miles   yet it took us five days with waggons and two Horses to each one to make the trip.

it was froze solid and in places quite icy but we had a fine yoke of oxen driveing in the yoke with the cows, so when we came to a place where it was a icy bank they would hitch the oxen on before the horses and they would fetch it out and we got through on Friday evening and Sunday we walked two miles to one of the neighbors to a class meeting, and Monday morning we settled down to business.

and now I was over fifteen years old and I determined to help my Father clear up that farm: we was only five in family one brother four years younger than my self and a little orphan boy five years younger than my brother. [*Keturah's two older sisters were away from home, either married or in domestic service.*] Mother was Strong and well so she could do the work in the house and I set out to work with the little boys   I soon found that I could make a prety good hand.

Father hired a man to grub and if I worked with the little boys we could pile the brush as fast as father could trim it Small enoughf to handle. and how we could all work to make big brush heeps to burn nights, but by the time the grubing was done the big trees had to be felled and prepared to burn and I soon found that I could trim up a tree soon as my Father could   so I made a hand all that spring and by June we had three acres ready to sow to buckwheat.

we worked in the clearing all the good weather and when it was to bad to be out, we fixed up about the house   in the Spring we made our own Sugar to last us all the year and if any thing was needed from town I got on old Philey and took some Butter and cheese and went to the town six miles away with only a blaised trail to follow and five miles without a house, through the swales knee deep in mud and water, [to] get the Mail and do my shoping and get back by noon.

this is how I carried my produce: our cheese weighed about 10 lbs. I put one in each end of a sack and put it across the saddle and set on the sack. then took the Basket of Butter in my lap about eight pounds Generaly, and with the right hand managed the bridle and was then off.

one very rainy day we was cutting out a place for a window and had chips all over the House and we saw a man rideing up and

132

we thought he looked like a Preacher. he got off his Horse and came in and introduced himself as David Burns the Preacher of Lyma circuit and was looking for a place to Preach and organise a class in that neighborhood.

so it was settled that we would have meeting at our house and the next week we had preaching on thursday and ever after as long as I staid their and I think as long as my father and Mother lived   our cabbin was 18 by 16 feet and we cooked and eat and slept all in the same room and then used it for a church. Sometime when the congregation would get out in the yard we could hardly believe that they could all have got in the house. then dinner was next but we always had plenty to eat. their was plenty of wild turkeys and venison and we had a thousand pounds of poark laid up for the first year.

sometimes we got Short of flower but we always had corn meal   we had to go to the old settlement for wheat or flower about seventy five miles was the nearest   one time we had no wheat bread and we wanted to have Roast Ducks for diner Preaching day but had nothing for stuffing so we took some nice mashed potatoes and filled them full and had nice gravey and they was fine I tell you with plenty of good Buckwheat pancakes and a skilit of fancy corn bread and plenty of Homemade Maple Syrup with other things needful we had a diner that any one might enjoy.

now I would like to tell of my first Deer chase—this was the first Deer I ever saw   we had been at our new home but a few days when one morning we heard a dog coming close to the House and we ran to the dore Just in time to see a fine Deer pass and a dog close to it made for the river and it was all frose up   when it struck the ice it fell and the dog caught it and we children gathered the ax and run to help the dog   Mother hollered after us to come back but we did not here. and by the time we got their the Deer was up and off.

it had one leg broken. but a little way farther it came to a smooth piece of ice and fell again perfectly exhausted and the dog was pawing at the hams when we came up with the ax and with what happened to be a well directed blow from my ax it lay senseless. and in less time than it takes to tell it I turned the ax and gave it a lick on the neck which almost severed its head from the body—then a few struggles and it was dead. Just then while we was keeping the old dog from tearing it up our batchelor neighbor came up very much pleased and said well well you ones caught it did you? so we stood around to see what he would do—thought sure he

would give us a piece. well he proceeded to take out the insides then took a strap from his belt and tied the legs together and put the strap over his head. now he says if you ones will give it a little boost so I can get my arm through, thats it I tell you he a fine un, and he was off without thanks or favours. well he was rich and afterward wanted to Marry me but I always thought of that Deer meat. but we had plenty of venison after as the Deer came in the clearing to brouse. . . .

And now we have been in Alen Co about five years   their is roads now and we have quite a little farm opened but its not a very healthy place and I was trying to support myself and help the family some. I found it pretty hard some times as wages wer very low. I got seventy five cents a week for doing common house work and some times a dollar for a hard Job and I would wash all day for twenty five cents and one time I worked a week for a family of eight to get the man to cradle my Fathers wheat crop and he done it all in one day.

so one day my mother had looked quite sober all day   I was getting ready to go to take care of a sick neighbor woman   toward evening we was getting supper (when I was going away Mother always got A good supper early so I could eat before I went) and we had got through the fryed chicken and short cake   Father had left the table and had gone to his work (him and Mother always worked in the garden after supper till time to milk)   I noticed Mother lingered over her tea and I thought she looked a little sad. Like she wanted to say something that was hard to say, so I said Mother, if you have anything you want me to do I wont go   She Said She did not need me. but said She, Kitt if I was you I [would] get married and be fixin up a home for myself and not be a drudge for the whole country   their is plenty of these fellows that wants you and could give you a good home, and with the tact you have you could soon have a nice place of your own. but says I Mother, I dont like this country and I dont want to leave you and pap alone   well, she Said, if I could better myself she had no objections. they could get along very well now they had land enoughf cleared to make them a good liveing on, and if I staid their till they died I would be an old broken down old Maid and maybe so cross nobody would want me and then would be kicked about from one place to another without any home.

So I told her then when the right one came along Ide think the matter over and let her know in time to get ready but now I must go if she had said her Say. So now I began casting about to see if their was anyone I thought I wanted (for their was about five single men to evry girl) so their was a young Preacher on the Circuit that year and he had all ready filed his intentions to go to conference a Married man so I thought that was my chance to do lots of good.

I was quite a good nurse and I thought we could visit the Sick and I could help them in two ways   by administering to their bodily wants I could lead them on to love the Lord, so I had almost decided to say yes at the next appointment, but before that time came his Presiding Elder informed me to go a little slow as Brother D did not belong to the conference and was only a supply and it was not recorded that he could get in for he would not study. So for my good he would advise me not to waste my talents on So unpromising a youth.

So that ended my romance of Marrying a Preacher and that I was so providencialy led out of the scrape but when his next appointment came he wanted to rush matters right through   as it was nearing the time for Conference the whole thing must be got through in a month. I told him that he must go acording to the laws of the church, had he counceled with his Presiding Elder? he said, no, nor would not. He was capable of doing his business and would not ask advice of anyone so I told him if he was that Smart that ended the matter, and we would quit friends   he said their was plenty of other girls, and I told him their was plenty of other men.

the next one that appeared on the sene was a rich young doctor but he was to lazy to practice and he did not know how to do anything else. he had been raised in the South and had Slaves to wait on him So he was no good.

the next was an old Batchelor with a head as red as fire. he had two Sections of Land and lots of money. he Said it was waiting to be at my disposal but he was too stingy to get himself a decent suit of cloaths   So he was Shiped pretyquick. but not long after one pleasant Sabbath morning we saw a man comeing walking up the road dressed up with a Stovepipe Hat on and I said to Mother, their he comes now   but we did not know who it was. but when he got a little nearer we Saw it was George Belknap.

Mother wondered how he came to come that five miles a foot for She knew their was meeting at his fathers that day. oh I said he wanted to hear Perkins preach. So after meeting father asked him to stay to diner and my brother had his girl their so after diner we all took a walk   we two girls Started out together but we did not get far till we paired off   we went out in the medow and sit on a log awhile then went to the house and pretty soon my brothers girl went home and he went with her and pretty soon Mr B went also   and we thought he had Just come up their for a change as Father had been to their house to hold meeting Several times.

but that was not the last of it   in two weeks their was preaching at one of our neighbors a mile and a half from us and as the roads was not very good we Generally went on Horseback or on foot   that day we all walked and about the same time we got their up rode Mr B and (verily) we thought he must like our meetings better than his own   but when meeting was out and I started home he met me in the yard and wanted to know if he could see me home and in my Surprise and excitement I said I had no objections   so i thought as he was on horseback he was going to ride a long to see that I did not stick in the mud or fall off of a log but I stopt a moment to speak with a girlfriend and there he was with Father on that fine black horse and he was telling Father that the horse was perfectly gentle. And he stepped up to me and we started out Some of the time we could walk side by side and sometimes we had to go Indian file and sometimes Coon it on the logs.

as I knew the way of course I went ahead and let him keep up if he could and it took a pretty good walker to get a head of me in them days   and from that [day] on the visits became more frequent and more interesting   About the middle of September he came one day and Said they was about to Sell their place and wanted to go west to a Prairie country and if we went along we must bring matters to a close pretty soon   So him and mother had a long talk out by the well that evening in the moonlight and before morning it was Settled that we would be Maried on the third of october 1839 so then we had to get ready for the wedding and also for the Journey.

George Belknap and Kitturah Penton were married Oct 3, 1839 both of Alen co. Ohio.

On Oct 17th we gathered up our earthly possesions and put them in a two horse wagon and started to find us a home in the far west. We had heard of the prairie land of Illinois but we had never seen anything but heavy timber land, so we set our faces westward. (there were no railroads then). We traveled thru part of Ohio and across Indiana and Illinois and crossed the Mississippi at Fort Madison into Iowa—was four weeks on the way and saw prairie to our hearts content, and verily we thot the half had never been told.

We camped out every night, took our flour and meat with us and were at home every night, cooked our suppers and slept in our wagon. We had a dutch oven and skillet, tea kettle and coffee pot and when I made bread I made "salt rising." When we camped I made rising and set it on the warm ground and it would be up about midnight. Id get up and put it to sponge and in the morning the first thing I did was to mix the dough and put it in the oven and by the time we had breakfast it would be ready to bake   then we had nice coals and by the time I got things washed up and packed up and the horses were ready the bread would be done and we would go on our way rejoycing.

When we wanted vegetables or horse food we would begin to look for some farm house along towards evenings and get a head of cabbage, potatoes, a dozen eggs or a pound of butter, some hay and a sack of oats. There were not many large towns on the way and there was no canned goods to get then. Where there were farms old enough to raise any thing to spare, they were glad to exchange their produce for a few dimes.

We stoped at Rushville, Ill. and stayed four weeks, expecting to winter there but we heard of a purchase of land from the Indians west of the Mississippi, and again we hitched up and mid-winter as it was we started never thinking of the danger of being caught on the prairies in a snow storm.

The second day we had to cross an 18 mile prairie and in the afternoon it turned cold and the wind from the northwest struck us square in the face. we had bought some cows at Rushville, had some boys driving them, and they would not face the storm so I had to take the lines and drive the team while my husband helped with the stock. I thot my hands and nose would freeze, when I got to the fire it made me so sick I almost fainted.

We came to a little house with a big family of children and they had plenty of wood for there was a point of timber run down into the prairie and in [later] years there was a town there called Westpoint. We got there about 4 oclock in the afternoon, had our provisions cooked up for the trip so we thawed it out a little and made some coffee and the kind lady put a skillet in the corner and made us a nice corn cake. We had bread, butter, good boiled ham and doughnuts and with good appetites we ate and were thankful.

When we had cleared up the woman hunted up the children and said, "Now children you get off to bed so these folks can have a show to make down their beds for if they cross that 20 mile prairie tomorrow they will have to start early and that little woman looks all pegged out now   now Honey, the best thing for you to do is to get good and warm and get to sleep." But, the "little woman" had

the tooth ache so [I] was not much sleepy. There was another family with us four of them and us two and eight of the household. We furnished our own beds and made them down on the floor. Tomorrow we cross the Mississippi into Iowa.

Up at 4 oclock in the morning, got our breakfast before the family was up, crossed the river just after noon, traveled till about 4 oclock, then came to another 18 mile prairie [and] put up for the night. the next day [we] started as soon as it was light [and I] had to drive the team again today and face the wind, it commenced snowing before we struck the timber. it was hard round snow and it seemed every ball that hit my face would cut to the quick. That night we had plenty of wood and a room to ourselves and the next day we went thru patches of timber and Oh my but it was cold.

Now were skirting the timber on the Demoin River and its tributaries. thot we could make it to our destination that day but the snow made it such heavy traveling that we could not quite make it so we camped again.

The next day we got to the place about noon   found the family living in the house yet to hold the claim and it was too cold for them to get out and their food was there for their stock.

The house was a double, hued log house. they let us have one room and we unloaded and commenced business. The folks we bought the claim [from] went back to Misurea so we made trades with them and got ploughs, foder, chickens and hogs. made us some home made furniture and went to keeping house. We had a quarter Section of land   we thot that sounded pretty big but it was not paid for yet. the land had just been bought [from] the Indians and had not been surveyed yet so it was not in the market yet, we could settle on it and hold our claims and make improvements, but we must have the cash to pay when it was surveyed and came [on the] market   if some land shark was ready to buy it from under us then we would lose improvements and all so we had to get in and dig to have the money ready.

The first thing was to get some land fenced and broke. Our timber land was 2 miles from the prairie. I would get up and get breakfast so as to have my husband off before it was fairly light and he would cut rail timber all day in the snow and bring a load home at night. [He] would take his dinner and feed for [the] horses, come in at night with his boots froze as hard as bones, strange to say he never had his feet frozen. Now we must save every dollar to pay for our land. we had clothes to last the first year, and we got a dollars worth of coffee and the same of sugar that lasted all winter and till corn was planted. We did not know anything about spring wheat then so our crop was all corn.

Then while the corn was growing, my husband made some rails for a man and got some more groceries   he had hauled the rail cuts and scattered them along where he wanted the fence and split the rails odd spells and laid up the fence when the frost was coming out of the ground.

We had 20 acres of broke land fenced to plant to corn the first spring   then we hired a man with a prairie team to break ten acres that was put into sod corn for foder, it was not tended any [and] did not get very big—was cut up in the fall and fed out ears and all. The breaking team was five yoke of oxen with a man to hold the plough and a good sized boy with a long whip to drive the oxen.

Now it was spring and we have got a few sheep on the shares and they are sheared. All this winter I have been spining flax and tow to make some summer clothes—have not spent an idle minute and now the wool must be taken from the sheeps back, washed and picked and sent to the carding machine and made into rolls then spun, colored and wove ready for next winter. I cant weave so I spin for my mother-in-law and she does my weaving.

Our part of the land had no house on it so we still live in the little kitchen and Father Belknaps live in the other room. Now its harvest time. George is off swinging the cradle to try to save a little something, while I am tending the chickens and pigs and make a little butter (we have two cows). butter is 12½¢ a pound and eggs 6½¢ a dozen. I think I can manage to lay up a little this year.

This year is about out. we sold some meat and some corn. fresh pork 5¢ per pound, corn 12½¢ per bushel in the ear   did not have to buy any clothes this year, so we have skimped along and have $20 to put in the box (all silver). We will put the old ground in wheat this fall and break some more land for corn. [We] will have twenty acres of wheat in and now its spring of 1840. The work of this year will be about the same. I have been spinning flax all my spare time thru the winter. made a piece of linen to sell, got me a new calico dress for Sunday and a pair of fine shoes and made me one home-made dress for every day. It was cotton warp colored blue and copper and filled with pale blue tow filling, so it was striped one way and was almost as nice as gingham.

It is now May and the sheep are sheared and the wool must be washed and picked and got off to the carding machine. So my summers work is before me. It is corn planting time now so the men have their work planned till harvest and now the corn is layed by. George and I are going to take a vacation and go about 10 miles away to a campmeeting. There are four young men and two girls going with us, but I made them promise there should be no sparking and they should all be in their proper places in time for service (for they were all members of the church, and if they did not set a good example before the world and show which side they were on they could not go with me, and they behaved to the letter), around the tent we were like one family but we were the head. This was the first campmeeting west of the Missisippi so far as I know. People came from far and near and I think there were about twenty clear conversions. Both the girls wer maried to two of the young men in the fall and lived to raise families who made good useful men and women in church and state.

Now we have had a rest and have got strengthened both soul and body—we will go at it again. We have thot of trying to get things together this year to build a house next summer as we have about all the land fenced and broke that one man can handle. The crops are fine—our wheat is fine. will have wheat bread now most of the time. The hogs did so well [we] can have our meat and quite a lot to sell. We more than make our living so we will have quite a lot to put in the box this year. We will get our wheat ground and get barrels to pack the flour in. then will have to haul it 60 miles to market and I think we got $3 a barrel. We took it to Keocuk on the Mississippi. then it was shiped off on steamboats.

It is now 1841 and we have most of the material together for the house. It will be a frame house the only one in sight on this prairie and its miles across. Now the coming generations will wonder how we will build a frame house and no sawmill within 50 miles and will have to go that far for nails as we can not get any large quantity at the little stores here. "Where theres a will theres a way." The timber is all hued out of oak trees that grow on Lick creek 4 miles away   everything from sills to rafters are hued with the broad axe. The timber is very tall and fine oak and hickory trees making as many as three or four rail cuts and splits so straight we can make anything we want of it. We found a carpenter who had some tools and he got to work two days and layed out the work. then George and his father worked at it after the corn was layed by till harvest [and] got the frame up and the roof on as there was one of our neighbors going to Burlington, after goods for a man who was starting a store in a little down on the Demoin about 4 miles from us   so we got them to bring us some shingles nails and we had made shingles in the winter. While I spun flax George brought in the shaving horse and shaves shingles and we burnt the shavings and both worked by the same light   we now have the roof on and it can stand awhile.

August the 20th, harvest is over and we have the sweetest little baby girl. [We] call her Hannah.

We will now work some more on the house. While my husband is staying round he will be putting on the siding, he made that himself, cut the trees and sawed off cuts 6 ft. long, then split them out and shaved them with the drawing knife to the proper thickness. [He] put it on like weather boarding and it looks very well. The house is 24 ft. long and 16 ft. wide—will take off 10 ft. and make two bedrooms   the balance is the living room with a nice stone chimney and fire place with a crane in one end to hang the pots on to cook our food. The house is to be lathed and plastered. will get the lath out this winter. there is plenty of lime stone and some men are burning lime kilns.

Oct. 1st, at the house again have it all enclosed and rocks on the ground for the chimney, now it is time to gather the corn so when it is dry they will be husking corn . . .   it will be husked out and stood up again and the foder fed to the hogs.

Nov. 10th, froze up and snowing will have winter now till the 1st of April. We will spend another winter in the little log house.

Dec. 1st, cold, and have had [to] go sleding for 6 weeks and the upstairs drifted full of snow twice. The roof is put on with slap-boards and weight poles.

Father Belknaps live in the large room of the same house we do and have meeting there. The 10th was Quarterly Meeting and Sat. night it snowed and blowed so the upstairs was so full of snow Sunday morning that we had to shovel it out and build big fires to get it dryed out so it would not drip before meeting time. We took up some of the boards and shoveled snow down and carried it out in the washtubs (barrels of it). Our room was not so bad [as it had a] loose floor and we had spread the wagon cover over it to keep out the cold so we rolled it up in a pile in the back corner and got breakfast in our room. The two families, the Presiding Elder and two preachers all joined in prayers and then all took breakfast in that little room   I think it was 14 by 16 ft. no one seemed crowded or embarassed and by the time breakfast was over the congregation began to gather.

We opened the middle door and the preacher stood in the door and preached both ways for both rooms were crowded. It was a grand meeting   by night the roads were broke and both rooms were crowded till there was not standing room. [We] had meetings again Mon. and Tues. nights   it was a happy time.

Time passes on and now it is time for the Holidays. What will we have for Christmas dinner? For company we will have Father Belknaps and the Hawley family and most likely the preacher—12 in all. and now for the bill of fare what shall it be? no fruit for mince pies, no red applies to eat, no nuts to crack.

They think Im too young to get up a big dinner under the circumstance. All have gone to bed so I will make out my bill of fare. firstly, for bread, nice light rolls, cake, doughnuts—for pie, pumpkin; preserves, crab apples and wild plums; sauce, dried apples; meat—first round, roast spare ribs with sausage and mashed potatoes and plain gravy; second round—chicken stewed with the best of gravy; chicken stuffed and roasted in the dutch oven by the fire, for then I had never cooked a meal on a stove.

I think I can carry that out and have dinner by two oclock if I get up early. I will cook in my room and set the table in the big room and with both of our dishes can make a good showing. Every thing went off in good style. [Someone] heard the old folks say they had no idea Kit could do so well.

May 1st Van Buren Co Iowa 1842. About the same routine of last year. Plant corn and tend it. we will be thru planting this month—then by the first of June what was planted first will need to be tended for it wont do to let the weeds get a start. so they will go thru it with the one horse plough, two furrows between every few and two or three boys with hoe to clean out the hills and pull out all the weeds (quite a tedious job if you have 50 or 60 acres)   but now it is all thru that suffering and now the sheep must be sheared.

Today the neighborhood all turns out to make a sheep pen on the bank of the Demoin River, wither they will drive their flocks to wash them before shearing. And now the fun begins for all the men and boys are there to help or see the fun. There were five men and their sheep and their boys. George's was the first ones in the pen (30). They were taken one at a time out in the river where they could not touch bottom with their feet—then hold their heads out of the water with one hand and with the other rub and souse them up and down till the water would look clean when they squeezed it out of the wool   then they took them out to a clean apartment and when they got one mans done they sent the boys home with them and put them in a little clean pasture to dry, and so on till all was done. They all took their dinner and had a regular picnic.

Now it is the 1st of June. The men are back in the corn except the sheep shearers. The sheep will be sheared this week. Then the wool will lay out for a few days to get the sheep smell off   then my work will begin. Im the first one to get at the wool— 25 fleeces, will sort it over, take off the poor short wool and put it by to card by hand for comforts, then sort out the finest for flannels and the courser for jeans for the mens wear. I find the wool very nice and white but I do hate to sit down alone to pick wool so I will invite about a dozen old ladies in and in a day they will do it all up.

June 20th. [I] have had my party—had 12 nice old ladies. they seemed to enjoy themselves fine. [We] had a fine chicken dinner. for cake I made a regular old fashioned pound cake like my mother used to make for weddings and now my name is out as a good cook so I am alright, for good cooking makes good friends.

July 1st. My wool came home today from the carding machine in nice rolls ready to spin. First I will spin my stocking yarn. can spin two skeins a day and in the evening will double and twist it while George reads the history of the U.S. then we read some in the bible together and have prayer and go to bed feeling that the sleep of the laboring man is sweet. My baby is so good she dont seem much in my way.

Times move on and here it is Sept and the new house is about ready to live in this winter, have been having meeting in it this summer so it has been dedicated and we will try to say "As for me and my house we will serve the Lord."

November. Everything is about done up and we have moved in our own house. have not got much to keep house with but it is real nice to have things all my own way. [I] have got my work for the winter pretty well in hand. have made me a new flannel dress colored blue and red—had it wove in small plaid. I am going to try and make me one dress every year then I can have one for nice and with a clean check apron I would be alright.

I made some jeans enough for two pair of pants . . . for George and have the knitting done so we have two good pair of stockings for all. It seems real nice to have the whole control of my

house. can say I am monarch of all I survey and there is none to dispute my right. I have curtained off a nice little room in one corner so we can entertain the preachers and they seem to enjoy it. Our house is right on the road going any way so I try to keep a little something prepared.

March 1843. The years have been much the same. this has been the most tedious winter I ever experienced. April 1st and everything frozen solid yet. We have a nice little baby boy now and I dont see as two babies are any more trouble than one. I put them both in their little cradle and the little girl amuses the baby till he gets sleepy   then I take them out, give the baby some attention while the little girl plays round the house and after they have exercised their muscles I fix up the little nest and lay the babe down to go to sleep. then the other comes running to be "pept in to by baby toseepens" and they are both soon asleep, I fix one in each end of the cradle and shove it to one side and then I just make things hum, for they are both babies, the oldest only a year and a half old.

We have got fixed up very nice in our new home. [We] have a good well close to the door, a nice little natural grove on the west—crab apples and wild plums.

The crabs are large and fine for preserves and the plums are fine too. Back of the house north is a piece of very rich soil   It is called hazel ruff   it has hazel bushes all over it but when grubbed out is very fine land, there we have prepared a place to raise melons and we have them in abundance and now I want to tell you how I make a substitute for fruit. Take the nice large watermelon. Cut them in two and scrape the inside fine to the hard rind and it will be mostly water and when you get a lot prepared strain it thru a seive or thin cloth   squeeze out all juice you can, then boil the juice down to syrup. I then took some good musk melons and crabapples about half and half and put them in the syrup and cook them down till they were done   being careful not to mash them, put in a little sugar to take the flat off and cook it down a little more and you have nice preserves to last all winter (and they are fine when you have nothing better and sugar 12½¢ a lb. and go 40 miles after it). On the east end of the house we have a garden.

Nov. 1843. I have experienced the first real trial of my life, after a few days of suffering our little Hannah died of lung fever so we are left with one baby   I expect to spend this winter mostly in the house but as we have prayer meeting Thursday here at our house, I can see all the neighbors twice a week for we have prayer meeting Thursday evenings.

Have commenced to build a church on our land, it will be brick. we are going to have Quarterly Meeting here about Christmas—if it gets very interesting protract it thru the holidays.

Jan. 5, 1844. The meeting is over and the house cleaned up. We had a good time and the house was packed every night. every body seemed to be interested. We had two beds in the house and a trundle bed that we could shove under one bed, then in the evening I would put both beds on one bedstead and take the other out doors till after meeting, then bring it in and shift the beds and make it up for the preachers. The one that was left in was used for a seat and to lay the sleeping babies on while the sisters were helping carry on the work and it was no uncommon thing for the noise to become so great that it would rouse some of the babes and a man would take it up and pass it along to the fire place where there was always a warm corner reserved for the sisters with little ones.

The meeting lasted for 10 days. [We] had over 20 conversions and I thot that was about the best time I ever had. I cooked by the fire place and our one room served for church, kitchen, dining room, bedroom, and study for the preachers, sometimes we had three or four as they came from adjoining circuits to help us thru the week.

January 1845. We have another little boy baby born Dec. 23, 1844, we call him Jesse Walker. The first name for his grandfather Belknap, the second for our family doctor who was also a local preacher and a fast friend and good neighbor.

We are still talking up the subject of building a church. have the lot on the west corner of our land near the burying ground. we gave 5 acres for that and two for the church. it is to be of brick, will do the [ground] work this winter. Tonight we have company—three neighbors and their wives have come to spend the evening and while they are talking about the [amount] of brick it will take to build the church, I am getting a fine supper in the same room by the same fire, took the chickens off the roost after they came and will have it ready about 10 oclock. have fried cakes (had fresh bread), stewed chicken, and sausage and mashed potatoes. had a fine time, had prayers before they left 15 min till twelve.

June 1846. Summer comes again with its busy cares. They have got to work at the church and I am boarding three men to get money to pay my subscription of $10 to the church.

I have had to pass thru another season of sorror   death has again entered our home   this time it claimed our dear little John for its victim, it was hard for me to give him up but dropsy on the brain ended its work in four short days. When our pastor was here a week before he said he thot that child was too good for this wicked world. but he little expected to be called to preach his funeral in less than one week. We are left again with one baby and I feel that my health is giving way. a bad cough and pain in my side is telling me that disease is making its inroads on my system.

Oct. 1st. We have got thru our summers work and now we are preparing for winter, have raised a good crop but will have to feed it all out this winter   will have a lot of hogs to fatten.

Nov. 10. Have had a month of cold frosty nights and now we expect a freeze up—cold northwest winds prevail. Im going to stay at home this winter and see if I will take so much cold.

We have another baby, such a nice little girl, only 6 lbs. at first and though it is a month old is not much bigger than at first. it has never been well so we have two children again for awhile, neither of them are very strong.

The church is not finished but the roof is on so it will stand over winter and meeting will still be at our house. We are fixed nicely in our home now have had a very pleasant winter and now it is spring time 1847 again and they all think I had better go on a visit to Ohio. The past winter there has been a strange fever raging here. it is the "Oregon fever." it seems to be contagious and it is raging terribly. nothing seems to stop it but to tear up and take a six months trip across the plains with ox teams to the Pacific Ocean.

May 1847. Some of our friends have started for Oregon—L.D. Gilbert, wife and six children, Oren Belknap, wife and four children, Ransom Belknap wife and two children, S.F. Starr, wife and two children. these were from our neighborhood   they will meet others at the crossing of the Missouri River and make laws and join together in a larger company.

May 15. Husband and I and two children start for Ohio to visit my father and mother. We go by wagon to Keocuck—there we take the steamer on the Mississippi of St. Louis, thence to Cincinatti   there we get a team to take us out 6 miles to my sisters stayed there one week then they took us out to Hamilton 30 miles to another sisters, stayed there three days, then took the canal boat for St Maries. got on the boat Mon evening, got off at the landing at three oclock Tues morning. there was a little shack there and as there was no one on the stir we had to stay there till day light. I took our wraps and made a bed for the children and we noded till people began to stir then we hunted up the town and found the hotel and got breakfast. While we were eating we saw an old man eating just on the other side of the table and we recognized Mr. Jones, one of our old neighbors, so we kept our eyes on him and when he left the table we made ourselves known to him and he said "And this is little Kittie Penton that you carried off from us a few years ago. Well! Well! she has got to be quite a woman."

He said he had just been in with a load of oats and was going home empty so he could take us to our journeys end it was 12 miles to my father so we thot we were in luck. We got to Mr. Jones at noon, so we stoped and fed the team and got a good warm dinner, then had about 4 miles to go yet. so the horses we hitched up again and about four oclock we drove up to my fathers gate. They were greatly surprised as we had not written them we were coming. We all seemed to enjoy the trip. the children seemed to be much better than when we left home but I was no better. Every one would say how changed I was till I realy thot I was sick and going into consumption, but my baby seemed better.

I knew it would be the last visit I would make there whether I lived or not I kept all those thots buried in my own breast and never told them that the folks at home were fixing to cross the plains while we were away, but taking it all around we had a good time. We were there a month then it came time to say good bye. The last few days the baby was growing weaker and I wanted to get home where it could be more quiet.

All the friends have visited us and Sunday we had a good social meeting and said goodbye to all the friends. It was hard for me not to break down but they all thot in about two years we would come again.

Tues. June 1st. we were ready to start for home. We went by wagon 25 miles to Springfield and there we struck the railroad that was just being built from Cincinatti to Columbus Ohio but was not finished any further than Springfield so we stayed there all night and in the morning got on the car for Cincinatti that was our first car ride and the first R.R. we had ever seen—we got to ride 75 miles. Our little boy was asleep when we got on and when he woke up he looked all around surprised and said "Where is the horses?"

At noon we were on the bank of the Ohio river if we had [gone] with a team it would have taken 3 days. There we found the same old steam boat that brought us down (the Victress) had made its trip and just steaming up to leave the wharf, so we got on board again for home—were on the water two days and one night then we were at the mouth of the Demoin River where we had arranged to get off and meet a team to take us home about 40 miles but it was a fine level road and by getting an early start we could make it in a day. Now we had been gone a month and traveled all kinds of ways.

Just as we landed Father Belknap drove up to meet us. We had friends there so we stayed all night with them and the next day we went home.

They thot I looked better for the trip but the baby was failing all the time. We found the folks all excitement about Oregon—some had gone in the spring of '47 . . . but they had not been heard from since crossing the Missouri River. Everything was out of place and all was excitement and commotion our home was sold, waiting our return to make out the papers and it was all fixed up for us to live with Father Belknaps as the man wanted the house on our place. Ransoms and Fathers had not been sold yet. It did not suit me to live with them so I told them it was out of the question so for the first time since our marriage I put my foot down and said "will and wont" so it was arranged for us to go on Rants place and live in their house till it was sold. I knew it would use me and the little sick baby up so to be in such a tumult. There was nothing done or talked of but what had Oregon in it and the loom was banging and the wheels buzzing and trades being made from daylight till bedtime so I was glad to get settled. My dear little girl Martha was sick all summer and the 30th of Oct she died one year and one month old. Now we have one puny boy left. So now I will spend what little strength I have left getting ready to cross the Rockies, will cut out some sewing to have to pick up at all the odd moments for I will try to have clothes enough to last a year.

Nov 15, 1947. Have cut out four muslin shirts for George and two suits for the little boy (Jessie) with what he has that will last him (if he lives) until he will want a different pattern.

The material for the mens outer garments has to be woven

yet. The neighbors are all very kind to come in to see me so I dont feel lonely   they dont bring any work, but just pick up my sewing so think I will soon get a lot done   then they are not the kind with long sad faces, but always leave me with such pleasant smiling faces that it does me good to think of them and I try not to think of the parting time but look forward to the time when we shall meet to part no more.

Now I will begin to work and plan to make everything with an eye to starting out on a six months trip. the first thing is to lay plans and then work up to the program   so the first thing is to make a piece of linen for a wagon cover and some sacks—will spin mostly evenings while my husband reads to me. The little wheel in the corner dont make any noise. I spin for Mother B. and Mrs. Hawley and they will weave now that it is in the loom   I must work almost day and night to get the filling ready to keep the loom busy. The men are busy making ox yokes and bows for the wagon covers and trading for oxen.

Now the New Year has come and Ill write 1848 . . . my health is better and I dont spend much time with housework   will make a muslin cover for the wagon as we will have a double cover so we can keep warm and dry   put the muslin on first and then the heavy linen one for strength. They both have to be sewed real good and strong and I have to spin the thread and sew all those long seams with my fingers. then I have to make a new feather tick for my bed   I will put the feathers of two beds into one tick and sleep on it.

Feb. 1st and the linen is ready to go to work on and six two bushel bags all ready to sew up that I will do evenings by the light of a dip candle for I have made enough to last all winter after we get to Oregon   and now my work is all planned so I can go right along. Have cut out two pairs of pants for Geo. (home made jeans)   a kind lady friend came in today and sewed all day on one pair then took them home with her to finish. Another came and wanted to buy some of my dishes and she took two shirts home to make to pay for them.

And now it is March and we have our team allready and in good condition—three good yoke of oxen and a good wagon. The company have arranged to start the 10 of April. I expect to load up the first wagon   George is practicing with the oxen. I dont want to leave my kind friends here but they all think it best so I am anxious

to get off. I have worked almost day and night this winter. have the sewing about all done but a coat and vest for George. he got some nice material for a suit and had a taylor cut it out and Aunt Betsy Starr helped me two days with them so I am about ready to load up. Will wash and begin to pack and start with some old clothes on and when we can't wear them any longer will leave them on the road. I think we are fixed very comfortable for the trip. There is quite a train of connection. Father Belknap has one wagon and 4 yoke of oxen. we have the same besides 3 horses and 10 cows. Now it is the 1st of April, and the stock is all in our corn field to get them used to running together. in ten days more we will be on the road. This week I will wash and pack away every thing except what we want to wear on the trip.

April 5. This week I cook up something to last us a few days till we get used to camp fare. Bake bread, make a lot of crackers and fry doughnuts, cook a chicken, boil ham, and stew some dryed fruit. There is enough to last us over the first Sunday so now we will begin to gather up the scatterings. Tomorrow is Sat. and next Tues. we start so will put in some things today. only one more Sunday here . . . We have had our farewell meeting so I wont go—dont think I could stand it   so George stays with me and we will take a rest, for tomorrow will be a busy day.

Mon. April 9th 1848   I am the first one up, breakfast is over [and] our wagon is backed up to the steps   we will load at the hind end and shove the things in front. The first thing is a big box that will just fit in the wagon bed that will have the bacon, salt, and various other things   then it will be covered with a cover made of light boards nailed on two pieces of inch plank about 3 inches wide. this will serve us for a table. there is a hole in each corner and we have sticks sharpened at one end so they will stick in the ground   then we put the box cover on, slip the legs in the holes and we have a nice table   then when it is on the box George will sit on it and let his feet hang over and drive the team. it is just as high as the wagon bed.

Now we will put in the old chest that is packed with our clothes and things we will want to wear and use on the way. The till is the medicine chest   then there will be cleats fastened to the bottom of the wagon bed to keep things from slipping out of place. Now there is a vacant place clear across that will be large enough to sit a chair—will set it with the back against the side of the wagon bed   there I will ride—on the other side will be a vacancy where little Jessie can play   he has a few toys and some marbles and some sticks for whip stocks, some blocks for oxen and I tie a string on the stick and he uses my work basket for a covered wagon and plays going to Oregon. He never seems to get tired or cross (but here I am leaving the wagon half packed and got off on the journey).

The next thing is a box as high as the chest that is packed with a few dishes and things we wont need till we get thru   and now we will put in the long sacks of flour and other things. The sacks are made of home made linen and will hold 125 pounds—4 sacks of flour and one of corn meal. Now comes the groceries—we will make a wall of smaller sacks stood on end, dried apples and peaches, beans, rice, sugar, and coffee—the latter being in the green state. we will brown it in a skillet as we want to use it. everything must be put in strong bags—no paper wrappings for this trip. There is a corner left for the washtub and the lunch basket will just fit in the tub   the dishes we want to use will all be in the basket. I am going to start with good earthen dishes and if they get broken have tin ones to take their place. [I] have made 4 nice little table cloths so am going to live just like I was at home.

Now we will fill the other corner with pick ups. The iron-ware that I will want to use every day will go in a box on the hind end of the wagon like a feed box   now we are loaded all but the bed. I wanted to put it in and sleep out but Geo said I wouldnt rest any, so I will level up the sacks with some extra bedding   then there is a side of sole leather that will go on first, then two comforts and we have a good enough bed for any one to sleep on. At night I will turn my chair down to make the bed a little longer so now all we will have to do in the morning is put in the bed and make some coffee and roll out.

The wagon looks so nice—the nice white cover drawn down tight to the side boards with a good ridge to keep from saging   its high enough for me to stand straight under the roof with a curtain to put down in front and one at the back end   now its all done and I get in out of the tumult. And now every thing is ready. I will rest a little, then we will eat a bite. Mother B. has made a pot of mush and we are all going to eat mush and milk to save the milk that otherwise would have to be thrown out   then we have prayers and then to bed.

Tues Apr 10, 1848. Daylight dawned with none awake but me. I try to keep quiet so as not to wake any one but pretty soon Father

Belknaps voice was heard with that well known sound: "Wife, wife, rise and flutter" and there was no more quiet for any one. breakfast is soon over—my dishes and food for lunch is packed away and put in its proper place. the iron things are packed in some old pieces of old thick rags   now for the bed (feather) nicely folded and the pillows laid smoothly on, reserving one for the outside so if I or the little boy get sleepy we have a good place to lie. the others are covered with a heavy blanket and now my chair and the churn and we will be all done.

Our wagon is ready to start   I get in the wagon and in my chair busy with some unfinished work, Jessie is in his place with his whip starting for Oregon. George and the boys have gone out in the field for the cattle. Dr. Walker calls at the wagon to see me and give me some good advice and give me the parting hand for neither of us could speak the word Farewell. He told me to keep up good courage and said "dont fret, whatever happens dont fret and cry. courage will do more for you than anything else." [then] he took the little boy in his arms and presented to him a nice Bible with his blessing and was off.

The cattle have come and most of the train are lined up here in the lane and many of the neighbors are here the last, so they will be behind today. We will take them in after we get a mile on the road at their place. Now we roll out—Father B is on the lead on old Polly. Rant is driving the team. Cory is on our old Lize, driving the loose stock   our wagon is number 2, G.W. Bethers number 3, J.W. Starr, 4, Uncle Brather two wagons, Chatman Hawley two wagons, and I think they all had one horse but Uncle John Starr   he had two yoke of oxen to each wagon   one wagon was a very shaky old thing   they had their provisions in it and when they got it lightened up, they would put everything in one wagon and leave the old shack by the road side. They started with a family of eight and had to take in an old man to drive one team.

Now were fairly on the road, it is one oclock   we got started at 10, will stop for an hour and eat a lunch and let the oxen chew their cuds. We have just got out of the neighborhood   the friends that came a piece with us [have turned back] and we will travel on. Jessie and I have had a good nap and a good lunch and now we will ride some more. Evening we come to water and grass and plenty of wood—what hinders us from camping here? They say we have come 15 miles. Every one seems hungry and we make fires and soon have supper fit for a king. I will make the first call and am the [only] one that has a table and—it has a clean white cloth on. I have my chair out, George piles up the ox yokes for a seat and Jessie has the wash tub turned upside down and will stand on his knees. Supper over and I fix the bed. The stock have all been looked after and are quietly chewing their cuds. Some of the men take bedding and will sleep out to see that none of the stock will get up and scatter off.

April 11th. All astir bright and early. breakfast is soon over—some of the men have gone to relive the night watch. My work is all done up—lunch prepared for noon and all put in its proper place. Here comes the oxen—our team is soon ready we have two yoke of well trained oxen all there is to do is to hold up the yoke and tell Old Buck and Bright to come under and they walk up and take their places as meek as kittens but now comes Dick and Drab a fine pair of black matched four year old steers—they have to be cornered. I am in the wagon sewing. Jessie is playing with his whips and now the word is "Roll out." The loose stock is started on ahead. Our wagon is in the lead today—will be behind tomorrow, so now we are on the wing. It is a fine spring morning. Noon we stop an hour to let the teams rest and eat our lunch.

We are in Missuri now, see once in awhile a log hut and some half dressed children running away to hide. Every man to his team now. This afternoon we pass along a little creek with fine timber the road is good and I am standing the rideing fine. Now we camp again I think all days will be about the same now. Sat evening we have a fine start—everything seems to move along nicely. Sunday morning we hitch up and move on a few miles to better grass, then camp for the Sabbath. Ten oclock we find a lovely spot—a fine little brook goes gurgling by with fine large trees and nice clean logs for seats and to spread our things on. We have cleaned up and put on clean clothes.

There are some fine farms along the creek bottom some of the ladies come out to visit us and brought some things along to sell to the immigrants but we had not been out long enough to get very hungry. I did get a nice dressed hen for 25 cents and 6 doz eggs, 6¢ a doz. I started with quite a box of eggs and found them handy.

Mon. morning April 17th. We start again. the next point is Missouri River, will cross at St. Joe. have moved every day for a week, have had fine weather good roads and all have been well. We have three good milch cows milk them at night and strain the milk in little buckets and cover them up and set on ground under the wagon and in the morning I take off the nice thick cream and put it in the churn. I save the strippings from each cow in the morning milking and put in the churn also and after riding all day I have a nice roll of butter as long as we have plenty of grass and water.

The 22. Are nearing the Missouri river—will camp here over Sunday.

Sunday. Breakfast over and the men come in from the stock and say there has been a band of sheep herded on the range for two days and they have spoiled the grass, so the stock wont feed on it so some of the men got on their horses and go to look for a better place 10 oclock and word is "Move on." About 10 miles there is plenty of water and grass—some want to stay, others are getting their teams ready to move. Mr. Jacksons voice is heard he says if we stay it will break the Sabbath worse than if we go on so we all started but had only gone about 5 miles when a little boy was run over by the wagon and instantly killed. We then stopped and buried the child we were near a settlement so he was not left there alone.

Monday. we are on the trail again, every man at his post. [We] made a big days drive—20 miles they say.

Tues. will get to the river tomorrow. Supper is over we have a nice place to camp. some have gone to bed and others have gone out with the stock. They say there are some Mormans here that give us some trouble with our stock they might want a good horse so we think it best to put a good guard out.

Wed. All are on the stir to get to the wharf before the other company gets here and now begins the scene of danger the river is high and looks terrific. one wagon and two yoke of oxen go over first so as to have a team to take the wagons out of the way—it is just a rope ferry. all back safe. Now they take two wagons and the loose horses. They say it will take about all day to get us over. Next the loose cattle must go as they are in a dry lot without any thing to eat. When they put the cattle on the boat they found that one of our cows was sick—she had got poisoned by eating the Jimson weeds. She staggered when she walked on the ferry and in the crowd she was knocked over board and went under but when she came up the boat man had his rope ready and throwed it out and lassoed her and they hauled her to land but she was to far gone to travel so

143

the boatman said he would take our wagon and stock over [in exchange for] her so they hauled her up to the house and the last we saw of her a woman had her wrapped in a warm blanket and had a fire and was bathing her and pouring milk and lard down her. She could stand alone the next morning so we bade farewell to the Missouri and old Brock.

The Watts company will stay here till the Jacksons get over the river and we will move on to fresh grass and water. Our next point will be the crossing of the Platte River near old Fort Laramie, there is life there now.

This is the 4th week we have been on the road and now we are among the Pawnee Indians. so we must get into a larger company so we can guard our selves and stock from the prowling tribes and renegade whites that are here to keep away from the law they seem to have their eyes on a good horse and follow [it] for days—then if they are caught will say they got him from the Indians. by paying them something they would give the horse up, [trying] to make us believe that they were sent out there to protect the emegrants.

Another week has past, had a nice road, will camp here till afternoon. At the Platte River will stay here all day and get ready to cross the river and do some work on the wagons—set tires mend chains, etc. We will now form a company and make some laws so all will have their part. Some of the oxen are getting tender-footed, they have been trying to shoe them but gave it up. I have washed and ironed and cooked up a lot—find our appetites improve the longer we are out, have baked a nice skillet of corn bread enough for two dinners for George, Jessie and I.

This morning the roll is called and every one is expected to answer to his name. They have quite a time with the election of officers—every man wants an office. George Jackson and Joe Watts are pilots. They have both been over the road before and have camping places noted down so now we take the trail again the order is for the first one hitched up to "roll out," so we are ahead on the lead today—then Beathers next but tomorrow we will be behind. Now we are getting on the Pawnee Indian hunting ground so we must make a big show. They are out after Buffalo so we have to keep out an advance guard to keep the herd from running into our teams. The road goes between the hills and it is just the time now when the buffalo are moving to the river bottom for grass and water. A herd passed us a few days ago—the guard turned them so they crossed the road behind us, they killed a nice young heifer, so we have fresh meat. It is very coarse and dark meat but when cooked right made a very good change. I cooked some and made mince pies with dried applies which was fine for lunch. During the hunt Dr. Baker lost his nice saddle horse and a fine saddle, he jumped off and threw down the bridle to give his game another shot and away went the horse with the buffalo. they hunted for [the horse] but didn't find him or the buffalo but in about two weeks the company that was behind us sent word to Dr. Baker that the horse had come to them with the saddle still on but turned under his belly the head part of the bridle was on him yet so old Dock got his horse—[it] never wanted to leave the train again. We have been on the route till its got to be June all days about the same.

We will now go down the noted Ash Hollow and strike the Sweet River, then will rest awhile.

We make the trip down the hollow all safe, went as far as we could with the team then took off some of the best teams and sent down so they could move the wagons out of the way—then they would take one wagon as far as they could with the team—unhitch and ruff-lock both hind wheels, then fasten a big rope to the axle of the wagon and men would hold to that to keep the wagon from going end over end some were at the tongue to steer it and others were lifting the wheels to ease them down the steps, for it was solid rock steps from six inches to two feet apart so it took all day but we all got thru without accident. We will stay here all night. I wash a little and cook some more, have a ham bone and beans. This is good sweet water—we have had alkali and nothing was good.

Just as we were ready to sit down to supper Joe Meek and his possie of men rode into camp. They were going to Washington D.C. to get the government to send soldiers to protect the settlers in Oregon and they told us all about the Indian Massacars at Walla Walla called the "Whitman Massacre." They had traveled all winter and some of their men had died and they had got out of food and had to eat mule meat so we gave them all their supper and breakfast. The captain divided them up so all could help feed them.

Father B. was captain so he and George took three so they made way with most all my stuff I had cooked up on the whole we are having quite a time—some want to turn back and others are telling what they would do in case of an attack. I sit in the wagon and write a letter as these men say if we want to send any word back they will take it and drop it in the first Post Office they come to so Im writing a scratch to a lady friend. While Im writing I have an exciting experience. Geo. is out on guard and in the next wagon behind ours a man and wife are quarreling she wants to turn back and he wont, so she says she will go and leave him—that these men will furnish her a horse and she will leave him with the children and he will have a good time with that crying baby. then he used some very bad words and said he would put it out of the way—just then I heard a muffled cry and a heavy thud as tho something was thrown against the wagon box and she said "Oh youve killed it" and he swore some more and told her to keep her mouth shut or he would give her some of the same.

Just then the word came "Change guards!" Geo came in and Mr Kitridge went out so he and his wife were parted for the night. The baby was not killed. I write this to show how easy we can be deceived.

We have a rest and breakfast is over. Meek and his men are gathering their horses and packing, but he said he would have to transact a little business with his men so they were all lined up and he court martialed them and found three guilty and made them think they would be shot for disobeying orders, but it was only a scare.

Now every man to his post and double quick till they reach The Hollow. The woman was out by the roadside with a little bag and her baby asleep in the wagon under a strong opiate. After that we had trouble with these folks as long as they were with us. They would take things from those that did the most for them and there were others of the same stripe. They seemed to think when they got on the plains they were out of reach of the law of God or man.

It is afternoon, we hitch up and drive till night. Here we are it is almost sun down we will have a cold lunch for supper then shake up the beds and rest after the excitement of the day is over. We will leave the sweet water in the morning and have a long dry drive—will fill our kegs and everything that will hold water so we will not suffer of thirst. We stop at noon for an hours rest its very warm—the oxen all have their tongues out panting. George took the wash pan and a bucket of water and let all our team wet their tongues and he washed the dust off their noses. Some laughed at him, but the oxen seemed very grateful.

George lays down to catch a little nap—if they start before he wakes the team will start up in their places. Time is up—the word along the line is "Move up." (Geo sleeps on.) that means 10 miles of dry hot dirt. I have a little water left yet—will have to let the thirsty ox drivers wet their parched lips. It will be hot till the sun goes down, then it will be dusk. That night we get to plenty of water. I think old Brights feet hurt—he is standing in the water. We eat a bite and go to bed we are coming near the Green River, will have to ferry it with the wagons. The cattle will be unyoked and swim over. some Mormans are here they have fixed up a ferry and will take us over for a dollar a wagon. It will take all day to get over it is the 4th of July . . .

Now we are on to the Pawnee Indians they say they are a bad set we must pass right thru their villiages. they come out by the thousands and want pay for us crossing their country they spread down some skins and wanted every wagon to give them something so they all gave them a little something and they set to dividing it amongst themselves. we rushed on to get as near Fort Hall as we could. There was a company of soldiers there to protect the immigrants. the scouts had been out and reported what the Indians were doing and the troops soon settled them and made them leave the road so we had no more trouble for us it was all for the best so that was all the time we had any trouble with the Indians tho it did look a little scary for awhile. The General at the Fort told us to make as big a show as possible.

For want of space I must cut these notes down [and] will pass over some interesting things. Watts and the sheep pulled out and fell behind. I got the blame for the split. The old mother Watts said after they got through "Yes Geo. Belknaps wife is a little woman but she wore the pants on that train" so I came into noterity before I knew it but to return to the trail, they say we are on the last half of the journey now.

My little boy is very sick with mountain fever and tomorrow we will have to make a long dry drive. We will stay here at this nice water and grass till about 4 oclock—will cook up a lot of provision, then will take what is known as "Green Woods Cut Off" and travel all night—must fill every thing with water. We are on the brink of Snake River but it is such a rocky canyon we could not get to it if ones life depended on it.

Its morning— I have been awake all night watching with the little boy he seems a little better—has droped off to sleep the sun is just rising and it shows a lot of the dirtest humanity ever was seen since the creation. We just stop for an hour and eat a bite and let the teams breath again. We divide the water with the oxen. George has sat on his seat on the front of the wagon all night and I have held the little boy in my lap on a pillow and tended him as best I could. I thot in the night we would have to leave him here and I thot if we did I would be likely to stay with him but at day light we seemed to get fresh courage. Some of the men went thru to Fort Hall on horse back and returned to meet us and say we can make it by noon.

The journal ends here and resumes when the Belknap party reached Oregon. The men stayed there just long enough to help establish their families in quickly built cabins before leaving in March of 1849 for the gold mines of California. By April, Keturah wrote, "We women folks began to realize that we were the providers for our families . . . we had to rustle for our families and [also] care for the church."

Eventually the men returned with minimal gains and they settled down in earnest to farm the land. Keturah continued on at the Belknap Settlement until 1871, striking up many friendships with the Indians that were always nearby, and acting as nurse and midwife to the neighbors. In 1874 they moved to Lane County, near Eugene, and, in 1879, they left Oregon and moved to Washington, homesteading a few acres near a one-cabin town named Latah.

In 1889 Keturah and George were honored at their golden wedding anniversary by forty friends and relatives who showered them with table linens, slippers, gold-banded dishes, and assorted tokens of their love and respect. Yet despite their precedence in the community, their farming luck apparently ran out in 1895, when, as granddaughter Katherine Christain Barrett reports, they lost their farm, sold their belongings, and went to stay with their children in Clackamas for the winter.

George Belknap died in 1897. Keturah lived with her grandson Walter and later with her son George, until the age of ninety-three. She was a spry woman who assisted in every household chore and regularly wrote to her remaining children.

She died August 19, 1913 leaving five surviving children and thirteen grandchildren. She had buried six children in Iowa and Oregon.

Emigrants stopping to lunch on a white tablecloth in Greenwood County, Kansas.

One room schoolhouse, probably in Colorado.

Sod schoolhouse, Custer County, Nebraska, 1886.

Pioneer schoolhouse somewhere in California, ca. 1890.

Mrs. Staples' class in Nome, Alaska, 1904

Two schoolgirls talking during lunch recess in Hadleyville, Oregon.

The Becker sisters branding cattle on their Rio Grande Ranch in the San Luis Valley, 1894.

Helen Wiser Stewart

Helen Jane Wiser of Sacramento met Archibald Stewart before her nineteenth birthday. She was gentle and unassuming; he a dour, though handsome, Scot who soundly met her parents' requirements that each of their daughters marry a successful older man. On April 6, 1873, they were wed, and returned to his thriving freight business in Pioche, Nevada.

For the next eight years Helen obligingly followed Archie through a successful round of cattle deals and land contracts, eventually finding herself on a newly purchased ranch fifty miles north of El Dorodo Canyon. She was pregnant with their fifth child, Eveline La Vega, and had grown increasingly anxious about her two sons' lack of education. Yet despite her misgivings, she accepted and made the best of her position on the remote Las Vegas ranch.

On September 22, 1882, her daughter was borne without midwife or nurse. On July 13, 1884, she suffered the slaying of her husband by an embittered ranch hand, Schyler Henry. The ledger used in their freighting business stated simply that Henry had told lies about Helen during Archie's absence, and although the specific lies are never mentioned, they so enraged Archie that he saddled his horse, took his rifle and departed for the nearby Kiel ranch—never to be seen alive again.

He died without a will, and the resultant threat to Helen's security forced her to a decision: either sell the land or manage it. She kept the land, and managed it so efficiently over the next twenty years that she became the largest landowner in Lincoln County, Nevada, with holdings of over two thousand acres.

Not only did she buy and sell cattle, raise crops, harvest fruit, and acquire more land, but she turned the dusty ranch into the social apex of the Las Vegas Valley; it was a haven for traveling cattlemen, prospectors, entomologists, archeologists, drifters—even outlaws.

In 1891, she persuaded James Ross Megarrigle, an Oxford-educated poet who had frequently taught school, to live at the ranch and tutor her children. This delighted the girls, but her older sons Hiram and Will could hardly be persuaded to give up ranching for the classroom. Helen, however, found in Megarrigle a true friend. He was a man of great knowledge who shared her lively interest in books and poetry. Their friendship blossomed during his five-year stay at the ranch, which ended with his death in the spring of 1894. Six years later she married one of her ranch hands, Frank Roger Stewart, who agreed in a prenuptial contract to forego any claim to the wealth she had already accumulated.

Because of the enormous burden of raising five children and managing a cattle ranch, Helen Stewart had little time for journal entries. Her writings in the day ledger between 1869 and 1890 are cryptic and reveal few clues to her personality. Yet later letters written to her growing children are phrased in such terms of tenderness and solicitude that her devotion to them is clear.

Although Helen Stewart often mused upon her isolation from "society," the entries in her day ledger track a ceaseless flow of activity between the ranch and El Dorodo Canyon, or the "Cañon." Intense beef and produce trading was conducted in the canyon, and many of those whose names appear in the following text pursued their business in the canyon via the Stewart ranch.

Among the most frequent visitors were James Wilson and George Allen, two neighboring ranchers who were close enough to Helen to be named appraisers of her estate after Archie's death. Also present from time to time was Ed Kiel, heir to the adjacent Kiel ranch, and suspect, along with his cohort Hank Parish, of plotting Archie's murder. Moore, Henderson, and Frazier must have been familiar to Helen Stewart; they simply came and went throughout the journal with little ado.

1884 Ledger #3

June 4	J. Wilson back from Cañon
June 6	G. Allen [back from Cañon]
June 8	G. Allen went down to burn coal
June 15	G. Allen came up from coal camp
June 17	G. Allen left for Cañon
June 18	Harry Henderson back from Cañon (Ed Kiel to Cañon with first vegetables.)
June 21	Archie & Willie with first fruits (to Cañon)
June 22	G. Allen back from Cañon
June 24	H. Henderson started from Muddy
June 24	G. Allen started for Cañon.

Helen Stewart dispassionately noted in her ledger the crucial steps leading to the murder of her husband, beginning with Archie's return from El Dorodo Canyon to find that Schyler Henry had quit and demanded his wages. Stewart then armed himself and left the ranch to find Henry and make him retract his lies about Helen.

July, 1884

July 3	Wilson came down, and the boys.
July 5	G. Allen started to Cañon. Told of H. Lying
July 6	Wilson went home; dried jerkey; Hank Parish went to Cañon.
July 7	Sick all day
July 9	Hank Parish back from Cañon
July 10	George Allen & Mr. Frazier came
July 11	Henry left—Baled hay for Mr. Moore from Pioche
July 13	Archie was murdered.
July 14	Archie was buried.

In spite of her grief, Helen Stewart showed great presence of mind in contacting a lawyer. Although she had stayed out of Archie's past business affairs, she seems to have known that his fast and successful dealings had created many enemies. She knew that legal counsel was the only way to protect herself against possible retaliation from disgruntled competitors.

July 16, 1884
Las Vegas Rancho Nev.

Mr. Sawyer, Sir.

I write to you in great distress of mind hoping you as a husband and father will aid me to the best of your ability—I am left alone here and my little children fatherless by the hand of a murderer. My beloved husband and only friend was murdered Sunday the 13th at Mr. Kiels one mile and half from here while defending the honor of his family from a black-hearted Slanderers tounge. The evidence is all circumstantial. The man had been working here and while Mr. Stewart was in the El Dorado Cañon left and went over to Kiels and was kept posted on every movement going on at the Vegas and was supplied with arms and a horse by men on the Ranch and vicinity. Archie came home Sunday about 10 o'clock after he had eaten dinner and rested a short time & told him of the Slander being talked about as it had been told to every one stopping on the place and passers by the day before. Mr. Stewart came home; they tried to frighten me into paying the man Schyler Henry off and letting him go. As he had got money and clothing of Mr. Stewart which I knew nothing of I could not settle as it was something I had never done before. About 2 O'Clock Willie the oldest boy saw his father saddle his horse and go down on the cattle range taking his Henry Rifle which is no unusual occurance, going in an opposite direction from Kiels. I supposed he was going down to see George Allen at his Coal camp on the road to the cañon 10 miles from here. Mr. Allen had been stopping here several days but left early Sunday morning for the cañon. The next I heard of my poor husband is this note which I copy as it was written by old man Kiel:

> Mrs. Stewart send a team and take Mr. Stewart away—he is dead—C Kiel

I left my little children with Mr. Frazier and went as fast as a Horse would carry me. The man that killed my husband ran as I approached as I got to the corner of the house I said Oh where is he Oh where is he and the Old Man Kiel and Hank Parish said here he is and lifting a blanket showed me the lifeless form of my husband. I knelt beside him, took his hands, placed my hand upon his heart and looked upon his face and saw a bullet hole about two inches above the temple and about one inch into the hair and looking more closely I saw where the Rifle had been placed directly under the right ear and fired off that side of his face to a crisp. (He must have received that shot after he fell) and across the cheek bone & forehead on the right side he had been hit with some heavy instrument breaking the cheek bone and forehead starting in the opposite direction from the way the bullet went in; they told me he was shot in the shoulder. The hired men came with the Spring waggon and I took him home and on examination found he had been shot right above the left breast coming out under the right arm. The men said it was a pistol shot. It is evident that Mr. Stewart was finally Killed in the house with no one as witness except this Henry and old man Kiel. They are both Archie's enemies and would not tell the truth but swear against Archie. I am here with a lot of roughs and my life and Husbands property in danger. If I have friends in Pioche I think—pray they will come and help me. George Allen & James Wilson are here; also Mr. Frazier whose health is very poor he being hardly able to wait on himself but he has done all he can for me. Mr. Allen and Mr. Wilson both have business to attend to but say they will help me all they can in the time they can leave their business both have inconvenienced themselves already.

PRIVATE

My friends here tell me I ought to be thinking of my children's interest. I do not know whether there is a will but think maybe there is but in case there is not I wish the guardianship of my children and to administer on the property. They tell me I will have to apply in 30 days from the 13th. They tell me I will have to go to Pioche right away. Write soon as possible and give me good legal instructions in regard to this matter. If there is a chance of anyone taking advantage of myself and childrens rights before I could get there I wish you to take measures to protect us. The man that murdered my husband is still at Kiels with a slight flesh wound in the hip. It is dangerous to say or do anything as we are overpowered by numbers and still threatened.

Yours in distress
Mrs. Archie Stewart
    you can give this to the public except what is marked private

Signed by,   These gentlemen sign their names here
Mr. Frazier   to corporate my statement—Mrs. Stewart
G. Allen
J. B. Wilson

The Las Vegas ranch was never without a full contingent of Indians who worked in the fields harvesting fruit and grain, or fetching supplies and running messages from one ranch to another. Here Helen Stewart briefly notes relationships of the Indians either in her employ or in the neighborhood.

Indian Ledger Book July 1886
    John Ontop (killed the mail rider)
    Ahuotes brother (killed Nelson Trandsen)
    Both brothers of To-go-mon-che
    Togomonche's wife to Bishop
    Happy Tune (Lew Betts child)
    Jim Wilson (Lew Betts child)
    Jim Wilson & Happy Tune half sisters and brothers
    Togomonche related to the Smith boys
    Kinginsmith's sons
    Loco killed Tommy Jennings
    Loco Vegas Joe's brother
    Ontop killed the stage driver, swam river.
    Torianoo, Button and Charley Keats: brothers

Helen Stewart's letter to her five children indicates that she has been at her parents' home in Galt, California, for several weeks. Perhaps she was talking to her father, Hiram Wiser, about his purchase of ranch land in the Muddy Valley; or discussing the offer of Pioche businessman A.G. Cambell to buy her ranch. All we know for certain is that Helen Stewart, alias "D.M. Widdr," had a piquant sense of humor, and loved nothing better than to send a humorous message of endearment to her children.

Galt Aug 15 1887

Dear Folks at the Vegas,

This leave[s] me at Galt anxiously waiting to hear from you. Have not heard from you since you sent few lines by Indian. Am afraid something has hapened.

Farmers all had pretty good crop, but complain of hard times. The first sales were good; $1.70 now, $1.40, but few buying

153

and every tavern is full. Jim Roach had 975 sacks. He think he will get 1.40 for his. I wish you would write and let me know what you are thinking of doing. I am thinking you will all let that *wine* get away with you all. If so, cursed be the *wine*.

I have writen two letters to you that I am waiting the answer. I have thought perhaps you have sold out . . . is the reason you do not write. If not, and you want to give me a chance as I propose in my last two letters, let me know.

What is Jim Wilson doing? Do you ever hear from Jim Patton? What are the Indians doing? What do they think of School? Don't think there is much use in trying to work up a school but don't say anything about it for it might come around yet. It might be more trouble than it is worth. Hiram why dont you write and tell me something, not always keep mum.

D.M. Widdr

Woman straddling a fence in Arizona.

Life, from her ledgers, seems to have been a constant round of buying beef and gathering crops, with all her spare time devoted to her family. The characters in her daily drama change with dizzying frequency. Employees and neighbors such as Billy, Charley, Mattison, and Shreve are identified only in the context of their work for her.

February, 1887

Feb. 1   Went up to Tule Spring

Feb. 2   Took meat from box and racked off 3 barrels of wine.

Feb. 3   Scraped and repacked meat; cleaned 2 barrels for wine. Willie and John Bradflute got home from Cañon.

Feb. 5   Uncle Johny plowing garden; John Bradflute tying up vines and staking; boys burning rubbish. Uncle Johny bought one pair of socks—50 cents.

Feb. 14   Rained all day; men didn't work.

Feb. 15   Grubbed mesquite all day

Feb. 20   Jim Patton's Indian came with a letter.

Feb. 19   Mattison and partner up to Corn Creek. Jim Wilson came down; *"oh do take care"* [*This inscription was lightly written in a tiny script on the original manuscript. Historian Carrie Townley believes this and a subsequent notation—"one egg passed safely"—indicate the possibility of a love relationship between Helen and neighboring rancher Jim Wilson during the years following Archie Stewart's death.*]

Feb. 1889

Feb. 16   Killed hogs; two men with donkeys came from Cañon. (Charley, for wine 50¢)

Feb. 18   Mattison and partner came; Billy got teeth pulled. (Billy, 1 bottle of wine) Salted meat away.

March 1889

Mar. 13   Charley Reube & Billy bale hay; light rain all day; put water on garden; small garden full.

Mar. 14   Charley fixing pig pen; Billy preparing tower; Reube irrigating lower Barley. (Billy, 75¢, wine.)

Mar. 29   Mr. Megarrigle, 50¢ for squaw washing; two men and pack horse from Cañon.

In order to start her father off in the cattle business, Helen offered Hiram Wiser and her brother-in-law Ed Meyer one-hundred head of female cattle from her ranch. The cattle would remain at Wiser's Muddy Valley holdings for two years, and after that time, Wiser would receive half of the increase in the herd. Wiser and Meyer were to pay all taxes on the cattle for the two years.

Sept. 14, 1889 To D.M.W.

The proposition to Ed & Pa is this: "100 heads of female cattle of different ages from 2 year olds up to the oldest cows for a term of two years & one-half the increase at that time; three horses furnished to be made good at the end of that time . . . and return of same [horses] if desired at that time, or expiration of two years, or a longer lease if agreeable to all parties interested."

In Helen Stewart's small ledger book, kept from December 1890–1892, the entry for January 2nd, 1891 is heavily underlined. We learn that Hank Parish was hung for the murder of a fellow miner, James B. Greenwood. Carrie Townley writes that Parish was probably responsible for the theft of two horses from the Stewart ranch a year-and-a-half before Archie's death—and so great was the suspicion that Parish himself had murdered Archie, that the Pioche Weekly Record of July 26, 1884, accused him of the crime. Though he was never convicted of the murder, or the horse theft, the mutual animosity between Helen Stewart and Hank Parish continued up until the time of his hanging.

Small Ledger Book

    Jan. 2d. 1891   Charles Smithson
        Three 2 year old steers, for $25–$30 in the next three years to come
        Christmas presents from the Carmens [*Sylvester and Mary carmen, long-time friends of the Stewarts*]
        First news of Hank Parishes Hanging
        Panton doing dishes today
    Jan. 3d.   Smithson still here, commenced sowing grain.
    Jan. 4th.   Smithson left. Streuve wants to quit, [says] $20 a month not enough. Red Nose Bob and another Indian [came] from Cañon. Iasic Howell here, and Attorney F. X. Murphy.
    Jan. 5th.   Jim's horses for one night's feed; Charley Morris & Reube harrowing and plowing. Hi & Toningo after the mare. They killed a colt lassoing her.
    Jan. 6th.   Henry T. Streuve. Paid him $45. Still due: $79.71.
    Jan. 7th   Indians still here . . . Kiels moved their cattle—51 head, 5 steer and quite a number of young cattle. Hiram and Toningo went as far as Mesquite—brought back 9 head of steers. Streuve went with Kiel and Horse Breaker.
    Jan. 12th.   Hiram home from Cañon—Toningo, Averall working.
    Jan. 14   [one] egg passed safe
    Jan. 20   Hiram started to the Cañon. Indians all quit work—'drunk. Indians all on drunk. Must pay for [it.] Jim Wilson came down.
    Jan. 21   Men working; Reube & Spats not at work; playing cards must pay for [their] meals. Reube pays for meals of Corn Creek Ben and one for Panton.
    Jan. 28   Johny commenced work I think. Johny Indian: Indians here are: Ben's squaw
        Pete & John's squaw
    Jan. 29   Hiram and Toningo from Cañon. Mr. Mills makes complaint of manner of cutting beef; wishes it cut down middle of back bone.

Ross Megarrigle began teaching the Stewart children on February 13, 1889, and his name appears frequently throughout the journals for the next five years.

    Feb. 13   Hiram Wiser pruning peach trees; Charley plowing garden, with Johny helping; Hiram Stewart making lasso rope; Megarrigle reading; Streuve back from Cañon and cattle camp, let Johny's squaw have 50¢ to buy beans over at Ed Kiels.
    Feb. 14   Hiram Wiser still pruning trees. Charley Morris's planting peas & onions & radishes; Spats & Grubbing John left for Muddy [Valley]. Settled with Spats for 21 days [work].

Feb. 15   Three strangers with mule team came; a real Sunday—Hiram Wiser, Charley Morris, J.R. Megarrigle, Willie Stewart, Hiram Stewart, Helen Stewart, Tiza, Eva, Archie Stewart here to dinner.

Feb. 16   Strangers left. Hiram Wiser pruning trees. Charley Morris put last sweet potatoes in bed. Planted beets, peas, lettuce.

March 1891

Mar. 1   Went to upper ranch, came home with sick headache. Kimonche hearding hogs. . . . Hiram Wiser preparing apple root grafts. Charley got blues.

Mar. 9   Willie's birthday—17 years old. Willie, Johny, Charley, burning grass. Johny working again today. Aaron Winters came. Wells Fargo money order, Jan. 23 '91 . . . Baily, Taxidermist, sort of a bughunter, Nelson, Botanist, Scoville, Skull hunter.

Mar. 13   Scoville, Nelson back from river, very much like Death Valley at [the] mouth of wash. Charley Morriss made some coal. Willie built chimney. Hiram sick.

Mar. 14   Entomologist left for Towners'

Mar. 15   Kiels man McBeth on a drunk

Mar. 16   Megarrigle commenced teaching again; Willie tried plowing—fixing plow. McBeth on a big drunk.

Mar. 17   St. Patrick's Day . . . Willie going to school.

Mar. 18   Willie, Hira, Tiza, Eve going to school. Spats in the mud. McBeth went to help him out.

The back pages of each ledger were covered with scrawled recipes, mixtures for horse medicine, herbal remedies, and snatches of popular songs and verse. Several of those that appear most worn, apparently thumbed-over until they were nearly illegible, are the following. They are taken from the 1895 and 1896 ledger books.

August 1895

RECEIPT FOR COLIC IN A HORSE

2 oz. Laudanum
2 oz. Chlorform
2 oz. Assoefiteda
1 oz. tb. essence of Jamaica Ginger

WORM ELIXIR DOCTOR GUNN'S

Take six halves each one ounce; Saffron, Sage leaves, and Tanzy leaves, each ½ ounce. Tincture in a pint of brandy two weeks, and give to children a tea spoonful once a week to once a month, as a preventative. They will never be troubled with worms as long as you do this.

EXCELLENT HAIR DRESSING

1 oz. of Borax
1 oz. of Ammonia
½ pt. of whiskey
1 qt. of water

PLUM PUDDING ANNIE CARMANS FAVORITE

To one pound dry flour add ½ pound stale bread crumbs, 1 pound raisens, 1 pound Beef Suet, ½ pounds currents, ½ pound Sugar, ½ pound citron, 6 eggs, One wine glass French Brandy, One wine glass Port Wine, cloves, all spice, nutmeg to taste. To Boil strong 5 hours. This recipt makes one extra pudding. Put in yeast powder cans, Fill about ⅔ full.

RECEIPT FOR SALT RISING BREAD

Scald ½ cupful of Sweet milk to boiling heat. Stir in enough cornmeal to make thin batter set away until morning then take ½ pint of warm water & pinch of salt, ½ teaspoonful of sugar stir in the cornmeal and thicken with flour about like cake batter set in a warm place. Mr. Sawyer adds a little ginger.

Megarrigle's death sadly interrupted the course of study Helen Stewart had in mind for her youngest children: Archie, Eva, and Tiza. Her oldest sons had disappointed her with their studies, and she determined to send the youngest ones to Los Angeles, to further their education. It is plainly evident from her letters that she missed them dreadfully, and she took every opportunity between cattle purchases and ranch obligations to visit them.

Nov. 24, 1897

Archie My Darling Boy,

See your teacher, learn all you can. Be good to the girls. Be neat and clean and orderly. Keep your room clean. Be sure to learn all you can. I will come soon as I can. Don't go with rough boys. Do all you can to learn so you can help me by and by. With a hug and kiss

Mamma
Goodbye Sweet Heart

Las Vegas, Nevada
Dec. 8, '97

Dear Tiza, Eva & Archie,

Midnight. There are two cattle buyers here tonight. They have been here two days. They offer for yearling $12; two year $15, three year $19, Dry cows $16 Hira wants $13 for 1 year; 2 year $17, 3 year $20, Dry Cows $17. It is a bad time to gather. We will see in the morning if we will make a deal or not. I feel almost tempted to sell anyway, if at some loss, so as to be sure of enough money for you to have what you need.

I am going to send you ten or fifteen in the morning. Do the best you can, learn all you can, and encourage Eva and Archie in doing their best. I know you will, so no need to write this to you.

I appreciate you more than your realize, Tiza. I know you are a little bundle of the truest womanly material that was ever put together. Others appreciate the same fact and know it—I cant just tell when I can come to you. I want to arrange before leaving here so as to know how the money is to come to keep us there, and to arrange for a regular supply of money.

It wont take so much when we get thoroughly established. After we get our first clothes. Now write and tell me just what you are doing. How Eva is doing and how she has arrainged for piano with Nellie. Is Archie going to his teacher Miss Culberwell?

Tell me just how your expenses are running. Be careful to turn off the gas in your rooms. Never forget and blow it out—you see, that would leave the gas jet open and fill the room with gas which, if the windows were closed, would be sure to cause your death. . . .

With love, Momma

Las Vegas, Nevada
Dec. 16th '97

Dear Archie; My Boy

I know you are dreadful lonesome and I wish I was with you; Because I love you more than any other boy I know of. You are the best boy I know of and I want you to learn so you can help me.

Are you going to the Normal school now? Do you go evenings to Miss Culberwell? Go to her and have each evening so you can learn even if you do not go to School.

My boy if you *love* me try and learn.

I know you are lonesome for me because I am lonesome for you. Soon as I can I will come to you. So do not make it any harder for me than you can. Go every Saturday and spend an hour or so with Mr. Madison Stewart—he is a good man. They hold him in high esteem. Do not mix with any men but the best, and you will only see and learn good things and you cant help but be a good, useful man.

Life is very short at the best, so make every moment of time count.

There are some Cattle men here from Wyoming we are going to sell them Our Hundred head of mixed cattle from the calves branded this year. . . . So if I wait until the sale is made you see, it will take me a little longer. I send you this time your little Purse with $3 in ten cent pieces for Christmas. They will go by freight and be at the Santa Fe Depot by the time you get this letter. So have Mr. Howell when he goes down to the Depot to have them sent up. Let Tiza read this letter. She and Eva too. Now be a good boy. Be good to the girls, do all you can to help yourself and your own loving Mamma.

Archie I send inside of this an envelope already adressed to me. Write a letter, put it inside the envelope, seal it up and drop it in the box at the corner and I will watch for it at this end of the line.

I would write the letter for you but I guess I wont. You might think of something I could not think of.

Good Night My Boy,
Your Loving Mamma

Las Vegas Nevada
Feb. 17, '98

My Dear Children,

How much I would like to see you tonight. We have sold the cattle and Hira has gone as far as the Muddy to see them through. . . . We will hear from them tonight by Denny. He will be here in about an hour. There is nothing for me to say only to tell you to be good children until I come. The folks on the Ranch now are Willie, Lena, Mr. Stewart, Uncle Ed, George Allen, Gann and myself. Denny just came in. The boys have sold the Muddy steers and it will be five or six more days before they come home. Have to wait untill the cattle man goes from the Muddy up to Cain Springs.

With Love to you each,

Be good and careful. Don't waste time nor be careless of your-selves. Read this slow not in a hurry.

Your Loving Mamma

Emeryville, Cal
Jan. 25th, '99

Dear Son Archie,

This is your birthday—you are fourteen years old. I wonder what course you will pursue. What you will do? What kind of a man you will be? I think you have pride and manliness about you to try and be one of the best. Remember always I love you and always think of you every day and wonder what you are doing.

Your Loving Mamma,
Helen J. Stewart

Dare to do right—
Dare to be true—
Dare to be good—
Everything will come right for you

Las Vegas, Nev.
June 21st 1899

Dear Tiza,

Archie has been very sick for four days—is some better tonight. I think he will be all O.K. in a few days. I got a letter from Mattie Shaw Sunday telling me she would leave San Francisco for this place Monday evening at the 19th. That would put her here . . . today at 11 O'Clock. She wanted me to meet her there. I could not so sent word to her to come to Good Springs on the stage and . . . Archie being very sick, I have to send Lena and Willie.

I got a letter from Aunt Flora . . . she seemed to think it was real nice you girls had decided to go to school and study. And I think so too . . . I see you presented your order and got the money . . . what did Eliza do with hers? It has not come back here marked paid yet. How much funds have you on hand . . . let me know. . . .

Archie is getting better I think. I hope you have a nice place and are doing well. I sent you by last Mail an Order on D.W. Earl & Co. for $25. I sent Eva an order for the same amount. . . . Now my darling girl, do the best you can, learn all you can and be good to Eva. I wish you could be together. I shall be uneasy until I learn where or who Eva will stay with until Mattie comes back..

Mr. Stewart was very kind to help me while Archie was sick and has been very kind since. He has helped me put up six gallons of Plum preserves and about five gallons of Apple jelly. Besides a lot of dried apples.

Tiza, you had ought to study Arithmetic and Book-keeping too. So you will understand business Methods. Do the best you can.

With Love,

Your Loving Mamma,
Helen J. Stewart, Las Vegas, Lincoln County Nevada

In July of 1899, Archie suffered a fatal fall from a horse, and was buried in the Stewart family plot near his father. This letter to her daughter Tiza, stating the grief she still felt over Archie's death, is partially obscured, as Carrie Townley noted, by "the marks of her tears."

Las Vegas Nev.
Jan 25th 1900

Dear Tiza,

Today Archie would have been fifteen years old. I have cried most all day through my work and all. I have had a dreadful time bringing myself to submit to what I know must be. I needed him so much. There has been strangers here every day lately; Charley Garull and Jack Smith and another fellow from the Meadow Valley Wash are here tonight. I have had extras to cook for all week.

I suppose by this time you have the $30 order I sent you. I want you to cash it and use it to fix yourselves so as to give all your time to beauty. I will send you an order in this for $20. Twenty dollars more so if you need it you can cash it immediately. If you have any old orders you can use them any time; write and let me know what you have. . . .

Tiza, I like the wrapper, I wish you would send me another one . . . apply yourself and learn all you can. Of course you can't learn everything you would like immediately, but you will be surprised how much you can learn if you keep trying..

I am rather tired tonight—with more love than this letter can carry,

Your Mamma

Helen Stewart sold the bulk of her property in 1902 to the San Pedro, Los Angeles, and Salt Lake Railroad, though she still retained a small area called Four Acres. In 1903, she married Frank Roger Stewart, a ranch hand she had employed for seventeen years. Her four remaining children—Will, Hiram, Tiza, and Eva— eventually married, leaving Helen more time for the social life in Las Vegas which she had always longed for. She wrote and lectured at women's clubs throughout Nevada and was the first woman elected to the Clark County School Board. She was active in the Nevada State Historical Society, and amassed an enormous collection of Indian baskets. Frank Stewart died on September 1, 1918. Helen lived for eight more years and died of cancer on March 6, 1926.

Helen Stewart, date unknown.

Cabin on the San Antonio, Jemez Cañyon, New Mexico, ca. 1885.

Mormon settlers in Arizona, ca. 1890.

Mrs. Clough and her daughter Nora in their kitchen in Arizona, ca. 1900.

Priscilla Merriman Evans

As handcart pioneers, Priscilla and Thomas Evans were part of an extraordinary mass migration of nearly three thousand poor Mormon immigrants—Germans, Welsh, English, Danish, Swedish, and Scottish converts—who trudged from Iowa City, Iowa, to Salt Lake City, Utah. They sometimes walked as much as fifteen miles a day, pulling their hickory carts behind them. Their personal belongings were few—only seventeen pounds of clothing and bedding were allowed per person. Any extra weight added to the four hundred pounds of flour and staples usually caused the cart axles to break and forced the party to stop to repair the damage.

The Evanses were members of Captain Edward Bunker's Third Handcart Party, which had the good fortune to reach Salt Lake City in October of 1856, only five months after its departure from Iowa City. Not so fortunate were the members of the two succeeding parties. The five hundred members of the Fourth company were caught in an early Wyoming blizzard. By the time supplies reached them, they were starving and had lost many. The Fifth party fared just as poorly, encountering winter weather as soon as it reached the Platte River. The immigrants died by the dozens each day, and the survivors managed to live on a barrel of hard bread and a beef carcass until the supply train from Salt Lake City brought relief.

Between the years 1856 and 1860 there were ten handcart companies to reach Salt Lake. As with all members of the first parties to get to Zion, the Evanses were greeted with prayers, hymns, and great exultation.

I, Priscilla Merriman Evans, born May 4, 1835 at Mounton New Marbeth, Pembrokeshire, Wales, am the daughter of Joseph and Ann James Merriman. About 1839, father moved his family from Mounton up to Tenby, about ten miles distant. Our family consisted of father, mother, Sarah, aged six, and myself, aged four. Tenby was a beautiful place, as are all those Celtic Islands, with remains of old castles, vine- and moss-covered walls, gone to ruin since the time of the Conqueror. . . .

When we were settled in our new home, we girls were sent to school, as children were put in school very young. There was a path leading up Castle Hill to the school, and another leading around the beautiful old moss-covered Castle down to the seashore, where the children played in the sand and gathered shells at intermission. The children also loved to wander around in the many rooms of the Castle, but shunned the lower regions, or basement rooms, for they had heard weird stories of dungeons and dark places, where in early times, people were shut up and kept until they died.

Besides reading, writing, spelling, and arithmetic, we were taught sewing and sampler making. The sampler work was done in cross stitch, worked in bright colors, on canvas made for that purpose. . . . We were also taught the Bible. I was greatly interested in school, but was taken out at eleven years of age, owing to the illness in our family. I was a natural student, and greatly desired to continue my studies, but mother's health was very poor, so I was taken out to help with the work. My sister, Sarah, continued school, as she did not like housework and wished to learn a trade. She went to Mrs. Hentin and learned the millinery trade. Mother's health continued [to be] poor, and she died at the birth of her eighth child, Emma, when I was sixteen. I had many duties for a girl so young, caring for my sisters and brothers. While Sarah was learning millinery, she would sometimes wake me in the night to try on a hat—one she was practicing on. She learned the millinery business and then went up to London, opened a shop of her own and was very successful. She married a gentleman . . . who was devoted to her, and followed her to London. She died at the birth of her fourth child.

[When] Mother died on the eighth of November 1851 . . . the responsibility of the family rested on my young shoulders. . . . After the death of my mother we were very lonely, and one evening I accompanied my father to the house of a friend. When we reached there, we learned that they were holding a cottage meeting. Two Mormon Elders were the speakers, and I was very much interested in the principles they advocated. I could see that my father was very worried, and would have taken me away, had he known how. When he became aware that I believed in the Gospel as taught by the Elders, I asked him if he had ever heard of the restored Gospel. He replied, "Oh, yes, I have heard of Old Joe Smith, and his Golden Bible." When my father argued against the principles taught by the Elders, I said, "If the Bible is true, then Mormonism is true."

My father was very much opposed to my joining the Church . . . as he thought the Saints were too slow to associate with. . . . But I had found the truth and was baptized into the Church of Jesus Christ of Latter-day Saints in Tenby, February 26, 1852. My sister Sarah took turns with me going out every Sunday. She would go where she pleased on Sunday, while I would walk seven miles to Stepaside and attend the Mormon meeting. My father was very much displeased with me going out every Sunday. He forbade me to

read the Church literature, and threatened to burn all I brought home. At the time I had a Book of Mormon borrowed from a friend, and when Father found out I had it, he began looking for it. It was in plain sight, among other books in the book case. I saw him handling it with the other books, and I sent up a silent prayer that he might not notice it, which he did not, although it was before him in plain sight. I do not think my father was as bitter against the principles of the Gospel as he seemed to be, for many times when the Elders were persecuted, he defended them, and gave them food and shelter. But he could not bear the idea of my joining them and leaving home.

About this time, Thomas D. Evans, a young Mormon Elder, was sent up from Merthyr Tydfil, Wales, as a missionary to Pembrokeshire. He was a fine speaker, and had a fine tenor voice, and I used to like to go around with the missionaries and help with the singing. Elder Evans and I seemed to be congenial from our first meeting, and we were soon engaged. He was traveling and preaching the restored Gospel without purse or script. Perhaps his mission will be better understood if I give a little account: [his father had died] and left his mother a widow with eight children, Thomas D. being four years old and the youngest. He was placed in a large forge of two-thousand men at the age of seven years to learn the profession of Iron Roller. At nine years of age, he had the misfortune to lose his left leg at the knee. He went through the courses and graduated as an Iron Roller. When I think of [when they met in 1852] it seems that we had put the world aside, and were not thinking of our worldly pleasures, and what our next dress would be. We had no dancing in those days, but we were happy in the enjoyment of the spirit of the Gospel. . . .

I was familiar with the Bible doctrine, and when I heard the Elders explain it, it seemed as though I had always known it, and it sounded like music in my ears. We had the spirit of gathering and were busy making preparations to emigrate.

About that time the Principle of Plurality of Wives was preached to the world, and it caused quite a commotion in our branch. One of the girls came to me with tears in her eyes and said, "Is it true that Brigham Young has nine wives? I can't stand that, Oh, I can't stand it!" I asked her how long it had been since I had heard her testify that she knew the Church was true, and I said if it was then, it is true now. I told her I did not see anything for her to cry about. After I talked to her awhile, she dried her eyes and completed her arrangements to get married and emigrate. She came with us. My promised husband and I went to Merthyr to visit his Mother, brothers, sisters, and friends, preparatory to emigrating. His family did all in their power to persuade him to remain with them. They were all well off, and his brothers said they would send him to school, support his wife, and pay all of his expenses but all to no avail. He bade them all goodbye, and returned to Tenby.

I think I would have had a harder time getting away, had it not been that my father was also going to be married again, and I do not suppose the lady cared to have in the home, the grown daughter who had taken the place of the mother for so many years.

Elder Thomas D. Evans, my promised husband, and I walked the ten miles from Tenby to Pembroke, where we got our license and were married, and walked back to Tenby. We were married on the third of April, 1856. On our return from Pembroke we found a few of our friends awaiting us with supper ready. We visited our friends and relatives and made our preparations to emigrate to Zion. We took a tug from Pembroke to Liverpool, where we set sail on the 17th of April, 1856, on the sailing vessel S.S. Curling. Captain Curling said he would prefer to take a load of Saints than others, as he always felt safe with Saints on board. We learned that the next trip across the water that he was loaded with gentiles and his vessel sank with all on board. We were on the sea five weeks; we lived on the ship's rations. I was sick all the way. [*Priscilla was then pregnant with their first child.*]

We landed in Boston on May 23rd, then travelled in cattle cars three hundred miles to Iowa City. We remained in Iowa City three weeks, waiting for our carts to be made. We were offered many inducements to stay there. My husband was offered ten dollars a day to work at his trade of Iron Roller, but money was no inducement to us, for we were anxious to get to Zion. We learned afterwards that many who stayed there apostatized or died of cholera.

When the carts were ready we started on a three-hundred-mile walk to Winterquarters on the Missouri River. There were a great many who made fun of us as we walked, pulling our carts, but the weather was fine and the roads were excellent and although I was sick and we were tired out at night, we still thought, "This is a glorious way to come to Zion."

We began our journey of one thousand miles on foot with a handcart for each family, some families consisting of man and wife, and some had quite large families. There were five mule teams to haul the tents and surplus flour. Each handcart had one hundred pounds of flour, that was to be divided and [more got] from the wagons as required. At first we had a little coffee and bacon, but that was soon gone and we had no use for any cooking utensils but a frying pan. The flour was self-raising and we took water and baked a little cake; that was all we had to eat.

After months of travelling we were put on half rations and at one time, before help came, we were out of flour for two days. We washed out the flour sacks to make a little gravy.

Our company was three-hundred Welsh Saints. There were about a dozen in our tent, six of whom could not speak the Welsh language, myself among the number. Don't you think I had a pleasant journey traveling for months with three-hundred people of whose language I could not understand a word? My husband could talk Welsh, so he could join in their festivities when he felt like it. [*Priscilla spoke no Welsh because English was the language she learned at home and Welsh was not taught in school.*]

There were in our tent my husband with one leg, two blind men . . . a man with one arm, and a widow with five chilren. The widow, her children, and myself were the only ones who could not talk Welsh. My husband was commissary for our tent, and he cut his own rations short many times to help little children who had to walk and did not have enough to eat to keep up their strength.

The tent was our covering, and the overcoat spread on the bare ground with the shawl over us was our bed. My feather bed, and bedding, pillows, all our good clothing, my husband's church books, which he had collected through six years of missionary work, with some genealogy he had collected, all had to be left in a storehouse. We were promised that they would come to us with the next emigration in the spring, but we never did receive them. It was reported that the storehouse burned down, so that was a dreadful loss to us.

Edward Bunker was the Captain of our Company. His orders of the day were, "If any are sick among you, and are not able to walk, you must help them along, or pull them on your carts." No one rode in the wagons. Strong men would help the weaker ones, until they themselves were worn out, and some died from the struggle and want of food, and were buried along the wayside. It was heart rending for parents to move on and leave their loved ones to such a fate, as they were so helpless, and had no material for coffins. Children and young folks too, had to move on and leave father or mother or both.

Sometimes a bunch of buffaloes would come and the carts

would stop until they passed. Had we been prepared with guns and ammunition, like people who came in wagons, we might have had meat, and would not have come to near starving. President Young ordered extra cattle sent along to be killed to help the sick and weak, but they were never used for that purpose. One incident happened which came near being serious. Some Indians came to our camp and my husband told an Indian who admired me that he could have me for a pony. He was always getting off jokes. He thought no more about it, but in a day or two, here came the Indian with the pony, and wanted his pretty little squaw. It was no joke with him. I never was so frightened in all my life. There was no place to hide, and we did not know what to do. The Captain was called, and they had some difficulty in settling with the Indian without trouble.

In crossing rivers, the weak women and the children were carried over the deep places, and they waded the others. We were much more fortunate than those who came later, as they had snow and freezing weather. Many lost limbs, and many froze to death. President Young advised them to start earlier, but they got started too late. My husband, in walking from twenty to twenty-five miles per day, [had pain] where the knee rested on the pad: the friction caused it to gather and break and was most painful. But he had to endure it, or remain behind, as he was never asked to ride in a wagon.

One incident shows how we were fixed for grease. My husband and John Thayne, a butcher, in some way killed an old lame buffalo. They sat up all night and boiled it to get some grease to grease the carts, but he was so old and poor, there was not a drop of grease in him. We had no grease for the squeaking carts or to make gravy for the children and old people.

We reached Salt Lake City on October 2, 1856, tired, weary, with bleeding feet, our clothing worn out and so weak we were nearly starved, but thankful to our Heavenly Father for bringing us to Zion. William R. Jones met us on the Public Square in Salt Lake City and brought us to his home in Spanish Fork. I think we were over three days coming from Salt Lake City to Spanish Fork by ox team, but what a change to ride in a wagon after walking 1330 miles from Iowa City to Salt Lake City!

We stayed in the home of an ex-bishop, Stephen Markham. His home was a dugout. It was a very large room built half underground. His family consisted of three wives, and seven children. . . . There was a large fireplace in one end with bars, hooks, frying pans, and bake ovens, where they did the cooking for the large family, and boiled, fried, baked, and heated their water for washing.

There was a long table in one corner, and pole bedsteads fastened to the walls in the three other corners. They were laced back and forth with rawhide cut in strips, and made a nice springy bed. There were three trundle beds, made like shallow boxes, with wooden wheels, which rolled under the mother's bed in the daytime to utilize space. There was a dirt roof, and the dirt floor was kept hard and smooth by sprinkling and sweeping. The bed ticks were filled with straw raised in Palmyra before the famine. [*Palmyra, on the river between Spanish Fork and Utah Lake, suffered the famine to which Priscilla Evans alludes shortly before the Evanses' arrival. Fifty families moved to Spanish Fork and lived in the dugouts she describes.*]

Aunt Mary [Markham] put her two children . . . in the foot of her bed and gave us the trundle bed. . . . How delightful to sleep on a bed again, after sleeping on the ground for so many months with our clothes on. We had not slept in a bed since we left the ship *Sam Curling.*

On the 31st of December, 1856, our first daughter was born. . . . My baby's wardrobe was rather meager: I made one nightgown from her father's white shirt, another out of a factory lining of an oilcloth sack. Mrs. Markham gave me a square of homemade linsey for a shoulder blanket, and a neighbor gave me some old underwear, that I worked up into little things. They told me I could have an old pair of jean pants left at the adobe yard. I washed them and made them into petticoats. I walked down to the Indian farm and traded a gold pen for four yards of calico that made her two dresses.

One day my husband went down in the field to cut some willows to burn. The ax slipped and cut his good knee cap. It was with difficulty that he crawled to the house. He was very weak from the loss of blood. My baby was but a few days old, and the three of us had to occupy the trundle bed for awhile.

Wood and timber were about thirty miles up in the canyon, and when the men went after timber to burn, they went in crowds, armed, for they never knew when they would be attacked by Indians. Adobe houses were cheaper than log or frame, as timber was so far away. Many of the people who had lived in the dugouts after coming from Palmyra got into houses before the next winter. They exchanged work with each other, and in that way got along fine. Mr. Markham had an upright saw, run by water. The next spring they got timber from the canyon, and my husband helped Mr. Markham put up a three-roomed house and worked at farming.

He worked for William Markham a year, for which he received two acres of land. I helped in the house, for which, besides the land, we got our board and keep. The next Spring we went to work for ourselves. We saved our two acres of wheat, and made adobes for a two-roomed house, and paid a man in adobes for laying it up. It had a dirt roof. He got timber from Mr. Markham to finish the doors, windows, floors, shelves, and to make furniture. My husband made me a good big bedstead and laced it with rawhides. There were benches and the frames of chairs with the rawhide seat, with the hair left on; a table, shelves in the wall on either side of the fireplace, which was fitted with iron bars and hooks to hang kettles on to boil, frying pans and bake oven. A tick for a bed had to be pieced out of all kinds of scraps, as there were no stores, and everything was on a trade basis.

If one neighbor had something they could get along without, they would exchange it for something they could use. We were lucky to get factory, or sheeting to put up to the windows instead of glass. We raised a good crop of wheat that fall, for which we traded one bushel for two bushels of potatoes. We also exchanged for molasses and vegetables. We had no tea, coffee, meat, or grease of any kind for seasoning. No sugar, milk, or butter. In 1855–1856 the grasshoppers and crickets took the crops and the cattle nearly all died. They were dragged down in the field west [and left to die].

Before my second baby, Jennie, was born, I heard that a neighbor was going to kill a beef. I asked her to save me enough tallow for one candle. But the beef was like the buffalo we killed crossing the plains—there was no tallow in it.

By this time we had two children, with no soap to wash our clothes. Grease of all kinds was out of the question, so I took an ax and gunny sack and went into the field where the dead cattle had been dragged, and I broke up all the bones I could carry home. I boiled them in saleratus and lime, and it made a little jelly-like soap. The saleratus was gathered on top of the ground.

My husband had never driven a team before he came to Utah. He had traveled and preached for the six years previous to coming to Utah, and he knew nothing about any kind of work but his profession of Iron Roller. His hands were soft and white, but he soon wore blisters . . . in learning to make adobes, digging ditches,

making roads, driving oxen, and doing what was required of pioneers in a new country.

The large bedstead [was good to have] for when my third child was born, two had to go to the foot of the bed, but it did not work. Jennie had to go to the foot alone. Caliline Louisa . . . was the third child, and although Emma was the oldest and just a baby herself, she could not be tempted to go to the foot of the bed, but was determined to sleep on her father's bosom, which she had done since the birth of Jennie. We went down to the marshy land and gathered a load of cattails, which I stripped and made me a good bed and pillows. They were as soft as feathers.

Our first fence around our lot was made of willows. Slender stakes were put in a certain distance apart, and the willows woven in back and forth. There was a board gate with rawhide hinges and flat rocks were laid on the walks, as we were located down under a long hill, and when it rained, it was very muddy. There were many mud walks in the early days of Spanish Fork, as the material in them cost nothing. The mud was mixed stiff enough with straw in it so it would not run, and a layer was put on, until high enough. Rock fences were also used, and were very durable.

There were no stores. Sometimes someone would come around with their basket of needles, pins, buttons, thread, and notions, but I had no money to buy with. Men who had no teams worked two days for the use of a team one day. Shovels were so scarce that when men were working in the roads and ditches, they had to take turns using the shovels.

My husband worked at Camp Floyd and got money enough to get him a good yoke of oxen. One day, while working in the canyon, a man above him . . . let a log roll down and broke the leg of one of the oxen. That was a calamity.

I traded for a hen . . . and got a setting of eggs somewhere else, and I have never been without chickens in all of my married life since. I could not get a thread to sew, so I raveled a strip of hickory shirting for dark sewing thread and factory for white, when I could get it. When we could get grease for light, we put a button in a rag, and braided the top, setting the button in the grease, after dipping the braided part in the grease.

On the 4th of August, 1861, our fourth child and first son, David T., was born. . . . In that year my husband's mother and step-father came [from Wales]. They drove their own team across the plains, two oxen, two cows, and they brought many useful things for their comfort. His parents lived with us, making eight in the family. Our rooms were small, and as grandma had left a good home and plenty, she became quite dissatisfied with our crowded condition.

We bought a lot on Main Street, and my husband gave his parents our first little home with five acres of land. They had a good ox team, two cows, a new wagon, and they soon got pigs, chickens and a few sheep. It wasn't long before they were well off. We moved up near our lot into a one-roomed adobe house with a garrett, so to be near while my husband was building our new house. While living in that one room, the Indians were quite bad, and he was broken of his rest by standing guard nights and working in the day time.

It was indeed comfortable to be in a good house with a shingled roof and good floors. He set out an orchard of all kinds of fruit; also currents and gooseberries, planted lucern . . . in a patch by itself for cows and pigs. We had a nice garden spot, and we soon had butter, milk, eggs, and meat. We raised our bread, potatoes, and vegetables. While our fruit trees were growing is when the saleratus helped. When I had the babies all about the same size, I could not get out to gather saleratus as others did; so we went with team and wagon, pans, buckets, old brooms, and sacks down on the alkali land, between Spanish Fork and Springville. The smallest children were put under the wagon on a quilt, and the rest of us swept and filled the sacks, and the happiest time was when we were headed for home. The canyon wind seemed always to blow and our faces, hands and eyes were sore for some time after. We took our saleratus over to Provo, where they had some kind of refining machinery where it was made into soda for bread. It was also used extensively in soap making. We got our pay in merchandise.

Another source of income before our fruit trees began to bear was the wild ground cherries. They grew on a vine or bush about six inches high, were bright yellow when ripe, were full of soft seed and about the size of a cherry. They made fine pies and all we had to spare sold readily at a good price when dried.

Most people who had land kept a few sheep which furnished them meat, light and clothing. We had no sheep, but I, and my oldest daughter, learned to spin and we did spinning on shares to get our yarn for stockings and socks, which we knitted for the family. Before this time my sister, Sarah, had sent me a black silk dress pattern, with other things, which I sold [and] I bought a cow and a pair of blankets. Before the building of the Provo factory, the people had wool-picking bees. The wool was greased and the trash picked out of it; then it was carded into rolls. We made our own cloth, which was mostly gray in color, for dresses, by mixing the black and white wool. If a light gray was wanted, more white than black was put in, and dark was added if a darker gray was wanted. The dresses for grown people were three widths, and for younger women two widths, one yard wide. There was a row of bright colors—red, blue, green—about half way up the skirt, which was hemmed and pleated onto a plain waist with coat sleeves. When our dresses wore thin in front, they could be turned back to front and upside down, and have a new lease on life. With madder, Indigo, logwood, copperas, and other roots, I have colored beautiful fast colors. We were kept busy in those days carding, spinning, knitting, and doing all of our own sewing by hand.

After getting settled in our new home, my husband went over to Camp Floyd, where he worked quite a bit. He found a friend who was selling out prior to leaving for California. He bought quite a number of articles, which greatly helped us. One thing was a door knob and lock. He also bought me a stepstove. Stoves were very scarce at that time in Spanish Fork. I had never cooked on a stove in my life, and I burned my first batch of bread. Where I came from people mixed their dough and had it baked in the public oven, and at home we had a grate with an oven at the side. When the soldier camp broke up, they left many useful things which helped the people.

On the 9th of July, 1863, our second son, J.J. Evans, was born. He was the first child born in our new home. After our fruit trees began to bear, we invited in our neighbor's young folks and had cutting bees. The peaches were spread on a scaffolding to dry, then sold at a good price. We kept some for our own use. On July 16, 1865, our daughter Sarah Amelia was born. . . . On May 4, 1867 Charles Abram was born. Thomas Isaac was born on May 8, 1869, and died when six months old. My husband farmed down on the river bottom, and between times he freighted produce to Salt Lake City, as he had come to Camp Floyd before the soldiers left, and brought some merchandise for the people. . . . My husband had poor luck farming. His farm was in the low land, near the river where the sugar factory now stands. Sometimes it would be high water, sometimes grasshoppers or crickets would take his crop; so he got discouraged with farming, sold his farm and put up a store. We had just got well started in the business and had got a bill of goods, when in the spring of 1875 my husband was called on another mission to England.

Before starting on his mission he sold his team and all available property, also mortgaged our home, for although he was called to travel without purse or scrip, he had to raise enough money to pay his passage and his expenses to his field of labor in Europe. He had too tender a heart for a merchant; he simply could not say no when people came to him with pitiful stories of sickness and privation. He would give them credit, and the consequence was that when he was suddenly called on a mission, the goods were gone and there were hundreds of dollars coming to us from the people, some of which we never got. Everything was left in my hands.

On the 24th of October 1875, after my husband's departure, our daughter Ada was born . . . I nursed her, along with my little grandaughter Maud, as twins, kept all the books and accounts . . . and was sustained as President and Secretary of the Relief Society Teachers, which office I held through many re-organizations.

During my husband's absence, we had considerable sickness. My little daughter, Mary, came near dying with scarlet fever. To help out, our eldest daughter, Emma, got a position as clerk in the Co-op store. I appreciated that action of the Board very much, as before that time they had not been employing lady clerks and she was the first girl to work in the store. . . .

My husband had a bottle green suit while on his mission. He had gotten so tired of seeing all gray suits that he asked me if I thought I could make him a bottle green suit. He bought the wool, and I had it carded into rolls, then I was particular to spin it very even. I scoured the yarn white, then with Indigo, yellow flowers and a liquid made from rabbit brush, the color was set. The yarn had to stay in this mixture for some time, and when it came out it was a pretty dark, bottle green. I took the yarn down to one of Pres. Hansen's wives who wove it into cloth. I ripped up an old suit for a pattern and made his suit all by hand, backstitching every stitch, until it was smooth on the right side as machine work. We did all of our sewing by hand. I took a large dinner plate and cut from the cloth the crown of a cap, lined it and put a band on it. He got a patent-leather visor in Salt Lake and when it was all finished, it was surely swell for those days, and would not look out of place in this day of caps.

In 1877, my twelfth child was born . . . I have had seven daughters and five sons. . . .

My husband's health was not good after his return from his mission. He had pneumonia twice. We sold our home on Main Street, paid off the mortgage and put up a little house on the five acres of land we had given his parents. They had left it to us when they died. We have some of our children as near neighbors and are quite comfortable in our new home.

At the conclusion of her account, Priscilla said that the motto of her life had been "Not to look back—but forward." She said that she had always "thanked the Lord for a contented mind, a home and something to eat."

Kitchen corner of the one room house on the Henderson ranch.

Mrs. Lippincott bathing her daughter Lucille, Silver City, Idaho.

Mrs. Sophie Walker in her kitchen at Benson, Arizona, ca. 1885.

Family in Oregon with newborn baby, names and date unknown.

Bethenia Owens-Adair

Bethenia Angelina Owens was one of nine children of a family that emigrated to Oregon. She married at the age of fourteen; within four years, however, she realized that the marriage was not successful and she petitioned for divorce. This in itself was highly unusual in pre-Civil War days. Her ensuing transformation from a semi-literate teenager into a determined and successful physician was even more unusual, and singles her out as a most resourceful woman.

She studied for a year at Philadelphia's Eclectic School of Medicine and practiced for several years in Oregon before continuing her medical studies at the University of Michigan. She obtained her medical degree in 1880, at the age of forty.

I was born February 7th, 1840, in Van Buren County, Missouri, being the second daughter of Thomas and Sarah Damron Owens.

My father and mother crossed the plains with the first emigrant wagons of 1843, and settled on Clatsop plains, Clatsop County, Oregon, at the mouth of the Columbia; the wonderful "River of the West," in sound of the ceaseless roar of that mightiest of oceans, the grand old Pacific. Though then very small and delicate in stature, and of a highly nervous and sensitive nature, I possessed a strong and vigorous constitution, and a most wonderful endurance and recuperative power. These qualities were inherited, not only from my parents, but from my grandparents, as well. My grandfather Owens was a man of exceptional financial ability. He had a large plantation in Kentucky, and owned many slaves, and many stores throughout the state. He was a grandson of Sir Thomas Owens, of Wales, of historic fame.

My grandmother Owens was of German descent, a rather small but executive woman, who took charge of, and ably administered the affairs of the plantation during my grandfather's absence, which was most of the time. . . .

My grandfather Damron was a man of equal worth. He was a noted Indian fighter, and was employed by the Government, during its wars with the Shawnees and Delawares, as a scout and spy. He performed many deeds of remarkable bravery and daring, one of which was the rescue of a mother and five children from the Indians, who had captured them, at the imminent risk of his own life.

My grandmother Damron was my grandfather's second wife. She was of Irish descent, and noted for her great personal beauty.

My father, a tall, athletic Kentuckian, served as sheriff of Pike County for many years, beginning as a deputy at the age of sixteen. It was often said of him: "Thomas Owens is not afraid of man or devil."

My mother was of slight build, but perfect form, with bright blue eyes, and soft brown hair. She weighed but ninety-six pounds when she was married, at the age of sixteen. . . .

I was a veritable "tom-boy," and gloried in the fact. It was father's custom to pat me on the head, and call me his "boy."

The regret of my life up to the age of thirty-five, was that I had not been born a boy, for I realized very early in life that a girl was hampered and hemmed in on all sides simply by the accident of sex.

Brother and I were always trying our muscular strength, and before I was thirteen, I bet him I could carry four sacks of flour, or two hundred pounds. I stood between a table and a box, on which we had put two sacks of flour each. Then brother placed a sack of flour on each of my shoulders, and held them steady, while I managed to get the other two sacks (one on the table and the other on the box on each side of me) under each arm, and then I walked triumphantly off, carrying all four sacks. . . !

I was the family nurse; and it was seldom that I had not a child in my arms, and more clinging to me. Where there is a baby every two years, there is always no end of nursing to be done; especially when the mother's time is occupied, as it was then, every minute, from early morning till late at night, with much outdoor as well as indoor work. She seldom found time to devote to the baby, except to give it the breast.

When the weather was fine we fairly lived out of doors, baby and all, I hauling the baby in its rude little sled, or cart, which bumped along, and from which baby was often thrown out, but seldom seriously hurt, and never killed; with a two-year-old on one hip, and a four-year-old hanging to my skirts, in order to keep up; but more often on brother Flem's back; so we went, playing here and working there, during all the pleasant weather. When it rained, we had access to the barn, where we could swing, play "hide-and-seek," and slide down the hay-mow, from the top to the bottom. Many a time I have carried the children to the top, from where, with the baby in my arms, and the two next younger clinging to me, I would slide to the bottom, to their great delight. . . .

When I was about twelve years old, a teacher by the name of Beaufort came to teach a three months' school in our neighbor-hood. School-books were extremely scarce, and sometimes whole families were taught out of one book. All the children over four years old attended the school, for children did not remain babies long when other babies came along so fast and crowded them out of the cradle. Boys and girls of fourteen and fifteen were expected to do a full day's work on the farm or in the house, and even the younger ones were all taught to be helpful and useful, and to do their full share in taking care of themselves.

The new teacher was a fine, handsome young man, who held himself aloof from the young people of his age, and kept his person so clean, neat and trim that the country young men disliked him.

Mr. Beaufort boarded at our house, and we children walked the two miles to school with him daily. He was greatly liked by the children, to whom he was most kind, playing with them, and often taking two or three of the little tots, or as many as could hang on, and thus handicapped, he would run races with the older children, to the hilarious joy of the little youngsters, who thought they had won the race.

I simply worshipped my handsome teacher, who taught me how to run, to jump, to lasso, to spring up on the horse's back, and so many other things that I appreciated. . . .

My love for my handsome, kind and intelligent teacher knew no bounds. . . . mother chided me for being so rude, saying, "You ought to know that he must get tired of you and the children sometimes."

However, I found many opportunities of being in his society, and I improved them all; especially as mother was so over-worked she was only too glad to be relieved of the care of the baby, and the two other smaller children. . . .

It was a sad, sad day when he left us. First, he bade father and mother good-bye; and then the children. He snatched up the baby from the floor, tossed her up, and kissed her. I was trying to keep back my tears. He smiled down on me with his handsome blue eyes, and said to mother, "I guess I'll take this one with me."

Mother answered, "All right, she is such a tom-boy I can never make a girl of her, anyway."

He took my little hand in his, and I went with him through the gate, and some distance down the road. Then he said; "Now little one, you must go back. You are a nice little girl, and some day you will make a fine woman; but you must remember and study your book hard, and when you get to be a woman everybody will love you; and don't forget your first teacher, will you?" He had gathered me up, and smiling, kissed me, and then set me down with my face toward home. I ran back, and seeing the children on the fence, all looking, I ran off around the back of the house, and hid, and cried a long time.

Of course they all laughed at me, and often times afterward, when I was especially rebellious and wayward, which was not infrequently, I would be confronted with, "I wish the teacher had taken you with him," to which I never failed to answer promptly and fervently, "I wish he had, too . . . !"

In 1853, finding that his 640 acres on Clatsop could no longer supply feed for his rapidly increasing herds, father decided to remove to Southern Oregon, where he could have an abundance of range for them.

He at once set about building a large flat-boat, or scow, in which to move his family, household goods, and what stock he could not, or did not wish to sell.

In the fall, after the crops were harvested, and everything disposed of that we did not want to move, father shipped his cattle and horses to St. Helens, and sent them on by the trail, to the valley. He then returned, and moved the family and our teams to Portland, then a very small town on the Willamette river.

After disposing of the boat, we loaded up the two wagons, and were ready to start for the valley. It had been raining, and I well remember what a terrific time we had getting through the dense timber west and south of Portland, father leading, driving one team, and my mother following, with the second. Mr. John Hobson, my brother-in-law, had, meantime, gotten the horses and cattle through the timber, and, leaving the other men to herd them, on good pasturage, came back and met us in the woods, for which we were very thankful. We came up with the herd near the Burton place, in North Yahhill, the next day, and bidding Mr. Hobson and one of the other two men good-bye, we proceeded on to Roseburg, arriving there without mishap.

Brother Flem and I, with the assistance of one man, who was not half equal to either one of us for the purpose, drove the herd.

Father said we were worth more than any two men he could hire. There was an abundance of grass; the weather was fine, and this part of the journey was really a picnic for us all. . . .

On reaching Roseburg, we found our old friend and neighbor Mr. Perry had a house all ready for us, and we moved right in. Father took up a claim just across the Umpqua river, from the then little village of Roseburg. This gave him a wide scope of range for all his stock. He at once bought lumber for a good house, and began hauling it on the building-spot, in order to be ready to build early in the spring. Then, during the winter, he built a ferry-boat for his own accommodation, and that of the public. As the river could not be forded during a part of the year, and was really dangerous, the ferry was quite a source of revenue to us. During the winter, Mr. Hill came to visit us. His parents and their family had come to Oregon the year before, and settled in the Rogue River valley, near the Siskiyou mountains.

It was now arranged that we should be married the next spring, when father's house was far enough completed to move in. During the winter and early spring, I put in all my spare time in preparing for my approaching marriage.

I had four quilts already pieced, ready for the lining; mother had given me the lining for them all, and the cotton for two, and we quilted and finished them all. She also gave me muslin for four sheets, two pairs of pillow-cases, two tablecloths, and four towels. I cut and made two calico dresses for myself, and assisted mother in the making of my wedding dress, which was a pretty, sky-blue figured lawn.

I had everything done, and neatly folded away long before the wedding day arrived. Mr. Hill came early in April, and assisted us in moving into the new house.

On May 4th, 1854, with only our old friends, the Perrys, and the minister present, beside our own family, we were married. I was still small for my age. My husband was five-feet eleven-inches in height, and I could stand under his outstretched arm. I grew very slowly, and did not reach my full stature until I was 25 years old, which is now 5-feet 4-inches.

Just prior to our marriage, Mr. Hill had bought a farm of 320 acres on credit, four miles from my father's home, for $600, to be paid for in two years.

The improvements on it consisted of a small cabin, 12x14 in dimensions, made of round logs, with the bark on them, each notched deeply enough at its end to dovetail into its neighbors above and below it. The cracks still remaining after this rude fitting were filled with mixed mud and grass, but this cabin had never yet been "chinked." It was covered with "shakes," (thick, hand-made shingles three feet long) which were kept in place by poles, tied down at each end. The door was so low that a man had to stoop to go in and out, and it was fastened with the proverbial latch and string. The cabin had neither floor nor chimney, and the wide cracks admitted both draughts and vermin. Later I gathered grass and fern, mixed them with mud, and filled these cracks, thus shutting out the snakes and lizards, which abounded in that region, and which had made me frequent and alarming visits. The window consisted of two panes of glass set in an opening made by sawing out a section of one of the logs for that purpose.

About twelve acres of land were fenced, and had been seeded to oats and wheat for one or two years. A rough, open shed sufficed to shelter six or eight head of stock, and surrounding it was a corral for milking cows, and a calf pen adjoining it.

Our furniture consisted of a pioneer bed, made by boring three holes in the logs of the wall in one corner, in which to drive the rails. Thus the bedstead required but one leg. The table was a mere rough shelf, fastened to the wall, and supported by two legs. Three smaller shelves answered for a cupboard, and were amply sufficient for my slender supply of dishes, which comprised mostly tinware, which, in those days, was kept scrupulously bright and shining. My sugar bowl, cream jug, steel knives and forks (two-tined) and one set of German silver teaspoons, I had brought with my own little savings before my marriage.

My cooking utensils were a pot, tea-kettle and bake oven (all of iron), a frying pan and coffee pot, a churn, six milk pans, a wash tub and board, a large twenty or thirty gallon iron pot for washing purposes, etc., and a water bucket and tin dipper. All these things, including a full supply of groceries, I got on my father's account, as he had told me to go to the store and purchase what I wanted. This I did in the afternoon of my wedding day, the ceremony having taken place at 10 a.m. He also gave me a fine riding mare, Queen, (my saddle I had already earned long before), one fresh cow and a heifer calf, which I selected; also one cow which would be fresh in the early fall, and a wagon and harness. In addition, mother gave me a good feather bed, and pillows, a good straw bed, a pair of blankets and two extra quilts. My husband's possessions were a horse and saddle, a gun, and less than twenty dollars in money; but I considered this a most excellent start in life. I knew what my father and mother had done, and I then believed that my husband was the equal of any man living. . . .

Consequently, I had high hopes and great expectations for the future. My husband was a strong, healthy man; I had been trained to work, and bred to thrift and economy, and everything looked bright and beautiful to me. My soul overflowed with love and hope, and I could sing the dear old home-songs from morning to night. My happy, buoyant nature enabled me to enjoy anything, even cooking out of doors, over a smoky fire, without even a covering over my head; for at first we had neither fireplace nor stove.

It was sweet, smiling spring—the season that I loved best. The hills were bedecked with the loveliest wild flowers, for the variety and abundance of which the Umpqua valley is especially noted.

And yet, from a child I was practical and methodical. I had everything packed, and ready to move to my new home as soon as we were married, and I insisted on going there the next morning, knowing that the garden ought to be in. Within a few days it was planted.

We depended on wild game for meat, and as my husband was a good marksman, he kept us well supplied. I always went with him, and we never came home empty handed. He often killed two grouse from one tree by shooting the under bird first. The upper one seldom flew, and the hunter could bag it at the next shot. This seemed to be characteristic of the grouse. It is not startled by the sound of the gun's discharge, but if the upper bird is killed, its fall alarms those under, who immediately take to flight. I have myself seen hunters who know this fact kill three grouse in one tree by shooting the lower ones first.

Mr. Hill was always ready to go hunting, no matter what work was pressing to be done.

One evening he proposed a deer hunt, so next morning we were off early. He decided to go to the top of the highest hill, as the wind coming from that direction would bear away our scent; so we rode our horses as far up as we could, and then staked them on good grass, and proceeded on foot to a point where he said we were sure to find deer. When near the summit, we crept with great caution, and peeped over. Sure enough! There, basking in the heat of the day, in the shade of the noble oak trees on that gentle, grassy slope, was a band of the soft eyed beauties.

All save one were lying down; while the king of the herd stood quietly by, leisurely chewing his cud, with his head toward us, all unconscious that his last hour had come.

We were behind a large tree, and my husband rested his rifle on one of its limbs, and took deliberate aim. At the click of the trigger, the royal buck sprang into the air, and fell dead. The herd was thrown into consternation; and, as the wind blew from them to us, they bounded toward us. In an instant the gun was reloaded, aimed, and a graceful doe succumbed. I now entreated that he shoot no more, and as it was then past noon, and we were a long way from home, he assented. We first went down to the big buck, and soon dismembered him, and cut off his head. After spending much time, and hard labor in tugging and pulling, we at last got him to the top of the hill, after which it was an easy task to carry the small deer up. Then we started down the long hill, he with the large animal, and I with the small one. In time we reached the horses, on which we lashed the carcasses. Then we led the horses to the foot of the hill, where we loaded both deer on one horse, and rode home ourselves on the other, getting home at dark. The early morning of the next day was spent in skinning and salting the meat. Then, taking the two large hams, we lost no time in riding over to father's for dinner, eager to tell of and talk over our hunting exploit. We well knew how much father and mother would enjoy the juicy steaks from those toothsome hams. Good coffee, hot buttermilk biscuits, or corn bread and fried venison, with cream gravy, and potatoes, was the favorite breakfast (or any other meal) of the southern man, and a hunter's delight. My mother was a cook worthy of the name. Breakfast foods were then unknown, and as little needed, as such a thing as a dyspeptic was never heard of, and the word, even, was scarcely comprehended.

In the beginning of our married life, my father had advised my husband to begin at once to fell trees, and hew them, and put up a good house before winter set in. There was an abundance of suitable timber on our land, near by, but he was never in any hurry to get down to work. In one way and another he managed to idle away the summer, going to camp meetings, reading novels, and hunting.

Bethenia's husband continued to hunt and fritter away his time, forcing her father to complete the house for them. Bethenia was not yet fifteen but recognized in Legrand Hill a "want of industry and perserverance." Unable to meet the first year's payment, the couple sold the farm and went to stay with Legrand's relatives in Jackson County, Oregon.

We moved into our new house in March, with the $150 mortgage hanging over us. On April 17th, 1856, our baby [George] was born, and then Aunt Kelly begged me to give him to her, addressing me thus:

"Now Bethenia, you just give him to me. I will take him, and educate him, and make him my heir. I will give him all I have, and that is more than his father will ever do for him. I know very well that Legrand will just fool around all his life, and never accomplish anything."

She seemed to think my consent to her having the child was all that was necessary. But my baby was too precious to give to anyone.

I continued to work with Aunt Kelly, who was always over-crowded with work, and as we were so near by each other, I could do much of it at my own home; so that, in time, I was able to get many little conveniences and comforts for the house, beside a good share of our groceries. Mr. Hill neither drank or used tobacco, but, as his aunt said, he simply idled away his time, doing a day's work here and there, but never continuing at anything. Then, too, he had a passion for trading and speculating, always himself coming out a loser; and thus the time dragged on, until September, 1857, when who should drive up, one glad day, but my father and mother. Father had heard how things were going with us, and had come, prepared to take us back with them in case we were willing to go, but he was too discreet to let this be known till later. He and mother wanted to see the country; the children were large enough to look out for things at home; and they especially desired to see my baby.

It did not take them long to understand that we were barely living "from hand to mouth," as it were, with most of the work coming on me, so father said:

"How would you like to go back to Roseburg? It is a growing town. I have several acres in it, and if you think you would like to make a change, I will give you an acre of land, and the material for a good house, which you can put up this fall. . . . The boys can help you, and there will always be plenty of work at carpentering in town.

To say that we were delighted with this proposal expresses it but faintly. We sold our house and lot in Yreka, realizing less than $100 out of the transaction, as the $150 mortgage and interest had to come out of the sum received for the property, but father said "A bird in the hand is worth two in the bush." We were soon packed, and ready to start again on our migrations. . . .

On reaching home, father told me I could go over and select my acre of land, and our building-spot, which I gladly did. He told

Mr. Hill he could have the team, and he and the boys could haul the lumber for our house, so that he could get to work on it at once.

They hauled the lumber, but, in the meantime, Mr. Hill had been talking with a man about burning brick. This man had some land a mile from father's, and a team, and he offered to go into equal partnership with Mr. Hill in the business of brickmaking there, each, beside his own work, furnishing one man to help, and I was to do the cooking for them all, for the use of the team.

Father endeavored, in every way, to dissuade him from going into this undertaking, telling him that it would be impossible, so late in the season, to prepare a yard, and burn a kiln of brick before winter; and that the soil had never been tested, and there was no certainty that it was suitable, for the purpose, etc., but the more he talked the more determined Mr. Hill was to put all the little money we had into the venture, and so he moved me and my young child into a tent in a low, damp valley, near the river, and their work and mine was begun. But it was never half completed, for when they had only a few hundred brick molded, it began to rain continuously, and put a stop to their work, and in addition to this ill-fortune, I was stricken down with typhoid fever. Father and mother came with the wagon, and moved us back to their home. It was now late in November; winter was upon us, and still our house was not touched.

When I became convalescent, father urged Mr. Hill to begin the house. He replied that he wanted a deed to the acre of land before beginning the house.

Father then told him that he and mother had talked it over, and had decided to deed the property to me and the boy; that he had given us one good start, and now, after three and a half years, we had nothing left but one horse, and that he thought it best to secure a home for me and the child in my own name.

This enraged Mr. Hill, who said he would not build on the lot unless the deed was made to him, as he was the head of his family. Father advised him to think it over, and not to act rashly.

He sulked for a time, and then bargained for a lot in town, after which he hired a team, and hauled the lumber off from the acre to the lot, and began to build the house. All this time we were living off father, who said nothing; but furnished the shingles, and told Mr. Hill to get nails, and anything he needed, at the store, on his account, which he did. In time, the roof was on, and the kitchen partly finished, and we moved in. The kitchen was so open that the skunks, which were very numerous in that region at that time, came

under the floor nights, and up into the kitchen, where they rattled around among the pots and pans, even jumping on the table, and devouring the food, if I did not keep everything securely covered, while I often lay and listened to their nocturnal antics, not daring to get up to drive them out, as the dire consequences of disturbing them suddenly were well known, and dreaded.

My health was poor. I had not been strong since the baby came, and I could not seem to recover from the effects of the fever. The baby was ill and fretful, much of the time, and things were going anything but smoothly. A short time before the climax, I went home and told my parents that I did not think I could stand it much longer. Mother was indignant, and told me to come home, and let him go; that "any man that could not make a living with the good starts and help he has had, never will make one; and with his temper, he is liable to kill you at any time."

Father broke down, and shed tears, saying:

"Oh, Bethenia, there has never been a divorce in my family, and I hope there never will be. I want you to go back, and try again, and do your best. After that, if you cannot possibly get along, come home." I went back, greatly relieved, for I knew that if I had to leave, I would be protected.

Our trouble usually started over the baby, who was unusually cross. He was such a sickly, tiny mite, with an abnormal, voracious appetite, but his father thought him old enough to be trained and disciplined, and would spank him unmercifully because he cried. This I could not endure, and war would be precipitated at once. A few days before our separation, his father fed him six hard boiled eggs at supper, in spite of all I could do or say. I slept little that night, expecting that the child would be in convulsions before morning. And thus one thing led to another until the climax was reached.

Early one morning in March, after a tempestuous scene of this sort, Mr. Hill threw the baby on the bed, and rushed down in town. As soon as he was out of sight, I put on my hat and shawl, and gathering a few necessaries together for the baby, I flew over to father's.

I found my brother ferrying a man across the river, and I went back with him. By this time, I was almost in a state of collapse, as I had ran all the way, about three fourths of a mile. Brother, seeing that something was wrong, and always ready to smooth out the wrinkles, took the baby with a smile, saying: "Give me that little 'piggywig,' and shall I take you under my other arm?

It seems to me you're getting smaller every year. Now, just hang on to me, and I'll get you up the hill, all right. Mother will have breakfast ready, and I guess a good square meal is what you need."

The next day father saw Mr. Hill, and found he had been trying to sell the house and lot. Father told him that he would come with me to get my clothes, and a few things I needed, and that he (Mr. Hill) could have the rest. That he (father) would take care of me from that time on, and that when he (Mr. Hill) sold the house and lot, I would sign the deed, as the lot was not paid for, and the unfinished house would, according to law, go with it.

However, before Mr. Hill found a purchaser, he had repented, and come several times to get me to go back to him. I said: "Legrand, I have told you many times that if we ever did separate, I would never go back, and I never will."

And now, at eighteen years of age, I found myself, broken in spirit and health, again in my father's house, from which, only four short years before, I had gone with such a happy heart, and such bright hopes for the future. . . .

It seemed to me now that I should never be happy or strong again. I was, indeed, surrounded with difficulties seemingly insurmountable; a husband for whom I had lost all love and respect; a divorce, the stigma of which would cling to me all my future life, and a sickly babe of two years in my arms, all rose darkly before me.

At this time I could scarcely read or write, and four years of trials and hardships and privations sufficient to crush a mature woman, had wrought a painful change in the fresh, blooming child who had so buoyantly taken the duties and burdens of wifehood and motherhood on her young shoulders. I realized my position fully, and resolved to meet it bravely, and do my very best.

My little George, too, felt the beneficial change fully as I did; for my mother's idea of raising children could not be improved upon; simply give them sufficient wholesome food, keep them clean and happy, and let them live out of doors as much as possible.

George was such a tiny creature, and so active in his movements that my young brothers and sisters felt him no burden, and always had him out of doors; so after pondering the matter for some time, I said one day:

"Mother do you think I might manage to go to school?"

"Why yes," she answered: "go right along. George is no trouble. The children will take care of him."

I joyfully accepted this opportunity, and from that day on, I was up early and out to the barn, assisting with the milking, and doing all the work possible in the house, until 8:30, when I went to school with the children, my younger brothers and sisters. Saturdays, with the aid of the children, I did the washing and ironing of the family, and kept up with my studies.

At the end of my first four months' term I had finished the third reader, and made good progress with my other studies of spelling, writing, geography, and arithmetic. . . .

Before going to Clatsop, in the fall of 1859, with my sister, I applied for a divorce, and the custody of my child and petitioned for the restoration of my maiden name of Owens. . . . The suit was strongly contested on account of the child. . . . My father employed Hon. Stephen F. Chadwick on my behalf, and he won my suit. . . . After the decree of the court was rendered giving me custody of my child, and my father's name, which I have never since discarded, and never will, I felt like a free woman.

The world began to look bright once more, as with renewed vigor and reviving hope, I sought work in all honorable directions, even accepting washing, which was one of the most profitable occupations among the few considered "proper" for women in those days.

My father objected to me doing washing for a living, and said:

"Why can't you be contented to stay at home with us: I am able to support you and your child?"

But no. No amount of argument would shake my determination to earn my own livelihood, and that of my child, so father brought me a sewing machine, the first that ever came into that town, and so, with sewing and nursing, a year passed very profitably.

Late in the fall of 1860, sister and I went over to Oysterville, Wash., to visit my old and much beloved girl friend, Mrs. S.S. Munson. . . . I told Mrs. Munson of my great anxiety for an education, and she immediately said:

"Why not, then, stay here with me, and go to school? We have a good school here, and I should like so much to have you with me, especially farther on."

To this generous offer I replied that I would gladly accept it if I could only find some way of earning my necessary expenses while attending school. Mrs. Munson replied:

"There are my brother and his hired man: I can get you their washing, which will bring you in from $1.00 to $1.50 per week, which will be all you will need."

To this I gratefully assented and I did their washing evenings. Work to me then was scarcely more than play.

Thus passed one of the pleasantest, and most profitable winters of my life, while, whetted by what it fed on, my desire for knowledge grew daily stronger. My sister, Mrs. Hobson, now urged me to come back to her, and I said to her: I am determined to get at least a common school education. I now know that I can support and educate myself and my boy, and I am resolved to do it: furthermore, I do not intend to do it over a washtub, either. Nor will I any longer work for my board and clothes alone. You need me, and I am willing to stay with you the next six months, if you will arrange for me to go to school in Astoria next winter. She agreed to this, and some time later I said to her: "Diane, don't you think I could teach a little summer school here on the plains? I can rise at four, and help with the milking, and get all the other work done by 8 a.m., and I can do the washing mornings and evenings, and on Saturdays."

She said: "You can try," so the following day I asked Mr. Hobson if he would not get up a little school for me.

He replied: "Take the horse and go around and among the neighbors and work it up yourself."

I lost no time in carrying out his suggestion, and succeeded in getting the promise of sixteen pupils, for which I was to receive $2 each for three months.

This was my first attempt to instruct others. I taught my school in the old Presbyterian church, the first Presbyterian church building ever erected in Oregon. Of my sixteen pupils, there were three who were more advanced than myself, but I took their books home with me nights, and, with the help of my brother-in-law, I managed to prepare the lessons beforehand, and they never suspected my incompetency.

From this school I received my first little fortune of $25; and I added to this by picking wild blackberries at odd times, which found a ready sale at fifty cents a gallon.

Fall found me settled at the old Boelling Hotel in Astoria, with my nephew, Frank Hobson, and my little son George. Our board was paid, I taking care of our small room, and our clothes, with the privilege of doing our washing and ironing on Saturdays. And now I encountered one of my sharpest trials, for, on entering school, and being examined in mental arithmetic, I was placed in the primary class!

Mr. Deardorff, the principal, kindly offered to assist me in that study after school, and, later, permitted me to enter both classes. Words can never express my humiliation at having to recite with children of from eight to fourteen years of age. This, however, was of brief duration, for in a few weeks, I had advanced to the next class above, and was soon allowed to enter the third (and highest) class in mental arithmetic.

At the end of the term of nine months, I had passed into most of the advanced classes; not that I was an apt scholar, for my knowledge has always been acquired by the hardest labor, but by sheer determination, industry and perseverance. At 4 a.m. my lamp was always burning, and I was poring over my books, never allowing myself more than eight hours of sleep.

Nothing was permitted to come between me and this, the greatest opportunity of my life.

The following summer was spent on Clatsop with my sister, milking, making butter, and assisting in all the laborious, and never ending work of a well managed farm. . . .

Bethenia then had two years of great success as a milliner and dressmaker, but was nearly driven out of business when a competitor moved in next door. She met the challenge by going to San Francisco to study with the best milliner there and returning with the latest fashions to become the best milliner in Roseburg. Her success as a businesswoman provided her with the money to send George through college and on to medical school.

In 1870 I placed my son in the University of California at Berkeley. I had always had a fondness for nursing, and had developed a special capacity in that direction by assisting my neighbors in illness. I was more and more besieged by the entreaties of my friends and doctors, which were hard to refuse, to come to their aid in sickness, often times to the detriment of business, and now that money came easily, a desire began to grow within me for a medical education. One evening I was sent for by a friend with a very sick child. The old physician in my presence attempted to use an instrument for the relief of the little sufferer, and, in his long, bungling, and unsuccessful attempt he severely lacerated the tender flesh of the poor little girl. At last, he laid down the instrument, to wipe his glasses. I picked it up, saying, "Let me try, Doctor," and passed it instantly, with perfect ease, bringing immediate relief to the tortured child. The mother, who was standing by in agony at the sight of her child's mutilation, threw her arms around my neck, and sobbed out her thanks. Not so the doctor! He did not appreciate or approve of my interference, and he showed his displeasure at the time most emphatically. This apparently unimportant event really decided my future course.

A few days later, I called on my friend, Dr. Hamilton, and confiding to him my plans and ambitions, I asked for the loan of medical books. He gave me Gray's *Anatomy*. I came out of his private office into the drug-store, where I saw Hon. S.F. Chadwick, who had heard the conversation, and who came promptly forward and shook my hand warmly, saying: "Go ahead. It is in you; let it come out. You will win."

The Hon. Jesse Applegate, my dear and revered friend, who had fondled me as a babe, was the one other person who ever gave me a single word of encouragement to study medicine.

Realizing that I should meet opposition, especially from my own family, I kept my own counsel.

I now began in good earnest to arrange my business affairs so that I could leave for the East in one year from that time, meantime studying diligently to familiarize myself with the science of anatomy, the groundwork of my chosen profession. . . .

In due time, I announced that in two weeks I would leave for Philadelphia, to enter a medical school. As I have said, I expected disapproval from my friends and relatives, but I was not prepared for the storm of opposition that followed. My family felt they were disgraced, and even my own child was influenced and encouraged to think I was doing him an irreparable injury, by my course. People sneered and laughed derisively. Most of my friends seemed to consider it their Christian duty to advise against, and endeavor to prevent me from taking this "fatal" step. I was literally kept on the rack. But as all things must have an end, the day of my departure was at last at hand. . . .

I had taken the decisive step, and I would never turn back. . . . My decision was now irrevocably made, and I was comforted.

Stage travel was no hardship for me, for, like the sailor on his ship, I felt at home in the stage. For several years I had gone to San Francisco spring and fall by land, when the nearest railroad connection was at Marysville, California. . . .

On reaching Philadelphia, I matriculated in the Eclectic School of Medicine, and employed a private tutor. I also attended the lectures and clinics in the great Blockly Hospital twice a week, as did all the medical students of the city. In due time I received my degree, and returned to Roseburg to wind up my business, which I had left in charge of my sister. A few days after my return, an old man without friends died, and the six physicians who had all attended him at various times, decided to hold an autopsy. At their meeting, Dr. Palmer, who had not forgotten my former "impudence" in using his instrument, made a motion to invite the new "Philadelphia" doctor to be present. This was carried, and a messenger was dispatched to me with a written invitation. I knew this meant no honor for me, but I said: "Give the doctors my compliments, and say that I will be there in a few minutes." The messenger left, and I followed close behind him. I waited outside until he went in and closed the door. I heard him say, in excited tones: "She said to give you her compliments, and that she'd be here in a minute." Then came a roar of laughter, after which I quietly opened the door and walked in, went forward, and shook hands with Dr. Hoover, who advanced to meet me, saying:

"Do you know that the autopsy is on the genital organs?"

"No," I answered; "but one part of the human body should be as sacred to the physician as another."

Dr. Palmer here stepped back, saying: "I object to a woman's being present at a male autopsy, and if she is allowed to remain, I shall retire!"

"I came here by written invitation," I said; "and I will leave it to a vote whether I go or stay: but first I would like to ask Dr. Palmer what is the difference between the attendance of a woman at a male autopsy, and the attendance of a man at a female autopsy?"

Dr. Hoover said: "Well, I voted for you to come, and I will stick to it." Another said: "I voted yes, and I'll not go back on it. . . ."

One of the doctors opened an old medicine case, and offered it to me.

"You do not want me to do the work, do you?" I asked, in surprise.

"Oh, yes, yes, go ahead," he said. I took the case and complied. The news of what was going on had spread to every house in town, and the excitement was at fever-heat.

When I had at last finished the dissection, the audience (not the doctors) gave me three cheers. As I passed out and down on my way home, the street was lined on both sides with men, women and children, all anxious to get a look at "the woman who dared," to see what sort of a strange, anomalous being she was. The women were shocked and scandalized! The men were disgusted, but amused, thinking it "such a good joke on the doctors. . . ."

And now, as I look back, I believe that all that saved me was the fact that my brothers, Flem and Josiah, lived there, and although they disapproved of my actions quite as much as the rest of the community did, yet "blood is thicker than water," and they would have died in their tracks before they would have seen me subjected to indignities, or driven out of town. And as everyone knew they would shoot at the drop of a hat, good care was taken to lay no violent hands on me.

As soon as possible after that autopsy, I closed up my business, and, taking my sister, and the remnant of my store goods, I removed to Portland, Oregon.

I first occupied the ground-floor of a two-story brick building on the east side of First street, between Taylor and Yahhill. There were no brick buildings in Portland south of there at that time. I had two rooms fitted up for electrical and medicated baths. This was a new process of treatment, and it, in connection with my other practice, proved both attractive and remunerative. I obtained the knowledge in a New York institution, which had been open but a short time.

There was but one man, a German, in Portland who seemed to have any knowledge of electrical batteries, and he found much trouble in keeping my batteries in running order.

I was now well settled, and notwithstanding occasional rebuffs here and there, and frequent slights from my brother M.D.s, I went steadily on, gaining a step here, and a point there, and constantly advancing, with money coming in faster and faster.

My son George was now nineteen, and I entered him in the Medical Department of the Willamette University. It was certainly one of the proudest days of my life when he was graduated from it, two years later. From the beginning, I had set my heart on making a physician of him, and at last my life's ambition was crowned with success. . . .

Time passed on. I was successful and prosperous, but not yet satisfied.

Again I was beginning to pine for more knowledge.

My sister asked for a course in Mills College, which I gave her. My son had his profession. "I have done my duty to those depending on me," I thought, "and now I will treat myself to a full medical course in the old school, and a trip to Europe. I shall then be equipped for business on an advanced scale. . . ."

Again my family and friends objected. They said: "You will soon be rich; why spend all you have for nothing. . .?"

But I was deaf to all entreaties—a better education I must have, and the best way to secure it was to go to the fountain head. . . .

My mind was made up, and, like the gambler who has won once, I would risk all at one throw again; and so, on September 1st, 1878, on a bright, sunny day, I left Portland, again *en route* for Philadelphia; not this time with a storm without and within, but surrounded by sunshine, and followed by the good wishes of many friends.

It was my intention, if possible, to gain admission to the then renowned Jefferson Medical College.

Armed with letters from U.S. Senators, Governers, Professors, and Doctors, on reaching Philadelphia, I at once called upon, and was entertained by Dr. Hannah Longshore, one of the first graduates of the Women's Medical School of Philadelphia, and sister of Professor Longshore, founder of and professor in the Eclectic Medical School of Philadelphia for men and women.

I told her plainly just what I desired.

"I have no faith that you can get into Jefferson College," she said, "but I want to see you try it. I believe the time will come when the doors of every medical school in our land will be forced open for women, as do the Eclectic and Homeopathic schools now. But the old schools, as you know, do not recognize them. If there is any man today who can open the doors of Jefferson College to women, it is Professor Gross."

"This is Saturday," I said, "and I will go at once to see him."

He received me with a gracious smile, requesting me to be seated, as I handed him the envelope containing my credentials.

While he was looking over the letters with a pleased expression on his fine face, I could scarcely realize that I was in the presence of the then greatest surgeon in the United States.

His slender, delicate hands were not suggestive of bloodletting.

I was lost in contemplation of this grand man, when he broke my reverie by saying, with the gentlest voice and manner:

"And now, my little lady, what can I do for you?"

"I have come to this grand old city in search of knowledge,"

I answered. "I hunger and thirst after it. I want to drink at the fountain-head. Can you not lead me into Jefferson College, you, her geatest professor?"

He gazed at me with moist and sympathetic eyes for an instant. Then, in the gentlest, softest tones, he said:

"My dear little woman, how gladly I would open the doors of Jefferson to you; but that privilege is denied to me. The deciding power lies in the hands of the board of regents, and they are a whole age behind the times. They would simply be shocked, scandalized, and enraged at the mere mention of admitting a woman into Jefferson College. Why not go to the Women's College? It is just as good. The examinations required to be passed are identically the same."

"I know that, Professor Gross," I responded, "but a Woman's College out West stands below par, and I must have a degree that is second to none."

"Then the University of Michigan is the school for you," he said. "It is a long-term school, and a mixed school, and it is second to none in America."

"Thanks, Professor, a thousand thanks!" I gratefully exclaimed; "I will follow your advice and go there at once. . . ."

Arriving there, I was soon settled, and in my seat for the opening lecture, on the next day but one. During the ensuing nine months, I averaged sixteen hours a day in attending lectures, in hard study, and in all the exercises required in the course, after which I put in ten hours a day (excepting Sundays) in study during the vacation. Most of this time was given to Professor Ford's Question-Book. It was a book of questions without answers, on anatomy. Anatomy has always been the bug bear of medical students.

I procured a blank book, and commencing at the beginning, I numbered each question, then looked up each answer, and wrote it out in full in my blank book. This book covered the anatomy, from beginning to end, and it was completed, with the exception of a few answers which I could not find.

At the opening of the next term, I took my book to Professor Ford for the correct answers to these, that I might fill in the blanks. Professor Ford took the book, and examined it carefully, and then said:

"You have done that which no other student in this University has ever done before, and more than I have expected one to do; and you have done it while the others have been enjoying a vaca-

tion. I shall not forget this. It will be of the highest value to you in the saving of time, and the fixing of these all-important facts in your memory."

It was my custom to rise at four a.m., take a cold bath, followed by vigorous exercise; then study till breakfast, at seven. (I allowed myself half an hour for each meal.)

After supper came "Quizzes," and then study till nine p.m., when I retired, to sleep soundly.

Between lectures, clinics, laboratory work, Quizzes, examinations, two good sermons on Sunday, and a church social now and then, the time was fully and pleasantly occupied. The constant change brought rest, and acted as a safety valve to our over heated brains.

At the close of the second year, in June, 1880, I received my degree. During all that time, I had not suffered from a day's sickness, and had been present at every class lecture save one, my absence from it being due to my having been so deeply absorbed in my studies that I failed to hear the bell. This lapse almost broke my heart, which had been set on being able to say, at the end of the course, that I had not missed a single lecture.

After graduating, having arranged for three years' absence from home, I went with one of my classmates to Chicago. Taking rooms, we devoted ourselves to hospital and clinical work.

While there, my son, Dr. Hill, joined me, and the first of October found us back at the University, where Dr. Hill entered for a post course, while I remained as a resident physician, which entitled me to all the lectures. I attended all the advanced lectures in my department, theory and practice in the Homeopathic School, and English literature and history in the Literary Department.

At the end of six months, with my son and two lady physicians, I sailed for Europe. We visited Glasgow, Hamburg, Berlin, Potsdam, Munich, Dresden, Paris, London, and other cities. . . .

When I landed at New York, the Customs Collector demanded $75 duty on my instruments, which I had purchased in Paris. I said: "These instruments are for my own use. I am a physician. Here is a letter from the President of the University of Michigan, and letters from U.S. Senators, Governers, etc. I know you have no right to collect duty on my instruments, and if you take my goods, I will employ an attorney."

"You stay right here," he said, "till I come back, and you'll find you will have to pay the duty." After two hours, he returned, and said: "Take your things, and go on."

I speedily obeyed, glad to get out of his clutches. In a few hours my ticket to San Francisco was secured and I was *en route* thither. . . .

A week or two after I was settled, Col. McC. called, and said:

"I am glad to welcome you back, and I thought I would take a few of your electrical medical baths. I have not really had an attack of rheumatism since that terrible time I had before, but I thought I had better take a few as a preventative."

I laughed again, saying: "I have no baths, and never expect to have again."

"Really; you have not lost faith in them, have you?"

"Oh no, I fully realize their worth; but you see, Colonel, I am now a full-fledged University physician of the old school, and I cannot afford to attach to myself the odium of the epithet, "Bath Doctor." One dollar and a half was considered a large price for those baths, by some of my customers, but no one expects to get a prescription for less than $2.00. Oh no, I expect to carry my stock in trade in my head from this time on."

Thus passed three of the happiest and most prosperous years of my life. Health, hosts of friends, and unbroken prosperity. What more could I ask, or desire?

When asked, as I often was, why I did not marry, I always responded; "I am married. I am married to my profession," and I was honest in that belief.

But the time came which is said to come to all, when I was ready and willing to add another name to mine, and it came about in this way: Oregon was about to vote on the Woman Suffrage Amendment. On an April morning, I saw C.W. Fulton's name in the list of arrivals from Astoria, and, knowing that he was a friend of the cause, I drove directly to his hotel. Stepping to the counter, I inquired of the clerk:

"Has Mr. C.W. Fulton breakfasted yet?"

I heard chairs moving behind me, and Mr. Fulton's voice saying:

"Yes, Doctor, I am here. And don't you know these three gentlemen?" He, with Col. John Adair, and his two brothers, were all having breakfast at the same table, and they urged me to join them. . . .

I had not seen any of the Adairs for years. General Adair and my father had been warm friends, as Kentuckians can be: and when I was thirteen, John was a large, handsome boy of his age, with the most beautiful curly auburn hair imaginable. I admired, and was quite fascinated with him, then. . . . He [had come] to my home occasionally with his father. . . . [*She mentions no more about Colonel Adair or their romance until the wedding.*]

Colonel Adair and I were married July 24, 1884, in the First Congregational Church of Portland, Oregon.

The church was filled by the invited guests, a number of whom were from Roseburg, two-hundred miles distant.

When we left the church, the street was lined on both sides with friends and uninvited people, and when the carriage rolled away, many called out: "Goodbye, Doctor, goodbye!"

After a month's absence, we returned to Portland, and I took up my work where I had left it.

More than twenty-one years have passed since I plighted my marriage vows. Many sorrows have been interspersed with the pleasures of my married life, and during all these years, I have been as active and determined as in former days. I have never flinched from any undertaking, and I hope I never shall, to the day of my death, but during these later years, I have often looked back over my past life not with a shudder, but to gain strength and courage to meet the financial difficulties that had accumulated, and threatened to engulf me.

My yearly income at the time of my marriage was fully $7,000.

Colonel Adair is an optimist of a happy and cheerful disposition, and, as I have frequently said, he is usually among the clouds, and rarely gets down to *terra firma*.

There were no dark shadows in his pictures, and my love for him knew no bounds. Soon after our marriage he induced me to invest in a large property, near Astoria, in which he saw millions in the near future.

A large portion of it was unreclaimed tide land. Reclamation at that time was very expensive, and little understood. I was earnestly advised not to invest in the property.

At the age of forty-seven I gave birth to a little daughter; and now my joy knew no limit, my cup of bliss was full to overflowing. A son I had, and a daughter was what I most desired. . . . For three days only, was she left with us, and then my treasure was taken from me, to join in the immortal hosts beyond all earthly pain and sorrow.

My grief was so excessive I felt it was more than I could bear, unsupported by the companionship of my husband, who, with the aid of twenty five Chinamen, were trying to reclaim the tide land, a task which did seem, as his brother once said, "like fighting the Pacific Ocean...."

My husband now urged me to go to [our] farm, saying: "Your health absolutely demands the change. In that pure, fresh air you can soon regain your health and strength. In less than two years railroad trains will be running across our land, and our fortunes will be assured, and you will never need work again."

In my weakened condition, I consented, and July 1st, 1888, found us on the farm, where we remained for eleven years.

Now, as I look back, I realize that that move was one of the greatest mistakes of my life. I soon, however, recovered my health, and accustomed vigor and energy, and was ready for business. During those eleven years, I carried on my professional work as best I could, in that out-of-the-way place; and at no time did I ever refuse a call, day or night, rain or shine. I was often compelled to go on foot, through trails so overhung with dense undergrowth, and obstructed with logs and roots, that a horse and rider could not get past; and through muddy and flooded tide lands in gum boots.

A few cases will better illustrate the nature of much of my practice, and the hardships which were entailed upon the physician in that locality.

One day a Mr. William Larsen came, saying: "My wife is sick. Come at once." There was a most terrific southwest storm raging, and we had a mile to go on foot over the tide-land before reaching the Lewis and Clark River. The land was flooded, the mud and slush deep, and the swollen sloughs had to be crossed on logs and planks. Nearly the whole distance was overgrown with enormous bunches of wire grass, many being three feet across. This long, intertwined grass was a great obstruction to walking, and I fell prone, again and again, before reaching the river. My boots were filled with water, and I was drenched to the skin. The wind was howling, and dead ahead. Mr. Larsen was a powerful man, and a master-hand with the oars. He sprang into the boat, throwing off his hat and two coats, and began to remove his outer shirt, saying: "You must excuse me, Doctor, but if I ever get you there, I shall have to strip near the skin."

I thoroughly understood the situation, and well knew that the odds were against us; and I fully expected that, notwithstanding his uncommon strength and skill, we would be compelled to land far below our starting point on the opposite side, and be forced to make our way over tide lands many times worse than that we had already crossed. However, before we had gone many rods from shore, the shrill whistle of his little steam milk launch was borne to us in that onrushing storm, and she now came shooting out of the big slough leading to his house, with the terrible storm at her stern forcing her onward.

In his anxiety and distress, Mr. Larsen's first thought was that his wife was dead, and in the anguish of his heart, with tears streaming over his face, he cried out:

"My God! My God! My wife is dead!"

"No, no, your wife is not dead," I said. "Captain Johnson has returned from Astoria, and knowing you could not get me there, has come for us." Which proved to be the fact.

As soon as the launch was in hailing distance, he called out: "How is my wife?"

"A-l-l r-i-g-h-t," instantly came the cheering reply. The sudden reaction of relief came near being too much for that strong man, who had a heart to match his powerful frame....

The worst storm, without exception, that I ever experienced on Clatsop occurred one dark winter night. It had been raining and blowing fiercely all day, but that night was truly fearful! The wind howled, and shrieked in fury: the house trembled, shook and swayed; the rain fell in a deluge. We could not sleep.

"This is such a night as I might expect a call from Seaside (fifteen miles distant)," I said; "and I feel as if I should be called any minute."

"Well, you'll not go, I'm sure of that," said my husband. I made no reply.

Sure enough, at four a.m. a lantern flashed across my window. (It was my custom to raise my window shade on retiring.) I was out of bed in an instant, hurrying on my clothes. The door bell rang, and the man said: "The Doctor is wanted at Seaside. I left there at ten last night. The storm has been at my back all the way, but I could not get here any sooner. There are trees down all through the woods. I had to leave my horse half a mile back, and come on foot. We shall have to cut our way out."

Colonel Adair said: "It is simply impossible for my wife to attempt this trip. It is really dangerous for anyone to be out in the woods in such a storm, with the trees falling all around."

"I promised to go, and I must go," I said. "There is no other doctor nearer than Astoria, and after this storm they might not be able to get one from there sooner than twenty four to forty eight hours: so saddle the horse; I will be down to the barn by the time you are ready."

I succeeded in reaching the barn without being blown off my feet, by taking the driveway under the hill. After I was in the saddle, a blanket with a hole in its center was drawn over my head, and its corners, sides and ends made fast to the saddle and cinch. Thus, in true Indian fashion, my wraps were held in place, and I could not be blown off. The messenger and my husband armed themselves with axes and lanterns, and we started for the woods. We found five trees in the road, and after two hours' hard work, we got around and past them. After we got out of the woods, the horses found great difficulty in facing the storm, and my good, sensible old horse wanted to go home. I was so bundled and tied up, I had little control of him, and the messenger had to come back and lead him for some miles. After daylight the storm began to abate, and by ten a.m. it was over, and the sun was shining. We found many more trees across the road, but we finally reached our destination at eleven a.m., and found the folks anxiously hoping for our arrival, and fearing they would have to dispatch a messenger to Astoria, which would have been a serious undertaking, as the railroad track was, in places, completely blocked with fallen timber.

I quickly relieved their anxiety, and was ready to return as soon as my horse was fed, and I had had my dinner, not having had any breakfast.

In addition to my professional duties, I worked early and late, in the house, and on the farm . . . but in time, the terrible mental and physical strain began to tell upon me. Rheumatism, which is hereditary in my family, had taken hold of me, and was fast undermining my health. . . . "I shall soon become a cripple if I continue to live in this wet climate [I told my husband]. Death, to me, would be preferable. . . ."

April 6th found us in North Yakima, Washington, where, in one week, we were comfortably settled in four lovely rooms. . . .

The following summer, instead of going to Seaside, I went to Chicago, and entered the Chicago Clinical School, for physicians only, and received a post-graduate degree. I found it exceedingly hard attending lectures and clinics from nine till six, and from eight to nine p.m., in that intense Chicago heat, where people were dying frequently from sunstroke. I left home July 1st, and returned September 11th, feeling well repaid, and equipped for going on with my professional work. I had reviewed my past work, and been brought up to date, just what I needed after those eleven years on the farm.

After another prosperous year, the summer found us again at the seaside, with my sign out . . . as my business increased, I found that my professional, social and household duties were pressing me very hard. I said: "Colonel, I cannot attend to my professional work which *must* not be neglected, and keep house any longer. You are in no business here, and I think you had better take John [*a child adopted by the Adairs in 1891*] and go back to Sunnymead. John's health is poor here, but he will get strong on the farm. . . . If you cannot get into business down there, you can certainly see that the place is kept up."

In June, 1902, he and John went to Sunnymead, and established themselves in our home there. . . . I still took my cold bath every morning, following it with vigorous physical exercise, which kept me in perfect health, and I had a large country practice, which I greatly enjoyed. I was not at all timid, and I never took my age into account.

Two years ago I set my stake, saying: "I shall be ready to retire in 1906—perhaps sooner. . . . The time came, sooner by several months than I had expected, and so, on October 10th, 1905 I closed my office door in North Yakima. After having received the kindest appreciation from friends, the public and the press, I bade the fair city adieu, and with my good horse, Pride, started in my carriage for the Dalles, much desiring to make the trip overland once more.

Bethenia Owens-Adair then became a determined lobbyist for the Women's Christian Temperance Union, addressing thousands of women, urging them through her speeches and her newspaper editorials to lead their men to temperance. "Where our girls go, there also will our boys be found," she wrote, "and they will make any sacrifice to obtain the good will of the young ladies." She also drew up a bill that restrained prostitution by raising the age of sexual consent from fourteen to sixteen. She found a sympathetic senator, Seymour W. Condo, to introduce it.

When not engaged in these struggles, she waged a heated campaign in favor of more exercise, shorter skirts, and against sidesaddle horse-back riding by women. In a rebuttal to an article by Dr. Montague Tallack, which was printed in the Seattle Times *in*

1904, she states: "Ladies should ride astride. . . . Mr. Tallack has but to visit a first-class circus and watch those beautiful muscular women riding and performing on the bars to have his little theory [that men's legs are long and flat and women's short and round] exploded . . . Nothing will preserve a woman's grace . . . so much as vigorous . . . exercise, and horse-back riding stands at the head of the list, provided [a woman has] a foot in each stirrup, instead of having the right limb twisted around a horn, and the left foot in a stirrup twelve or fifteen inches above where it ought to be."

In her retirement, Bethenia was surrounded by the people most affected by her loving energy: her family and the scores of her former patients who continued to correspond and visit until her death on September 11, 1926.

Dr. Bethenia Owens-Adair, date unknown.

Families enjoying a picnic, ca., 1885.

Family gathering at a Sunday dinner in Montana.

Sleigh ride, 1894.

Climbing Mt. Hood, 1913.

Tennis court at Congress Mine, Arizona, 1889.

Cowgirl band at the round-up, Pendleton, Oregon, 1910.

Family camping, probably on the Fourth of July.

Children fishing in Beaver Canyon, ca. 1905.

Unidentified group camping in Colorado.

Unidentified group cooling off at Camp Gardiner, 1894.

Telephone operators in Oregon, date and city unknown.

Anna Harder Ogden

Anna Friederike Luise Harder was born in Berlin, on December 16, 1867, the youngest of four sisters. When the family emigrated to Wisconsin in 1880, she worked as a chambermaid, laundress, baby-tender and domestic servant, both there and in their later home in Berkeley, California, in an effort to support herself and help her family.

She was twenty-one when she began her journal. The frequency with which she changed employment, and her often disparaging comments about herself or her work, reflected basic feelings about the drudgery of her lot. Though she claimed that she was uneducated and unfit for any better station in life, she had learned English by keeping a journal, and answering matrimonial ads in the classifieds. Her entries are written both in German and English in a flawless hand. She also refers repeatedly to a steady stream of books she enjoyed reading.

She kept this journal between October 24, 1888, and December 25, 1895. The first place of employment recorded in her journal was as general hotel chambermaid at Camp Capitola, a resort in California run by a Mrs. Lewis.

Tuesday, December 4, 1886. Was very much provoked with Mrs. Lewis. She mentioned casually how hard she had worked all day and questioning further, I found out she has swept all the carpet up on the Hill. Well, she deserves to be tired. Couldn't she have told me to come up instead? I never heard of such a thing in my life! I am expected to smell everything that has to be done!!!

Thursday, December 6, 1886. Worked hard all day on the Hill, cleaning windows. Feel very lame in my arms. Expected a letter from home to-day, but got none. Intend to work to-morrow.

Friday, December 7, 1888. Large washing to-day. Loaned some whiting material to Mr. Bryant, which he promised to return. Monday. No letter. Hope there is nothing the matter at home.

Saturday, December 8, 1888. Letter from home to-day. Will answer it tomorrow, for I have got a terrific headache to-night. I must go and see the Doctor about my Head and Heart when I go home: Most of the moving done to-day. It looks very much like rain all day.

Sunday, December 9, 1888, 11:45 a.m. Answered Mother's & Hermines letter. . . . Spent a little while with Pearl Van Sycle, as she showed me the interior of the house. It is very homelike, but I feel sorry for Pearl, having to associate with such a girl as Mame Silva. I wonder who Mr. Frank Downing, is, whom she went to meet? Must ask the girls whether they know him.

Monday, December 10, 1888, 8:10 p.m. Have been moving furniture on the Hill. Ought to iron my clothes, but have had no time as yet. Mr. Delaney arrived to-night and asked me if I wouldn't give him some Blankets! I acquiesced & promised to bring them to him about 6:30. He must have misunderstood it, for I hunted for him without success. No letter.

Tuesday, December 11, 1888, 8:10 p.m. Probably the last night down here. Worked dreadful hard all day & am about worn out. Mrs. Lewis does not seem to think so though!

Wednesday, December 12, 1888, 7 p.m. First night on the Hill. Have moved some of my things up already.... Mr. Delaney left to-day and gave me [$1.50] from Mrs. B.

Friday, December 4, 1888. Mrs. Lewis went to San Jose on the 2 p.m. More rain to-day. I should like to wash tomorrow, so I won't have so much Monday. No letters.

Saturday, December 15, 1888. 7 p.m. Letter from home included a few lines from Mother. Hermine has received another letter from Grebs [apparently Anna's grandfather], so she intends to leave for Europe in April/May. Is trying to sell her house with all the belongings. I only wish I were in possession of about $400, for I should like to accompany her ever so much, but perhaps it is all for the best that I cannot. Who knows!! Tomorrow!—Last year Mrs. Norton, the year before with Mrs. Titus. Happy then & ignorant of the fact! Am never content! Never appreciate good days and homes until they are a thing of the past! What a dissatisfied thing Mankind is in general! How I wish I were home to-night with Vater and Mütter! But one week will soon pass and then I dare say Mrs. Lewis would rather have me stay.

    But, I am only a servant, and not expected to have any feelings of my own. Although she wants all her children around Christmas, she does not think other mothers feel the same way. Still, I may be wrong! At least, I hope I am! Well, my only hope is, I'll get all the money coming to me. I never cared so much for money in my life, as I do since Father and Mother have come.

Sunday, December 16, 1888. 3 p.m. Mrs. Lewis has told me that I could stay at home for one week, if I go Thursday before Christmas, I am to come back the Thursday after. So I have concluded to go home on Monday the 24, and stay until the first day after New Year, if she'll let me.

Tuesday, December 18, 1888, 9:15 p.m. Worked very hard to-day, washing & ironing. Mrs. Lewis went to Santa Cruz this afternoon, & is going to San Jose tomorrow. I asked Charley to wake me & hope he won't forget it. I think . . . that Mrs. Lewis is trying to get

money. Poor little woman! I feel so sorry for her. If it was not for Father and Mother, I should work for $5 a month.

Wednesday, December 19, 1888, 9:00 p.m. Got up at 5:30 and saw Mrs. Lewis to the depot. . . . Washing again this morning — ironing in the afternoon. . . . If that Chinaman doesn't stop his nonsense! I feel very much inclined to stay home. I don't think she cares very much, for one Girl is as good as another & they never seem satisfied with what I do, always expect more. Yes, yes! This is a very queer world.

Thursday, December 20, 1888, 9:40 p.m. Cleaned up the Patterson House to-day. Very hard work. Intend to iron tomorrow as the stove is now up in the laundry. . . . I think Will is a little bit gone on Gina. . . .

Friday, December 21, 1888, 9:00 p.m. . . . Sweeping in the forenoon and ironing in the afternoon. They have given up trading with Mr. Angell. Why? I wonder!

Saturday, December 22, 1888, 8:30 p.m. Washing & Ironing in the forenoon & to my own surprise, crocheting in the afternoon. . . . No letter. Ought to have one from home.

Sunday, December 23, 1888, 3:00 p.m. No letter from Home, am very much disappointed. Headache ever since morning, can't account for it. One who lives as simple and steady as I do, ought not to be troubled with such things. If only Mrs. Lewis would give me my money unasked! I do hate to go & beg for it every time I want a penny. I feel as though something will prevent me from going to-morrow. . . .

Modesto, March 1, 1889, 5 p.m. Arrived here at the Ross house, this afternoon at 2 o'clock. Capacity: chambermaid. Proprieter: Mr. A. C. Bilieke; Germans. They are thinking of transferring me to their Hotel in Dunsmuir. Well, I don't care, as long as he is paying the fare. I only hope I'll like it and stay with them for some time, so I'll get a little money ahead. I also hope Mr. Graber [her attorney] can get the money from Mrs. Lewis in a quiet way, without going to Court. Such a long time has elapsed since I last wrote in this Book, and so many things have happened in the meantime! Spent one month at the Los Gatos Hotel, one month at home, and now here.

God knows where I'll be next month! I only hope I'll give satisfaction. I will try my best.... I am dreadful hungry, not having had my dinner.

Saturday, March 2, 1889. 8:15 p.m. xxx [*This mark is a record of her menstrual cycle.*] Worked *very* hard all day and am completely tired out. Have been put in another room, which is right over the Kitchen and therefore, extremely hot. I don't know what it will be in the summer. It is suffocating now! And only Spring....! I have an idea there are bedbugs in this room. If so, I'll have a lovely night. I hope they will send me to Dunsmuir for the landlady is awfully fussy and cranky. *There* I'll be by myself! I wonder what sort of man the son is?

Sunday, March 3, 1889. 2:45 p.m. Passed the most miserable, sleepless night in all my life. The heat was something dreadful.... Hope they will get a girl to-morrow, so I can go on to Dunsmuir. I am afraid if I stay here much longer I, too, will have trouble with Mrs. Rogers. Her physiognomy is that of a cross, deceitful body. Mrs. Bilieke gave me a warning this morning about her. I wish I had been left in my other room, for this one is fearful warm, beside the rats.
7:10 p.m. The book-keeper, Mr. Clive, I believe his name is, a'int a little too smart! He invited himself up here to-night. I do hope he will behave himself.

No chance for Dunsmuir now, as Mr. Bilieke got a letter from there this afternoon. They have a girl up there. I am awfully provoked, too! But will have to make the best of the bargain! If only I could get another room, I would be satisfied, I think. But perhaps not! I've always something to wish. . . .

Monday, March 4, 1889, 9:50 p.m. Have been reading all evening a book I found this afternoon. Very interesting. Mr. Clive paid me a visit again to-night. Why will he persist in sitting on the bed when I offer him a chair?

Tuesday, March 5, 1889, 9:45 p.m. House cleaning commenced upstairs.... Had quite a little fuss with Mrs. Bilieke. She is certainly very ill-bred in my opinion, always seeks an occasion to prove her authority, something I do not like at all! I think I shall do splendid if I stay here one month, least of all two!!! Well, we shall see.

Friday, March 8, 1889, 8:30 p.m. More house-cleaning, and rain today. Mr. Clive paid me a visit and brought me some papers. He is a very common-place old Bachelor, always dwelling on his good qualities and points; seems to think that every girl who looks at him wants to marry. Still, I think I'll miss him; He is better than nobody, and when he is gone, I shall have nobody to talk to, which, I don't think I can stand very long.

March 9, 1889. I hope this will be my last night in Modesto, and that I'll get away tomorrow morning....

Berkeley, Tuesday, March 12, 1889, 9:15 a.m. Left Modesto Sunday ... arrived at Berkeley just in time for supper. Everybody was very much surprised of course, to see me back so soon. Went to the City yesterday to look for a place. Was engaged as waitress at Ward's, in the International Hotel, in Sacramento for $25 per month. It is not certain however, and I will have to go over again to-morrow. I should like to go to Sacramento on account of Blanche [*Blanche was Anna's moody and often judgmental friend*] being there, although I don't suppose she cares very much to have me so near her.... Mother and Hermine are washing to-day and everything is up-set.

Berkeley, March 13, 1889, 2:15 p.m. Went to the City on the 11 a.m. train.... I leave for Sacramento at 4:55 p.m. I only hope it will be a good place and that I shall be able to stay 2-3 months for Father's sake. [*Anna borrowed money from her parents which she hoped to be able to repay. She also wanted to give them financial support.*] Met Billy Marriott going over. He says his wife is dead, which is very doubtful, and also, that he has a shop in Sacramento, which I don't believe either. Borrowed $5 from Mother & have not got enough yet—!!!

Woodland, March 15, 1889, 9:15 p.m. Left Sacramento this morning at 10:40. After leaving the International yesterday 4 p.m. Stayed with Blanche all night and had supper and breakfast with her.... Am working at the Craft Hotel. The other girl, May, seems rather tough.

Sunday, March 17, 1889, 2:30 p.m.... Prospects of doing my washing at the house. Mrs. Reynolds has hired a Chinaman to do the laundry work for the house. I feel as though I ought to write home, but think it best not, for I may not stay longer than a week and I don't want Mother to know where I am until I can send her my first month's wages. May seems to be of German descent too, for her last name is Huber. But she is a disgrace to our Nation, she is *so* tough.

Will wait a little longer too, before I write to Blanche. She talked as though she had not time to answer my letter. Mr. Thomas Reynolds has just paid me a visit, also leaving a bag of candy for the girls. Had to go down and get supper for 2 more men that came in on the late train. Mr. Joseph R. reminds me somewhat of _____ in face as well as manner. He tries to be a little smart. . .! I have an idea May has taken a look at my writings. If so, it cannot be helped. Do not feel well to-night. Have a slight headache.

Monday, March 18, 1889. The new laundryman installed. Must go down and see if there is a chance for me to wash. . . . May is writing a letter to her parents. She told me today that they had been separated four different times, and are still so at the present. I am anxious to write to Mother, but I have made up my mind to wait until I can send $20. If only Mr. Graber gets the money from Mrs. Lewis, I should be quite content!! Well, I hope he will, although the chances are very slight indeed. Kitty, at the Byrus Hotel, told me that Mrs. L. owes $40 to her sister for 3 years, and has never paid her. And mine is so much more!

Wednesday, March 20, 1889, 2:30 p.m. . . . May is terribly giddy, to be sure, but nothing bad about her. . . . I am beginning to take a liking to her. Johnny and her are having a great time fooling around. The pantry is being enlarged downstairs, and everything is in a dreadful mess. Must write to Blanche sometime this week, although she did not seem very anxious to get a letter from me!

Monday, March 25, 1889, 11:15 a.m. Mr. Hinkley kindly informed me just now that I would leave to-day, in fact this very afternoon. I think I'll go to Sacramento again, and try to obtain another situation. It is the queerest thing that I can not stay in any place. Something turns up every time. Here I had such good intentions of saving money and sending it home. Disappointed again! What in the world shall I do next? I do not know. I am glad, though, I did not write home yet. I am more determined than ever not to do so until I am able to send her $20. What in the world will Blanche say? I shall get a very cool reception, of that I am positive. Well, this time it is not my fault! I should think they might have told me that

Susie intended to return so I could have been on the look-out for another place!

No home, and no place to go where anybody cares to see. . . . I'll surely commit suicide some of these days—Must go over to the Byrus [Hotel] and bid some good-byes.

Over the next several months Anna moved from job to job. At one point she asked herself in despair, "What was I born for anyhow?" Her sister suggested that she learn telegraphing and offered to loan her the money for the school.

Monday, July 1, 8:10 p.m. Went to the office on Clay St., also Healds Business College. Engaged to take a course of telegraphing at the latter. Payment: $10 per month. . . . Mrs. Banuel was here to-night. She wanted me to work for her.

Tuesday, July 2, 1889, 8:30 p.m. first lesson in telegraphing to-day. Paid $10. Commutation ticket $3. Writing material, 90 cts. Returned with a bad headache. Have almost mastered the A-B-C. Also numbers. Am taking penmanship, too.

Wednesday, July 10, 1889. 8 p.m. Mr. Merrick said I did very well to-day. Intend to buy me a book on shorthand.

Wednesday, July 17, 1889, 8:50 p.m. . . . Miss Whitman left school to-day. I am disgusted myself. I am reading the *Strange Adventures of Lucy Smith*. Almost finished.

Friday, July 19, 1889, 8:10 p.m. Left school to-day at 3 p.m. Went to see the operator at the stock yards. She refused to let me stay there and receive, saying she was not allowed to do so. Am quite disgusted. Wish I had somebody that would send.

Friday, July 26, 1889, 9:30 p.m. Did some good receiving to-day. . . . Mr. Merrick too thinks I am doing well. Headache and pain in my heart to-day. Bought tea for Bertha and Pork for Mother.

Saturday, July 27, 1889, 8:45 p.m. . . . Have figured out to-day how much my bill will be when through learning. It will be by learning 5 months; $168. Hope it won't take me long to repay it.

Monday, July 29, 1889, 8:15 p.m. . . . Brought back my book to-day. Mr. Merrick took it and locked it up. The whole of the young fellows are getting too smart in talking as well as actions. Am reading Cooper's *Pathfinder* now—like it very much. . . .

Tuesday, July 30, 1889, 9:20 p.m. Made the acquaintence of Mr. Rivers, a brother to a brakeman on the Berkeley Line. He is very anxious to learn [*telegraphing*]. I have been writing for him most of to-day. Miss Hushaw wrote some for me. Was very tired to-day.

Wednesday, July 31, 1889, 8:20 p.m. . . . Missed the 2 o'clock boat by a few minutes on account of Mr. Biggs walking down to the ferry with me. He is quite a gentlemanly young fellow, blond, of medium stature, which means, of course, smaller than myself, and is the happy possessor of a handsome pair of eyes. He is only 24 years of age and seems to have better common sense than the average. Mr. Rivers is 26, but looks much younger, being of slight build and delicate looking. Am not improving very rapidly, at least, not as fast as I should like to. Earthquake this morning at 4:50 A.M. Quite a severe one, too. . . . Where shall I be next year, this time????!!!

Friday, August 2, 1889, 9:30 p.m. Took the 5 P.M. boat, Mr. Biggs walked down to the ferry with me. He asked me to go to the California Theater with him, but I refused! Did some good receiving from Mr. Merrick. . . .

Monday, August 5, 1889, 9:10 p.m. Was dreadfully stupid all day. . . . Met Mr. Rivers on the 7:30 train this morning. Was provoked with Mr. B. . . . He and Mr. Rivers intend to meet Saturdays and practice. I wish I could join them, or had some one to practice with. It would help me along so much. . . . I think I will have to change my behaviour and soon, too. People all get disgusted with me. Must remember to-morrow and try and be more reserved and ladylike. It will be very hard, but it must be done. Am old enough to be sure! I want to be so boisterous. People form very queer opinions and especially boys. So there. To-morrow! Will see to-morrow what progress I have made!

Tuesday, Aug. 6, 1889, 9:15 p.m. Tried my best to be good and hope I have succeeded. . . . Mr. B. walked to the ferry with Mr.

Rivers & I. We have concluded to meet at Mr. Rivers' place. Still, I am going to propose to them to come down here.

Saturday, August 10, 1889, 8:30 p.m. Went to Mr. Rivers' place this noon to practice. Mr. B. was there too. Came back with the 4:30 p.m. Tried my level best to be prim, but without success. Will have to give it up as a bad job.

Friday, Aug. 28, 1889, 8:15 p.m. . . . Mr. B. is mad yet. It makes me so uncomfortable. I like to be on speaking terms with everyone. Still, it would not do for me to make advances when he chooses to sulk. It serves him right, though why should I care whether he is angry or not? What am I to him? Nothing!! The trouble is I take a fancy to people too quick, but it always takes a long time to get over it. That has been my misfortune, if it could be called that name, twice; after getting bravely over the second, I vowed it should be the last! Here I am again. If the men were only worth their while to fret about, but they are not. . . . Well, I am sure, my intentions were good enough. . . . This is the way it will always be! Still, I should not mind that in the least if all the men would only leave me alone and not talk to me at all (at least the blonds) then I would not notice them, not even come in contact with them. Well, I'll have to stand it now, although it is very hard. I must try and be more reserved. Why was I not born a flirt like other girls!

What a difference there is in this Saturday and last week! Then I was happy and now!! Now I am rattling on. Have studied shorthand to sharpen my mind. I must let out my thoughts to someone and this is the safest way because nobody would think of reading it. If I tell anything to Bertha or Hermine, they laugh, poke fun at me and tell it all over the place. This book is my only refuge, and I am indeed thankful to possess it. Very warm all day.

Saturday, August 24, 1889, 10 p.m. Letter from Blanche to-day. She thinks and advises me to give up Mr. B. altogether, on account of being a Welshman, which are never good at their best! Suppose I must, at least will try very hard. . . . I've not felt well all day, a bad pain in my heart. Expect I'll die soon!

Sunday, August 25, 1889, 10:40 p.m. I've not felt well all day. Went down to practice this morning, also in the afternoon. Mr. B. got over his sulking spell, and spoke. He and I took a long walk on the track from 10 St. to B St. and back. I am so glad we are on speaking terms. It made me feel quite miserable. He said I was very peculiar! I don't see why!

Tuesday, August 27, 1889, 8:45 p.m. Had a tiff with Mr. Rivers. I dare say he thinks himself smart. He behaved pretty well to-day. I think Mr. B. is in love with Miss Reynolds. She is very homely. He makes me weary. He acts like a boy of 17. In fact, I don't think he is very bright. Why can't people stay the way they are when we first get acquainted with them? But no! They *will* be familiar! Something I detest. I am sure I have never given those boys the least cause of encouragement to act in such a manner as they do now! At first Mr. B. was courteous and gentlemanly. The same with Mr. Rivers, and how they have changed!

Monday, September 9, 1889, 8 p.m. Admission day . . . very few scholars came. Mr. B. called. He is as ridiculous as ever, surely more so. He will never get over his conceit. Took my handkerchief along with him. Met Blanche on Market St. She gave me some bananas, which Mr. Rivers got away with. Received my first train dispatch today.

Friday, October 11, 1889, 8:30 p.m. . . . was very stupid in school, I don't know what is the matter with me lately. I can't receive anything at all. Saw Mammy Pleasant coming off of the boat tonight, but did not speak to her. . . .

Tuesday, October 15, 1889, 8:45 p.m. . . . I am really disgusted with myself. . . . All the young ladies have positions as soon as qualified, only I have to be out in the cold. It is enough to disgust anybody. Ought to go and see some other superintendent, but am too discouraged since Mr. Wilder refused to grant me an office. Well, I must go back to my old occupation. It will be the only chance ever to earn an honest penny!

Sunday, April 27, 1890, 4:15 p.m. Have just been re-reading my notices of a year ago. Was worrying about my debts, which often only amounted to about $40. I had prospects of earning and getting that amount in a few months. Now I have $640 [in debts] and no work!! It is getting worse with me all the time. How will it end? Last year I was tired of working out, tired of being treated like a mere machine or an animal. Now I will have to begin all over again. It shall be a different plan, though how long it will take me to save up enough to pay for that amount! Very very discouraging. I shall

feel the treatment the poor [working] girls receive all the more now than before, but it must be. Month after month slipped by and nothing is done. If only I had some help. . . .

There is no record of what Anna may have written from 1891 to 1894.

Berkeley, Calif., January 18, 1895. Never wrote one line in the whole year of 1894. But, of course, what was there to write? Nothing pleasant. Nothing but sickness, want of money and worry of every kind from beginning to end. . . . I wonder if I will ever be able to pay all my debts. They are growing more and more instead of less and less. Received from Fritz in 1892 $45 altogether. When I look at these debts my courage sinks within me. No work and unable to do any hard work. Oh dear, if I could only get work at telegraphing, I would be all right, and able to pay them off in one year. But as things are not, it will take me at least 10 years. Am crocheting all the time, just to make enough money for medicine.

September 4, 1896. Sent $100 to Bertha today. The last of the money I owed her. At last, I have paid my debts, after so many weary years. It almost seems as if I had nothing to work for now. . . .

Anna Harder married Kansas farmer John Quincy Adams Ogden in 1899 after thirteen years of working as a domestic. At one time she had been a maid-of-all-work for Mammy Pleasant, the controversial black heiress and landowner in San Francisco.

Anna and her husband lived in Berkeley until 1917; they later bought a farm in Contra Costa County, California. Her son remembers her as being a great socialist—an ideology she and her husband shared. They had met at a socialist picnic and Anna once said, "There were only three real socialists in the world: Anna Ogden, John Ogden, and George Bernard Shaw."

Anna Harder Ogden died in 1960 at the age of ninety-three, leaving a vast network of penpals throughout Europe, Australia, and the Far East—she corresponded with them until the day she died.

County Clerk's Office, Idaho Court House, Rathdrum, Idaho, 1908.

Anna Harder, date unknown.

Assembly line of women packing biscuits at the Merchants Biscuit Co., Denver, 1905.

Women sorting ripe olives at the Sylmar Olive Factory, California, 1910-1915.

The Red Rock Stage, near the Continental Divide, on the Montana side en route to Salmon, Idaho, August, 1903.

Elinore Pruitt Stewart

Elinore Pruitt was born in 1876 in Fort Smith, Arkansas, one of nine children in a family so poor that Elinore didn't own a pair of shoes until she was six years old. Her parents died when she was fourteen, and she assumed the care of her eight brothers and sisters, working for the railroad at a time when others were going to high school.

But by following the newspapers and asking a steady stream of questions, she fashioned her own education. Her marriage to Mr. Rupert at the age of twenty-two lent her the support she needed to begin writing short articles for the Kansas City·Star, *and even after his untimely death in a railroad accident four years later, she continued to write.*

By then she had a daughter, Jerrine, and had found employment cooking and stoking the coal furnace for Mrs. Coney, in Denver. Mrs. Coney was a genteel woman, and the recipient of all Elinore's future letters, which make up the two volumes Letters of a Woman Homesteader *and* Letters on an Elk Hunt.

At the age of thirty-three Elinore decided to answer an ad placed by a Wyoming sheep rancher, Clyde Stewart. She was hired as his housekeeper and six weeks later they married, though she in no way let their life interfere with her dream of owning her own land in Wyoming and homesteading it alone, under her own name. The following letters were written to Mrs. Coney between April of 1909 and November of 1913, and describe Elinore Pruitt's life in Burnt Fork, Wyoming.

Burnt Fork, Wyoming,
April 18, 1909

Dear Mrs. Coney,

Are you thinking I am lost, like the Babes in the Wood? Well, I am not and I'm sure the robins would have the time of their lives getting leaves to cover me out here. I am 'way up close to the Forest Reserve of Utah, within half a mile of the line, sixty miles from the railroad. I was twenty-four hours on the train and two days on the stage, and oh, those two days! The snow was just beginning to melt and the mud was about the worst I ever heard of.

The first stage we tackled was just about as rickety as it could very well be and I had to sit with the driver, who was a Mormon and so handsome that I was not a bit offended when he insisted on making love all the way, especially after he told me that he was a widower Mormon. But, of course, as I had no chaperone I looked very fierce (not that that was very difficult with the wind and mud as allies) and told him my actual opinion of Mormons in general and particular.

Meantime my new employer, Mr. Stewart, sat upon a stack of baggage and was dreadfully concerned about something he calls his "Tookie," but I am unable to tell you what that is. The road, being so muddy, was full of ruts and the stage acted as if it had the hiccough and made us all talk as though we were affected in the same way.

At last we "arriv," and everything is just lovely for me. I have a very, very comfortable situation and Mr. Stewart is absolutely no trouble, for as soon as he has his meals he retires to his room and plays on his bagpipe, only he calls it his "bugpeep." It is "The Campbells are Coming," with variations, at intervals all day long and from seven till eleven at night. Sometimes I wish they would make haste and get here.

There is a saddle horse especially for me and a little shotgun with which I am to kill sage chickens. We are between two trout streams, so you can think of me as being happy when the snow is through melting and the water gets clear. We have the finest flock of Plymouth Rocks and get so many nice eggs. It sure seems fine to have all the cream I want after my town experiences. Jerrine is making good use of all the good things we are having. She rides the pony to water every day.

I have not filed on my land yet because the snow is fifteen feet deep on it, and I think I would rather see what I am getting, so will wait until summer. They have just three seasons, winter and July and August. We are to plant our garden the last of May. When it is so I can get around I will see about land and find out all I can and tell you.

I think this letter is about to reach thirty-secondly, so I will send you my sincerest love and quit tiring you. Please write me when you have time.

Sincerely yours,

Elinore Rupert

May 24, 1909

Dear, Dear Mrs. Coney,

Well, I have filed on my land and am now a bloated landowner. I waited a long time to even *see* land in the reserve, and the snow is yet too deep, so I thought that as they have but three months of summer and spring together and as I wanted the land for a ranch anyway, perhaps I had better stay in the valley. So I have filed adjoining Mr. Stewart and I am well pleased. I have a grove of twelve swamp pines on my place, and I am going to build my house there. I thought it would be very romantic to live on the peaks amid the whispering pines, but I reckon it would be powerfully uncomfortable also, and I guess my twelve can whisper enough for me; and a dandy thing is, I have all the nice snow-water I want; a small stream runs right through the center of my land and I am quite near wood.

A neighbor and his daughter were going to Green River, the county-seat, and said I might go along, so I did, as I could file there as well as at the land office; and oh, that trip! I had more fun to the square inch than Mark Twain or Samantha Allen *ever* provoked. It took us a whole week to go and come. We camped out, of course, for in the whole sixty miles there was but one house, and going in that direction there is not a tree to be seen, nothing but sage, sand, and sheep. About noon the first day out we came near a sheepwagon, and stalking along ahead of us was a lanky fellow, a herder, going home for dinner. Suddenly it seemed to me I should starve if I had to wait until we got where we had planned to stop for dinner, so I called out to the man, "Little Bo-Peep, have you anything to eat? If you have, we'd like to find it." And he answered, "As soon as I am able it shall be on the table, if you'll but trouble to get behind it." Shades of Shakespeare! Songs of David, the Shepherd Poet! What do you think of us? Well, we got behind it, and a more delicious "it" I never tasted. Such coffee! And out of *such* a pot! I promised Bo-Peep that I would send him a crook with pink ribbons on it, but I suspect he thinks I am a crook without the ribbons.

The sagebrush is so short in some places that it is not large enough to make a fire, so we had to drive until quite late before we camped that night. After driving all day over what seemed a level desert of sand, we came about sundown to a beautiful cañon, down which we had to drive for a couple of miles before we could cross. In the cañon the shadows had already fallen, but when we looked up we could see the last shafts of sunlight on the tops of the great bare buttes. Suddenly a great wolf started from somewhere and galloped along the edge of the cañon, outlined black and clear by the setting sun. His curiosity overcame him at last, so he sat down and waited to see what manner of beast we were. I reckon he was disappointed for he howled most dismally. I thought of Jack London's "The Wolf."

After we quitted the cañon I saw the most beautiful sight. It seemed as if we were driving through a golden haze. The violet shadows were creeping up between the hills, while away back of us the snow-capped peaks were catching the sun's last rays. On every side of us stretched the poor, hopeless desert, the sage, grim and determined to live in spite of starvation, and the great, bare, desolate buttes. The beautiful colors turned to amber and rose, and then to the general tone, dull gray.

Then we stopped to camp, and such a scurrying around to gather brush for the fire and to get supper! Everything tasted so good! Jerrine ate like a man. Then we raised the wagon tongue and spread the wagon sheet over it and made a bedroom for us women. We made our beds on the warm, soft sand and went to bed.

It was too beautiful a night to sleep, so I put my head out to look and to think. I saw the moon come up and hang for a while over the mountains as if it were discouraged with the prospect, and the big white stars flirted shamelessly with the hills.

At length a cloud came up and I went to sleep, and next morning was covered several inches with snow. It didn't hurt us a bit, but while I was struggling with stubborn corsets and shoes I communed with myself after the manner of prodigals, and said; "How much better that I were down in Denver, even at Mrs. Coney's, digging with a skewer into the corners seeking dirt which *might* be there, yea, even eating codfish, than that I should perish on this desert—of imagination." So I turned the current of my imagination and fancied that I was at home before the fireplace, and that the backlog was about to roll down. My fancy was in such good working trim that before I knew it I kicked the wagon wheel, and I certainly got as warm as the most "sot" Scientist that ever read Mrs. Eddy could possibly wish.

After two more such days I "arrived." When I went up to the office where I was to file, the door was open and the most taciturn old man sat before a desk. I hesitated at the door, but he never let on. I coughed, yet no sign but a deeper scowl. I stepped in and modestly kicked over a chair. He whirled around like I had shot him. "Well?" he interrogated. I said, "I am powerful glad of it. I was afraid you were sick, you looked in such pain." He looked at me a minute, then grinned and said he thought I was a bookagent. Fancy me, a fat, comfortable widow, trying to sell books!

Well, I filed and came home. If you will believe me, the Scot was glad to see me and didn't herald the Campbells for two hours after I got home. I'll tell you, it is mighty seldom any one's so much appreciated.

No, we have no rural delivery. It is two miles to the office, but I go whenever I like. It is really the jolliest kind of fun to gallop down. We are sixty miles from the railroad, but when we want anything we send by the mail-carrier for it, only there is nothing to get.

I know this is an inexcusably long letter, but it is snowing so hard and you know how I like to talk.

Baby has the rabbit you gave her last Easter a year ago. In Denver I was afraid my baby would grow up devoid of imagination. Like all the kindergartners, she depended upon others to amuse her. I was very sorry about it, for my castles in Spain have been real homes to me. But there is no fear. She has a block of wood she found in the blacksmith shop which she calls her "dear baby." A spoke out of a wagon wheel is "little Margaret," and a barrel stave is "bad little Johnny."

Well, I must quit writing before you vote me a nuisance. With lots of love to you,

Your sincere friend,

Elinore Rupert

September 11, 1909

Dear Mrs. Coney,

This has been for me the busiest, happiest summer I can remember. I have worked very hard, but it has been work that I really enjoy. Help of any kind is very hard to get here, and Mr. Stewart had been too confident of getting men, so that haying caught him with too few men to put up the hay. He had no man to run the mower and he couldn't run both the mower and the stacker, so you can fancy what a place he was in.

I don't know that I ever told you, but my parents died within a year of each other and left [nine] of us to shift for ourselves. Our people offered to take one here and there among them until we should all have a place, but we refused to be raised on the halves and so arranged to stay at Grandmother's and keep together. Well, we had no money to hire men to do our work, so had to do it ourselves. Consequently I learned to do many things which girls more fortunately situated don't even know have to be done.

Among the things I learned to do was the way to run a mowing-machine. It cost me many bitter tears because I got sunburned, and my hands were hard, rough, and stained with machine oil, and I used to wonder how any Prince Charming could overlook all that in any girl he came to. For all I had ever read of the Prince had to do with his "reverently kissing her lily-white hand," or doing some other fool thing with a hand as white as a snowflake.

Well, when my Prince showed up he didn't lose much time in letting me know that "Barkis was willing," and I wrapped my hands in my old checked apron and took him up before he could catch his breath. Then there was no more mowing, and I almost forgot that I knew how until Mr. Stewart got into such a panic. If he put a man to mow, it kept them all idle at the stacker, and he just couldn't get enough men. I was afraid to tell him I could mow for fear he would forbid me to do so. But one morning, when he was chasing a last hope of help, I went down the barn, took out the horses, and went to mowing. I had enough cut before he got back to show him I knew how, and as he came back manless he was delighted as well as surprised. I was glad because I really like to mow, and besides that, I am adding feathers to my cap in a surprising way. When you see me again you will think I am wearing a feather duster, but it is only that I have been said to have almost as much sense as a "mon," and that is an honor I never aspired to, even in my wildest dreams.

Woman driving grain binder.

I have done most of my cooking at night, have milked seven cows every day, and have done all the hay-cutting, so you see I have been working. But I have found time to put up thirty pints of jelly and the same amount of jam for myself. I used wild fruits, gooseberries, currants, raspberries, and cherries. I have almost two gallons of the cherry butter, and I think it is delicious. I wish I could get some of it to you, I am sure you would like it.

We began haying July 5 and finished September 8. After working so hard and so steadily I decided on a day off, so yesterday I saddled the pony, took a few things I needed, and Jerrine and I fared forth. Baby can ride behind quite well. We got away by sunup and a glorious day we had. We followed a stream higher up into the mountains and the air was so keen and clear at first we had on our coats. There was a tang of sage and of pine in the air, and our horse was midside deep in rabbit-brush, a shrub just covered with flowers that look and smell like goldenrod. The blue distance promised many alluring adventures, so we went along singing and simply gulping in summer. Occasionally a bunch of sage chickens would fly up out of the sagebrush, or a jack rabbit would leap out. Once we saw a bunch of antelope gallop over a hill, but we were out just to be out, and game didn't tempt us. I started, though, to have just as good a time as possible, so I had a fish-hook in my knapsack.

Presently, about noon, we came to a little dell where the grass was as soft and as green as a lawn. The creek kept right up against the hills on one side and there were groves of quaking aspen and cottonwoods that made shade, and service-bushes and birches that shut off the ugly hills on the other side. We dismounted and prepared to noon. We caught a few grasshoppers and I cut a birch pole for a rod. The trout are so beautiful now, their sides are so silvery, with dashes of old rose and orange, their speckles are so black, while their backs look as if they had been sprinkled with gold-dust. They bite so well that it doesn't require any especial skill or tackle to catch plenty for a meal in a few minutes.

In a little while I went back to where I had left my pony browsing, with eight beauties. We made a fire first; then I dressed my trout while it was burning down to a nice bed of coals. I had brought a frying-pan and a bottle of lard, salt, and buttered bread. We gathered a few service-berries, our trout were soon browned, and with water, clear, and as cold as ice, we had a feast. The quaking aspens are beginning to turn yellow, but no leaves have fallen. Their shadows dimpled and twinkled over the grass like happy children. The sound of the dashing, roaring water kept inviting me to cast for trout, but I didn't want to carry them so far, so we rested until the sun was getting low and then started for home, with the song of the locusts in our ears warning us that the melancholy days are almost here. We would come up over the top of a hill into the glory of a beautiful sunset with its gorgeous colors, then down into the little valley already purpling with mysterious twilight. So on, until, just at dark, we rode into our corral and a mighty tired, sleepy little girl was powerfully glad to get home.

After I had mailed my other letter I was afraid that you would think me plumb bold about the little Bo-Peep, and was a heap sorrier than you can think. If you only knew the hardships these poor men endure. They go two together and sometimes it is months before they see another soul, and rarely ever a woman. I wouldn't act so free in town, but these men see people so seldom that they are awkward and embarrassed. I like to put them at ease, and it is to be done only by being kind of hail-fellow-well-met with them. So far not one has ever misunderstood me and I have been treated with every courtesy and kindness, so I am powerfully glad you understand. They really enjoy doing these little things like fixing our dinner, and if my poor company can add to any one's pleasure I am too glad.

Sincerely Yours,

Elinore Rupert.

September 28, 1909

Dear Mrs. Coney,

Your second card just reached me and I am plumb glad because, although I answered your other, I was wishing I could write you, for have had the most charming adventure.

It is the custom here for as many women as care to, to go in a party over into Utah to Ashland (which is over a hundred miles away) after fruit. They usually go in September, and it takes a week to make the trip. They take wagons and camp out and of course have a good time, but, the greater part of the way, there isn't even the semblance of a road and it is merely a semblance anywhere. They came over to invite me to join them. I was of two minds—I wanted to go, but it seemed a little risky and a big chance for discomfort, since we would have to cross the Unita Mountains, and

a snowstorm likely any time. But I didn't like to refuse outright, so we left it to Mr. Stewart. His "Ye're nae gang" sounded powerful final, so the ladies departed in awed silence and I assumed a martyr-like air and acted like a very much abused woman, although he did only what I wanted him to do. At last, in sheer desperation he told me the "bairn canna make the treep," and that was why he was so determined.

I knew why, of course, but I continued to look abused lest he get it into his head that he can boss me. After he had been reduced to the proper plane of humility and had explained and begged my pardon and had told me to consult only my own pleasure about going and coming and using his horses, not only to "expoose" the bairn, why, I forgave him and we were friends once more.

Next day all the men left for the round-up, to be gone a week. I knew I never could stand myself a whole week. In a little while the ladies came past on their way to Ashland. They were all laughing and were so happy that I really began to wish I was one of the number, but they went their way and I kept wanting to go somewhere. I got reckless and determined to do something real bad. So I went down to the barn and saddled Robin Adair, placed a pack on "Jeems McGregor," then Jerrine and I left for a camping-out expedition.

It was nine o'clock when we started and we rode hard until about four, when I turned Robin loose, saddle and all, for I knew he would go home and some one would see him and put him into the pasture. We had gotten to where we couldn't ride anyway, so I put Jerrine on the pack and led "Jeems" for about two hours longer; then, as I had come to a good place to camp, we stopped.

While we had at least two good hours of daylight, it gets so cold here in the evening that fire is very necessary. We had been climbing higher into the mountains all day and had reached a level tableland where the grass was luxuriant and there was plenty of wood and water. I unpacked "Jeems" and staked him out, built a roaring fire, and made our bed in an angle of a sheer wall of rock where we would be protected against the wind. Then I put some potatoes into the embers, as Baby and I are both fond of roasted potatoes. I started to a little spring to get water for my coffee when I saw a couple of jack rabbits playing, so I went back for my little shotgun. I shot one of the rabbits, so I felt very like Leather-stocking because I had killed but one when I might have gotten two. It was fat and young, and it was but the work of a moment to dress it and hang it up on a tree.

Then I fried some slices of bacon, made myself a cup of coffee, and Jerrine and I sat on the ground and ate. Everything smelled and tasted so good! This air is so tonic that one gets delightfully hungry. Afterward we watered and restaked "Jeems," I rolled some logs on to the fire, and then we sat and enjoyed the prospect.

The moon was so new that its light was very dim, but the stars were bright. Presently a long, quivering wail arose and was answered from a dozen hills. It seemed just the sound one ought to hear in such a place. When the howls ceased for a moment we could hear the subdued roar of the creek and the crooning of the wind in the pines. So we rather enjoyed the coyote chorus and were not afraid, because they don't attack people. Presently we crept under our Navajos and, being tired, were soon asleep.

I was awakened by a pebble striking my cheek. Something prowling on the bluff above us had dislodged it and it struck me. By my Waterbury it was four o'clock, so I arose and spitted my rabbit. The logs had left a big bed of coals, but some ends were still burning and had burned in such a manner that the heat would go both under and over my rabbit. So I put plenty of bacon grease over him and hung him up to roast. Then I went back to bed. I didn't want to start early because the air is too keen for comfort early in the morning.

The sun was just gilding the hilltops when we arose. Everything, even the barrenness, was beautiful. We have had frosts, and the quaking aspens were a trembling field of gold as far up the stream as we could see. We were 'way up above them and could look far across the valley. We could see the silvery gold of the willows, the russet and bronze of the currants, and patches of cheerful green showed where the pines were. The splendor was relieved by a background of sober gray green hills, but even on them gay streaks and patches of yellow showed where rabbit brush grew. We washed our faces at the spring—the grasses that grew around the edge and dipped into the water were loaded with ice. Our rabbit was done to a burn, so I made some delicious coffee. Jerrine got herself a can of water, and we breakfasted. Shortly afterwards we started again. We didn't know where we were going, but we were on our way.

That day was more toilsome than the last, but a very happy one. The meadowlarks kept singing like they were glad to see us. But we were still climbing and soon got beyond the larks and sage

chickens and up into the timber, where there are lots of grouse. We stopped to noon by a little lake, where I got two small squirrels and a string of trout. We had some trout for dinner and salted the rest with the squirrels in an empty can for future use. I was anxious to get a grouse and kept close watch, but was never quick enough.

Our progress was now slower and more difficult, because in places we could scarcely get through the forest. Fallen trees were everywhere and we had to avoid the branches, which was powerful hard to do. Besides, it was quite dusky among the trees long before night, but it was all so grand and awe-inspiring. Occasionally there was an opening through which we could see the snowy peaks, seemingly just beyond us, toward which we were headed. But when you get among such grandeur you get to feel how little you are and how foolish is human endeavor, except that which reunites us with the mighty force called God. I was plumb uncomfortable, because all my own efforts have always been just to make the best of everything and to take things as they come.

At last we came to an open side of the mountain where the trees were scattered. We were facing south and east, and the mountain we were on sheered away in a dangerous slant. Beyond us still greater wooded mountains blocked the way, and in the cañon between night had already fallen. I began to get scary. I could only think of bears and catamounts, so, as it was five o'clock, we decided to camp. The trees were immense. The lower branches came clear to the ground and grew so dense that any tree afforded a splendid shelter from the weather, but I was nervous and wanted one that would protect us against any possible attack. At last we found one growing in a crevice of what seemed to be a sheer wall of rock. Nothing could reach us on two sides, and in front two large trees had fallen so that I could make a log heap which would give us warmth and make us safe. So with rising spirits I unpacked and prepared for the night.

I soon had a roaring fire up against the logs and, cutting away a few branches, let the heat into as snug a bedroom as any one could wish. The pine needles made as soft a carpet as the wealthiest could afford. Springs abound in the mountains, so water was plenty. I staked "Jeems" quite near so that the firelight would frighten away any wild thing that tried to harm him. Grass was very plentiful, so when he was made "comfy" I made our bed and fried our trout. The branches had torn off the bag in which I had my bread, so it was lost in the forest, but who needs bread when they have good, mealy potatoes? In a short time we were eating like Lent

208

was just over. We lost all the glory of the sunset except what we got by reflection, being on the side of the mountain we were, with the dense woods between. Big sullen clouds kept drifting over and a wind got lost in the trees that kept them rocking and groaning in a horrid way. But we were just as cozy as we could be and rest was as good as anything.

I wish you could once sleep on the kind of bed we enjoyed that night. It was both soft and firm, with the clean, spicy smell of the pine. The heat from our big fire came in and we were warm as toast. It was so good to stretch out and rest. I kept thinking how superior I was since I dared to take such an outing when so many poor women down in Denver were bent on making their twenty cents per hour in order that they could spare a quarter to go to the "show." I went to sleep with a powerfully self-satisfied feeling, but I awoke to realize that pride goeth before a fall.

I could hardly remember where I was when I awoke, and I could almost hear the silence. Not a tree moaned, not a branch seemed to stir. I arose and my head came in violent contact with a snag that was not there when I went to bed. I thought either I must have grown taller or the tree shorter during the night. As soon as I peered out, the mystery was explained.

Such a snowstorm I never saw! The snow had pressed the branches down lower, hence my bumped head. Our fire was burning merrily and the heat kept the snow from in front. I scrambled out and poked up the fire; then, as it was only five o'clock, I went back to bed. And then I began to think how many kinds of idiot I was. Here I was thirty or forty miles from home, in the mountains where no one goes in the winter and where I knew the snow got to be ten or fifteen feet deep. But I could never see the good of moping, so I got up and got breakfast while Baby put her shoes on. We had our squirrels and more baked potatoes and I had delicious black coffee.

After I had eaten I felt more hopeful. I knew Mr. Stewart would hunt for me if he knew I was lost. It was true, he wouldn't know which way to start, but I determined to rig up "Jeems" and turn him loose, for I knew he would go home and that he would leave a trail so that I could be found. I hated to do so, for I knew I should always be powerfully humble afterwards.

Anyway, it was still snowing, great, heavy flakes; they looked as large as dollars. I didn't want to start "Jeems" until the snow stopped because I wanted him to leave a clear trail. I had sixteen loads for my gun and I reasoned that I could likely kill enough food to last twice that many days by being careful what I shot at. It just kept snowing, so at last I decided to take a little hunt and provide for the day. I left Jerrine happy with the towel rolled into a baby, and went along the brow of the mountain for almost a mile, but the snow fell so thickly that I couldn't see far. Then I happened to look down into the cañon that lay east of us and saw smoke. I looked toward it a long time, but could make out nothing but smoke, but presently I heard a dog bark and I knew I was near a camp of some kind. I resolved to join them, so went back to break my own camp.

At last everything was ready and Jerrine and I both mounted. Of all the times! If you think there is much comfort, or even security, in riding a pack horse in a snow storm over mountains where there is no road, you are plumb wrong. Every once in a while a tree would unload its snow down our backs. "Jeems" kept stumbling and threatening to break our necks. At last we got down the mountain-side, where new danger confronted us—we might lose sight of the smoke or ride into a bog. But at last, after what seemed hours, we came into a "clearing" with a small log house and, what is rare in Wyoming, a fireplace. Three or four hounds set up their deep baying, and I knew by the chimney and the hounds that it was the home of a Southerner. A little old man came bustling out, chewing his tobacco so fast, and almost frantic about his suspenders, which it seemed he couldn't get adjusted.

As I rode up, he said, "Wither, friend?" I said "Hither." Then he asked, "Are you spying around for one of them dinged game wardens after that deer I killed yisteddy?" I told him I had never even seen a game warden and that I didn't know he had killed a deer. "Wall," he said, "Are you spying around arter that gold mine I diskivered over on the west side of Baldy?" But after a while I convinced him that I was no more nor less than a foolish woman lost in the snow. Then he said, "Light, stranger, and look at your saddle." So I "lit" and looked, and then I asked him what part of the South he was from. He answered, "Yell County, by gum! The best place in the United States, or in the world, either." This was my introduction to Zebulon Pike Parker.

Only two "Johnny Rebs" could have enjoyed each other's company as Zebulon Pike and myself did. He was so small and so old, but so cheerful and so sprightly, and a real Southerner! He had a big, open fireplace with backlogs and andirons. How I enjoyed it all! How we feasted on some of the deer killed "yestiddy," and real corn-pone baked in a skillet down on the hearth. He was so full of happy recollections and had a few that were not so happy! He is, in some way, a kinsman of Pike of Pike's Peak fame, and he came west "jist after the wah" on some expedition and "jist stayed." He told me all about his home life back in Yell County. . . .

I got home at twelve and found, to my joy, that none of the men had returned, so I am safe from their superiority for a while, at least.

With many apologies for this outrageous letter, I am,

Your ex-Washlady,

Elinore Rupert

June 16, 1910

My Dear Friend,

Your card just to hand. I wrote you some time ago telling you I had a confession to make and have had no letter since, so thought perhaps you were scared I had done something too bad to forgive. I am suffering just now from eye-strain and can't see to write long at a time, but I reckon I had better confess and get it done with.

The thing I have done is to marry Mr. Stewart. It was such an inconsistent thing to do that I was ashamed to tell you. And, too, I was afraid you would think I didn't need your friendship and might desert me. Another of my friends thinks that way.

I hope my eyes will be better soon and then I will write you a long letter.

Your old friend with a new name,

Elinore Stewart.

August 15, 1910

Dear Mrs. Coney

. . . If you traveled due north from my home, after about nine hours' ride you would come into an open space in the butte lands, and away between two buttes you would see the glimmer of blue water. As you drew nearer you would be able to see the fringe of willows around the lake, and presently a low, red-roofed house with corrals and stables. You would see long lines of "buck" fence, a flock of sheep near by, and cattle scattered about feeding. This is Cora Belle's home. On the long, low porch you would see two old folks rocking. The man is small, and has rheumatism in his legs and feet so badly that he can barely hobble. The old lady is large and fat, and is also afflicted with rheumatism, but has it in her arms and shoulders. They are both cheerful and hopeful, and you would get a cordial welcome. . . .

When you saw Cora Belle you would see a stout, square-built little figure with long flaxen braids, a pair of beautiful brown eyes and the longest and whitest lashes you ever saw, a straight nose, a short upper lip, a broad, full forehead—the whole face, neither pretty nor ugly, plentifully sown with the brownest freckles.

She is very truly the head of the family, doing all the housework and looking after the stock, winter and summer, entirely by herself. Three years ago she took things into her own hands, and since that time has managed altogether. Mrs. O'Shaughnessy, however, tells her what to do.

The sheep, forty in number, are the result of her individual efforts. Mrs. O'Shaughnessy told her there was more money in raising lambs than in raising chickens, so she quit the chickens as a business and went to some of the big sheep-men and got permission to take the "dogie" lambs, which they are glad to give away. She had plenty of cows, so she milked cows and fed lambs all day long all last year. This year she has forty head of nice sheep worth four dollars each, and she doesn't have to feed them the year round as she would chickens, and the wolves are no worse to kill sheep than they are to kill chickens.

When shearing time came she went to a sheep-man and told him she would help cook for his men one week if he would have her sheep sheared with his. She said her work was worth three dollars, that is what one man would get a day shearing, and he could easily shear her sheep in one day. That is how she got her sheep sheared. The man had her wool hauled to town with his, sold it for her, and brought sixty dollars. She took the money to Mrs. O'Shaughnessy. She wanted some supplies ordered before she went home, because, as she gravely said, "the rheumatiz would get all the money she had left when she got home"—meaning that her grandparents would spend what remained for medicine.

The poor old grandparents read all the time of wonderful cures that different dopes accomplish, and they spend every nickel they can get their hands on for nostrums. They try everything they read of, and have to buy it by the case—horrid patent stuff! They have rolls of testimonials and believe every word, so they keep on trying and hoping.

When there is any money they each order whatever medicine they want to try. If Mrs. Edmonson's doesn't seem to help her, Grandpa takes it and she takes his—that is their idea of economy. They would spend hours telling you about their different remedies and would offer you spoonful after spoonful of vile-looking liquid, and be mildly grieved when you refused to take it. Grandma's hands are so bent and twisted that she can't sew, so dear old Grandpa tries to do it. . . .

Well, we had a large room almost empty and Mr. Stewart liked the idea of a party, so Mrs. Louderer, Mrs. O'Shaughnessy, and myself planned for the event. It was to be a sewing-bee, a few good neighbors invited, and all to sew for Grandma. . . . So Mrs. O'Shaughnessy went to Grandma's and got all the material she had to make up. I had saved some sugar-bags and some flour-bags. I knew Cora Belle needed underwear, so I made her some little petticoats of the larger bags and some drawers of the smaller. I had a small piece of white lawn that I had no use for, and of that I made a dear little sunbonnet with a narrow edging of lace around, and also made a gingham bonnet for her.

Two days before the time, came Mrs. Louderer, laden with bundles, and Mrs. O'Shaughnessy, also laden. We had all been thinking of Cora Belle. Mr. Stewart had sent by mail for her a pair of sandals for everyday wear and a nice pair of shoes, also some stockings. Mrs. Louderer brought cloth for three dresses of heavy Dutch calico, and gingham for three aprons. She made them herself and she sews so carefully. She had bought patterns and the little dresses were stylishly made, as well as well made. Mrs. O'Shaughnessy brought a piece of crossbar with a tiny forget-me-not polka dot, and also had goods and embroidery for a suit of underwear. My own poor efforts were already completed when the rest came, so I was free to help them.

Late in the afternoon of the 29th a funny something showed up . . . Cora Belle's team would bring a smile to the soberest face alive. Sheba is a tall lanky old mare . . . Balaam, a little donkey . . . has to trot his best to keep up with Sheba's slowest stride. . . . That is the kind of layout which drew up before our door that evening.

Cora Belle was driving and she wore her wonderful pink dress which hung down in a peak behind, fully six inches longer than anywhere else. The poor child had no shoes. The winter had tried the last pair to their utmost endurance and the "rheumatiz" had long since got the last dollar, so she came with her chubby little sunburned legs bare. Her poor little scarred feet were clean, her toe-nails full of nicks almost to the quick, broken against rocks when she had been herding her sheep.

In the back of the wagon, flat on the bottom, sat Grandma and Grandpa, such bundles of coats and blankets I can't describe. After a great deal of trouble we got them unloaded and into the house. Then Mrs. Louderer entertained them while Mrs. O'Shaughnessy and I prepared supper and got a bath ready for Cora Belle. We had T-bone steak, mashed potatoes, hominy, hot biscuits and butter, and stewed prunes. Their long ride had made them hungry and I know they enjoyed their meal.

After supper Cora Belle and I washed the dishes while Mrs. O'Shaughnessy laid out the little clothes. Cora Belle's clothes were to be a surprise. The postmistress here also keeps a small store and has ribbon, and when she heard of our plans from Mr. Stewart she sent up a couple of pairs of hair-ribbon for Cora Belle.

Soon Mrs. O'Shaughnessy called us, and Cora Belle and I went into the bedroom where she was. I wish you could have seen that child! poor little neglected thing, she began to cry. She said, "They ain't for my birthday, it's Granny's." Nevertheless, she had her arms full of them and was clutching them so tightly with her work-worn little hands that we couldn't get them. She sobbed so deeply that Grandma heard her and became alarmed. She hobbled to the door and pounded with her poor twisted hands, calling all the while, "Cory, Cory Belle, what ails you?" She got so excited that I opened the door, but Cora Belle told her to go away. She said, "They ain't for you, Granny, and they ain't for me either."

People here observe Decoration Day faithfully, and Cora Belle had brought half a wagon-load of iris, which grows wild here. Next morning we were all up early, but Cora Belle's flowers had wilted and she had to gather more, but we all hurried and helped. She said as she was going to see her mother she wanted to wear her prettiest dress, so Gale and Mrs. O'Shaughnessy helped her to get ready.

The cemetery is only about two miles away, so we were all down quite early. We were obliged to hurry because others were coming to help sew. Cora Belle went at once to the graves where her parents lie side by side, and began talking to her mother just as if she saw her. "You didn't know me, did you, Mother with my pretty new things? But I am your little girl, Mamma. I am your little Cora Belle." After she had talked and had turned every way like a proud little bird, she went to work. And, ooh, how fast she worked! Both graves were first completely covered with pine boughs. It looked like sod, so closely were the little twigs laid. Next she broke the stems off the iris and scattered the blossoms over, and the effect was very beautiful.

Then we hurried home and everybody got busy. The men took Grandpa off to another part of the ranch where they were fanning oats to plant, and kept him all day. That was good for him because then he could be with the men all day and he so seldom has a chance to be with men. Several ladies came and they all made themselves at home and worked like beavers, and we all had a fine time. . . .

Your sincere friend,

Elinore Rupert Stewart

December 2, 1912

Dear Mrs. Coney,

Every time I get a new letter from you I get a new inspiration, and I am always glad to hear from you.

I have often wished I might tell you all about my Clyde, but have not because of two things. One is I could not even begin without telling you what a good man he is, and I didn't want you to think I could do nothing but brag. The other reason is the haste I married in. I am ashamed of that. I am afraid you will think me a Becky Sharp of a person. But although I married in haste, I have no cause to repent. That is very fortunate because I have never had one bit of leisure to repent in. So I am lucky all around.

The engagement was powerfully short because both agreed that the trend of events and ranch work seemed to require that we be married first and do our "sparking" afterward. You see, we had to chink in the wedding between times, that is, between planting the oats and other work that must be done early or not at all. In Wyoming ranchers can scarcely take time even to be married in the springtime.

That having been settled, the license was sent for by mail, and as soon as it came Mr. Stewart saddled Club and went down to the house of Mr. Pearson, the justice of the peace and a friend of long standing. I had never met any of the family and naturally rather dreaded to have them come, but Mr. Stewart was firm in wanting to be married at home, so he told Mr. Pearson he wanted him and his family to come up the following Wednesday and serve papers on the "wooman i' the hoose." They were astonished, of course, but being such good friends they promised him all the assistance they could render. They are quite the dearest, most interesting family! I have since learned to love them as my own.

Well, there was not time to make wedding clothes, so I had to "do up" what I did have. Isn't it queer how sometimes, do what you can, work will keep getting in the way until you can't get anything done? That is how it was with me those few days before the wedding; so much so that when Wednesday dawned everything was topsy-turvy and I had a very strong desire to run away. But I always did hate a "piker," so I stood pat. Well, I had most of the dinner cooked, but it kept me hustling to get the house into anything like decent order before the old dog barked, and I knew my moments of Liberty were limited. It was blowing a perfect hurricane and snowing like midwinter. I had bought a beautiful pair of shoes to wear on that day, but my vanity had squeezed my feet a little, so while I was so busy at work I had kept on a worn old pair, intending to put on the new ones later; but when the Pearsons drove up all I thought about was getting them into the house where there was fire, so I forgot all about the old shoes and the apron I wore.

I had only been here six weeks then, and was a stranger. That is why I had no one to help me and was so confused and hurried. As soon as the newcomers were warm, Mr. Stewart told me I had better come over by him and stand up. It was a large room I had to cross, and how I did it before all those strange eyes I never knew. All I can remember very distinctly is hearing Mr. Stewart saying, "I will," and myself chiming in that I would, too. Happening to glance down, I saw that I had forgotten to take off my apron or my old shoes, but just then Mr. Pearson pronounced us man and wife, and as I had dinner to serve right away I had no time to worry over my odd toilet. Anyway the shoes were comfortable and the apron white, so I suppose it could have been worse; and I don't think it has ever made any difference with the Pearsons, for I number them all among my most esteemed friends.

It is customary here for newlyweds to give a dance and supper at the hall, but as I was a stranger I preferred not to, and so it was a long time before I became acquainted with all my neighbors. I had not thought I should ever marry again. Jerrine was always such a dear little pal, and I wanted to just knock about foot-loose and free to see life as a gypsy sees it. I had planned to see the Cliff-Dwellers' home; to live right there until I caught the spirit of the surroundings enough to live over their lives in imagination anyway. I had planned to see the old missions and to go to Alaska; to hunt in Canada. I even dreamed of Honolulu. Life stretched out before me one long, happy jaunt. I aimed to see all the world I could, but to travel unknown bypaths to do it. But first I wanted to try homesteading.

But for my having the grippe, I should never have come to Wyoming. Mrs. Seroise, who was a nurse at the institution for nurses in Denver while I was housekeeper there, had worked one summer at Saratoga, Wyoming. It was she who told me of the pine forests. I had never seen a pine until I came to Colorado; so the idea of a home among the pines fascinated me. At that time I was hoping to pass the Civil Service examination, with no very definite idea as to what I would do, but just to be improving my time and opportunity.

I never went to public school a day in my life. In my childhood days there was no such thing in the Indian Territory part of Oaklahoma where we lived, so I have had to try hard to keep learning. Before the time came for the examination I was so discouraged because of the grippe that nothing but the mountains, the pines, and the clean, fresh air seemed worth while; so it all came about just as I have written you.

So you see I was very deceitful. Do you remember, I wrote you of a little baby boy dying? That was my own little Jamie, our first little son. For a long time my heart was crushed. He was such a sweet, beautiful boy. I wanted him so much. He died of erysipelas. I held him in my arms till the last agony was over. Then I dressed the beautiful little body for the grave. Clyde is a carpenter; so I wanted him to make the little coffin. He did it every bit, and I lined and padded it, trimmed and covered it. Not that we couldn't afford to buy one or that our neighbors were not all that was kind and willing; but because it was a sad pleasure to do everything for our little first-born ourselves.

As there had been no physician to help, so there was no minister to comfort, and I could not bear to let our baby leave the world without leaving any message to a community that sadly needed it. His little message to us had been love, so I selected a chapter from John and we had a funeral service, at which all our neighbors for thirty miles around were present. So you see our union is sealed by love and welded by great sorrow.

Little Jamie was the first little Stewart. God has given me two more precious little sons. The old sorrow is not so keen now. I can bear to tell you about it, but I never could before. When you think of me, you must think of me as one who is truly happy. It is true, I want a great many things I haven't got, but I don't want them enough to be discontented and not enjoy the many blessings that are mine. I have my home among the blue mountains, my healthy, well-formed children, my clean, honest husband, my kind, gentle milk cows, my garden which I make myself. I have loads and loads of flowers which I tend myself. There are lots of chickens, turkeys, and pigs which are my own special care. I have some slow old gentle horses and an old wagon. I can load up the kiddies and go where I please any time. I have the best, kindest neighbors and I have my dear absent friends. Do you wonder I am so happy? When I think of it all, I wonder how I can crowd all my joy into one short life. . . .

With much love to you, I am
"Honest and truly" yours,

Elinore Rupert Stewart

January 23, 1913

Dear Mrs. Coney,

. . . When I read of the hard times among the Denver poor, I feel like urging them every one to get out and file on land. I am very enthusiastic about women homesteading. It really requires less strength and labor to raise plenty to satisfy a large family than it does to go out to wash, with the added satisfaction of knowing that their job will not be lost to them if they care to keep it. Even if improving the place does go slowly, it is that much done to stay done. Whatever is raised is the homesteader's own, and there is no house-rent to pay.

This year Jerrine cut and dropped enough potatoes to raise a ton of fine potatoes. She wanted to try, so we let her, and you will remember that she is but six years old. We had a man to break the ground and cover the potatoes for her and the man irrigated them once. That was all that was done until digging time, when they were ploughed out and Jerrine picked them up. Any woman strong enough to go out by the day could have done every bit of the work and put in two or three times that much, and it would have been so much more pleasant than to work so hard in the city and then be on starvation rations in the winter.

To me, homesteading is the solution of all poverty's problems, but I realize that temperament has much to do with success in any undertaking, and persons afraid of coyotes and work and loneliness had better let ranching alone. At the same time, any woman who can stand her own company, can see the beauty of the sunset, loves growing things, and is willing to put in as much time at careful labor as she does over the washtub, will certainly succeed; will have independence, plenty to eat all the time, and a home of her own in the end.

Experimenting need cost the homesteader no more than the work, because by applying to the Department of Agriculture at Washington he can get enough of any seed and as many kinds as he wants to make a thorough trial, and it doesn't even cost postage. Also one can always get bulletins from there and from the Experiment Station of one's own State concerning any problem or as many problems as may come up.

I would not, for anything, allow Mr. Stewart to do anything toward improving my place, for I want the fun and the experience myself. And I want to be able to speak from experience when I tell others what they can do. Theories are very beautiful, but facts are what must be had, and what I intend to give some time.

Here I am boring you to death with things that cannot interest you! You'd think I wanted you to homestead, wouldn't you? But I am only thinking of the troops of tired, worried women, sometimes even cold and hungry, scared to death of losing their places to work, who could have plenty to eat, who could have good fires by gathering the wood and comfortable homes of their own, if they but had the courage and determination to get them.

I must stop right now before you get so tired you will not answer. With much love to you from Jerrine and myself, I am

Yours affectionately,

Elinore Rupert Stewart

In 1926, Elinore was seriously injured when a covey of quail scattered in front of her horses, causing them to bolt and her to fall beneath the hay mower she had been driving. She never really recovered from those injuries, and died in 1933.

Living room of the ranch house of I. L. Killie, with handmade furniture and Christmas decorations.

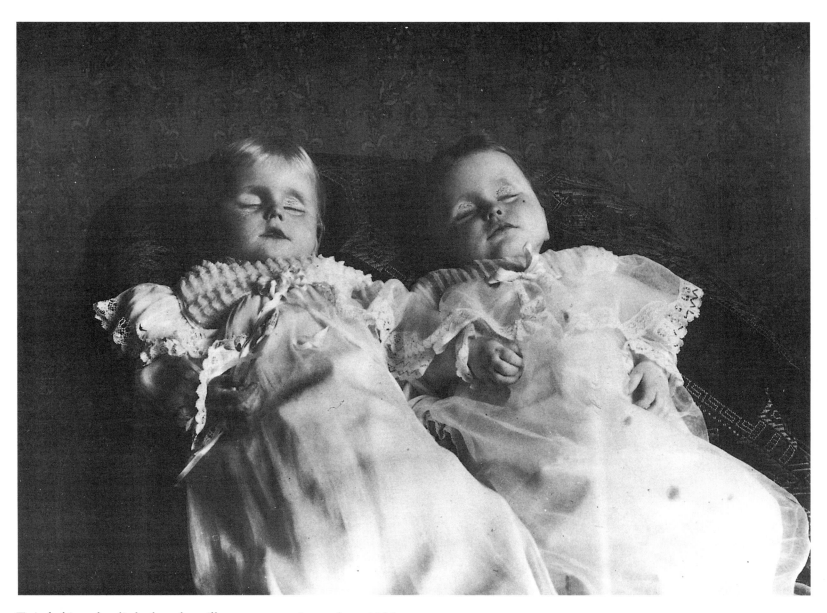

Twin babies who died when the milk cow ate a toxic weed, ca. 1906.

Appendix

1811-1897	Mary Richardson Walker
1817-Unknown	Miriam Davis Colt
1813-1903	Sister Mary Catherine Cabareaux
1844-1891	Sarah Winnemucca
1850-1894	Pauline Lyons Williamson
1820-1913	Keturah Penton Belknap
1854-1926	Helen Wiser Stewart
1840-1926	Bethenia Owens-Adair
1835-1914	Priscilla Merriman Evans
1867-1960	Anna Harder Odgen
1876-1933	Elinore Pruitt Stewart

1820	Public lands in the West are offered for sale at $1.24 per acre
1825	Erie Canal opens
1826	Lowell textile mills open with jobs for women
1831	Underground railway is begun
1833	Coeducational Oberlin College is founded Philadelphia Female Anti-Slavery Society is organized
1834	Cyrus McCormick patents the reaping machine
1838	Mary Richardson Walker and her husband Elkanah set out on horseback for Oregon
1839	Sister Mary Catherine and her companions reach the shores of Oregon after sailing from Antwerp
1842	Col. John C. Fremont explores the Wind River Mountains in Wyoming
1846	Donner Party is trapped in the snows near Truckee, Calif. Elias Howe's sewing machine is patented Oregon is acquired from Great Britain and becomes a state Texas's war of independence from Mexico begins
1847	First settlement in the Salt Lake Valley is established Keturah Penton Belknap and her husband George emigrate across the plains to Oregon
1848	Married Woman's Property Bill is introduced

Dates in the Development of the West

1848	First Women's Rights Convention is held
	Gold is discovered near Sutter's Mill in California
	Department of the Interior is created
1851	Cherokee National Female Academy is established in Oklahoma
	Bloomer costume is first introduced
	Uncle Tom's Cabin is published
1852	Antioch becomes second college to admit women
1854	Bethenia Owens-Adair marries at fourteen and sets up housekeeping in Oregon
1855	First convention of the Colored Citizens of the State of California is held
1856	Miriam Colt moves to Kansas with her family
	Priscilla Merriman Evans and her husband Thomas walk to Utah as Mormon handcart pioneers
1857	Gold is discovered near Pike's Peak, Colorado
1858	Iowa State University is third college to admit women
1860	Sarah Winnemucca and her Paiute tribe settle on the first of several government reservations near Pyramid Lake, Nevada
1873	Elizabeth Cady Stanton advocates birth control
1875	Mary Baker Eddy founds the Church of Christ, Scientist

1876	Telephone is patented
1878	Clara Foltz is admitted as first woman lawyer to the California Bar
1879	Belva Lockwood is admitted to practice before the Supreme Court
1882	American Red Cross is founded
1884	Helen Stewart's husband Archie is murdered
1885	Pauline Lyons Williamson comes to Oakland, California, with her son
1886	Anna Harder begins her journal in Oakland, California, at the age of twenty-one
1887	Dawes Act terminates tribal government and communal ownership of tribal lands
1888	Scott Act prohibits immigration of Chinese laborers
1890	Army battles Plains Indians at Wounded Knee
1896	Klondike gold rush begins
1903	National Women's Trade Union League is established
1909	Elinore Pruitt Stewart comes to Wyoming to homestead
	Model T Ford is manufactured
1911	First transcontinental plane flight takes place
1920	18th and 19th Amendments—Prohibition and Women's Suffrage—are passed

Five generations of Montana women in the Mary Wells Yates family.

The Stewart family in Spokane, Washington, taken July 5, 1889.

Footnotes

The opening quote, "Work is love made visible," is from *The Prophet*, by Kahlil Gibran, Copyright 1944, published by Alfred A. Knopf, reprinted here with permission of the publisher.

[1]Bill Hosokawa, *Ni Sei, The Quiet Americans* (New York: William Morrow & Co., 1969), pp. 90–91. Harry S. Linfield, *The Jews in the United States: A Study of Their Numbers and Distribution* (New York: American Jewish Committee, 1929). *Historical Statistics of the United States: Colonial Times to 1952* (Washington: U.S. Department of Commerce, Bureau of Statistics).

[2]Helen Carpenter, "A Journey Across the Plains in an Ox Cart, 1857," Henry E. Huntington Library, San Marino, California.

[3]Diary of Mrs. Byron J. Pengra, Lane County Historical Society, Eugene, Oregon.

[4]Lavinia Honeyman Porter, *By Ox Team to California: a Narrative of Crossing the Plains in 1860* (Oakland, California: Oakland Enquirer Publishing Company, 1910).

[5]LeRoy R. and Ann W. Hafen, *Handcarts to Zion* (Glendale, California: The Arthur H. Clark Company, 1976), p. 105.

[6]Gloria Ricci Lothrop, "The Not-So-Shady Ladies of the West" (Lecture, Scripps College, Claremont, California, Feb. 20, 1981).

[7]Ibid.

[8]Claire Noall, *The Guardians of the Hearth* (Utah: Horizon Publishing Company, Bountiful, Utah), p. 31.

Maude Park churning butter, 1905.

Adeline Hall churning butter on her ranch house porch, 1910.

[9]Mary A. Jones, "Recollections of Mrs. Mary A. Jones, 1825-1918, Alamo, Contra Costa County," The Bancroft Library, Berkeley, Calif.

[10]Frank Hoyt, ed., "Hoyt-Bobenyer and Thompson-Sidles Genealogy and Early History," Lincoln, Nebraska, p. 22.

[11]Rebecca Hildreth Nutting (Woodson), "A Sketch of the Life of Rebecca Hildreth Nutting (Woodson) and Her Family, Dec. 6, 1835-1907," Bancroft Library, University of California, Berkeley, CA.

[12]Ibid, p. 29.

[13]Lothrop, "Not-So-Shady-Ladies of the West."

[14]Mrs. Arthur Cowan, Journal of Mrs. Arthur Cowan, Jan. 1, 1895-Jan. 4, 1896, Montana State Historical Society.

[15]Rebecca Hildreth Nutting (Woodson)'s "Sketch."

[16]Tommie Clack, "Recollections of Miss Tommie Clack," *Pioneer Days . . . Two Views*, Katharyn Duff, Betty Kay Seibt, eds. (Abilene, Texas: Reporter Publishing Co., 1979), p. 162.

[17]Sarah E. Olds, *Twenty Miles From a Match: Homesteading in Western Nevada* (Reno: University of Nevada Press, 1978), p. 119.

[18]Ibid., p. 75.

[19]Kate Nye Starr, "Letters of Kate Nye Starr," Bancroft Library, University of California, Berkeley, CA.

[20]Luzena Stanley Wilson, *49'er* (Oakland, California: Mills College, Eucalyptus Press, 1937), p. 27.

[21]Sarah Winnemucca Hopkins, *Life Among the Piutes: Their Wrongs and Claims*, Mrs. Horace Mann, ed. (Boston: for sale by Cupples, Upham & Co., G.P. Putnam's Sons, N.Y. and by the author, 1883), p. 5.

[22]Mary Stewart Bailey, "A Journal of Mary Stuart Bailey, 1852," Henry E. Huntington Library, San Marino, California.

[23]Margaret M. Hecox, *California Caravan: The 1846 Overland Trail Memoir of Margaret M. Hecox*, Richard Dillon, ed. (San Jose, California: Harlan-Young Press, 1966).

[24]Ibid., p. 74.

[25]Tommie Clack, "Recollections," p. 169.

[26]Fred Lockley, *Conversations with Pioneer Women*, Mike Helm, ed. (Eugene, Oregon: Rainy Day Press, 1981), p. 65.

[27]Ibid, pp. 168–169.

[28]Joanna L. Stratton, *Pioneer Women* (New York: Simon and Schuster, 1981), p. 117.

[29]Patience Cooper, "Letters of Jeremiah B. Sanderson," Jeremiah Sanderson Collection, Bancroft Library, University of California, Berkeley, CA.

[30]Lockley, *Conversations with Pioneer Women*, p. 33.

[31]Catherine Sanderson, "Letters of Jeremiah B. Sanderson," Jeremiah B. Sanderson Collection, Bancroft Library, University of California, Berkeley, CA.

[32]Norman L. Crockett, *The Black Towns* (Lawrence: The Regents Press of Kansas), pp. 68–69.

[33]Linfield, *The Jews in the United States*, p. 35.

[34]Levi, John Newmark Sr., "This is the Way We Used to Live," *Western States Jewish Historical Quarterly*, vol. IV, nos. 1–4, Oct. 1971-July 1972, p. 76.

[35]Rudolf Glanz, *The Jews of California* (New York, 1960), p. 112.

[36]Henry Mayer, "Reminiscences of Henry Mayer," personal collection.

[37]Levi's "This is the Way," p. 76.

[38]"American Israelite," Vol. 25, 1875, No. 7, p. 5.

[39]Claire (Hofer) Hewes, "Reminiscences of Claire (Hofer) Hewes," 1898, Special Collections Library, University of Nevada, Reno.

[40]Harriet Lane Levy, *920 O'Farrell Street* (Garden City, New York: Doubleday & Co., 1947), p. 20.

[41]Flora Spiegelberg, "Spiegelberg Brothers' Papers," State Records Center and Archives, Santa Fe, New Mexico.

[42]Hosokawa, *Ni Sei, The Quiet Americans*, p. 89.

[43]"Seventeenth Annual Report of the Occidental Board of the Women's Foreign Missions, 1887," Library of the San Francisco Theological Seminary, San Anselmo, California, p. 44.

[44]"Seventh Annual Report, 1880," p. 44.

[45]"Eleventh Annual Report, 1886," p. 80.

[46]"Report," 1900, p. 162.

[47]"Eleventh Annual Report, 1886," p. 32.

[48]"Thirteenth Annual Report, 1886," p. 65.

[49] Ibid.

[50]Gee, Emma. "Issei: The First Women," *Counterpoint: Perspective on Asian Americans*. (Los Angeles: Asian American Studies Center, 1973), p. 12.

[51]Ibid.

[52]Ibid.

[53]Kazuko Hayashi, "Life of Kazuko Hayashi," Michiyo Laing, Carl Laing, Heihachiro Takarabe, Asako Tokuno, Stanley Umeda, eds. *Issei Christians* (Sierra Mission Area: Synod of the Pacific, United Presbyterian Church, 1977), p. 106.

Unidentified women washing in California.

Bibliography

Alderson, Nannie T. and Helena Huntington-Smith. *A Bride Goes West*. Lincoln: University of Nebraska Press, 1969.

Aloysia, Sister Mary. *Notice Sur la Territoire et Sur à la Mission de l'Oregon Suivie du Queles Lettres des Soeurs de Notre Dame*. Brussels: The Sisters of Notre Dame de Namur, 1847.

Backes, Reverend Mother Pia, O.P. *Her Days Unfolded*. St. Benedict, San Jose, Calif.: Benedictine Press, 1853.

Bancroft, Hubert. *History of California, Vol. 23, 1848–1859, Vol. 24, 1860–1890; History of Nevada, Colorado, and Wyoming, Vol. 25, History of Arizona and New Mexico, Vol. 27 1530–1888*, The Works of Hubert. H. Bancroft. San Francisco: The History Company Publishers, 1888–1890.

Barth, Gunther. *Bitter Strength: A History of the Chinese in the United States, 1850–1870*. Boston: Harvard University Press, 1964. Second Printing, 1971.

Baum, Charlotte, Paula Hyman, Sonya Michl. *The Jewish Women in America*. New York: The Dial Press, 1976.

Beasley, Delilah. *The Negro Trail Blazers of California*. Los Angeles: 1919.

Bender, Flora I. *Diary, 1863*. Typescript. Reno: Nevada State Historical Society.

Blair, Kay. *Ladies of the Lamplight*. Timberline Books, 1978.

Brooks, Elisha. *A Pioneer Mother of California*. San Francisco, 1922.

Brown, Dee. *The Gentle Tamers*. New York: Bantam Books, Inc., 1974.

Brownlee, W. Elliot, and Mary M. Brownlee. *Women in the American Economy: A Documentary History, 1675 to 1929*. New Haven and Yale: Yale University Press, 1976.

Bryson, Nettie Korb. *Prairie Days*. Los Angeles: Times-Mirror Press. 1939.

Burchell, R.A. *The San Francisco Irish, 1848–1880*. Berkeley: University of California Press, 1980.

Cayuse twins.

Burlend, Rebecca. *A True Picture of Emigration.* Chicago: Lakeside Press, 1936.

Bushman, Claudia L. *Mormon Sisters.* Salt Lake City, Utah: Olympus Publishing Company, 1976.

Chase, A.W., M.D. *Dr. Chase's Recipes for Information for Everybody.* Ann Arbor, Mich.: A.W. Chase, 1866.

Clack, Tommie, and Mollie Clack. *Pioneer Days . . . Two Views.* Abilene, Texas: Reporter Publishing Company, 1979.

Clark, Harry. "Their Pride, Their Manners, and Their Voices; Sources of the Traditional Portrait of the Early Californians." *California Historical Quarterly.* 53 (1974): 71-82.

Cleaveland, Morely. *No Life for a Lady.* Santa Fe, N.M.: W. Gannon, 1976. Reprint of ed. by Houghton-Mifflin, Boston: Life in America series.

Cogan, Sara G. *Pioneer Jews of the California Mother Lode.* Berkeley, Calif.: Western Jewish History Center, 1968.

Coolidge, Mary Roberts. "Jane Fourr, A Pioneer Mother." *Arizona Quarterly,* 1:3 (1945): 27-33.

Cornelius, Mrs. *The Young Housekeeper's Friend.* Cambridge: Allen & Farnham, 1859.

Cowan, Mrs. Arthur. Journal, 1895, typescript of MS. Missoula: Montana State Historical Society.

Custer, Elizabeth Bacon. *Tenting on the Plains.* Williamstown, Mass.: Corner House Publishers, 1973.

Daniels, Douglas Henry. *Pioneer Urbanites.* Philadelphia: Temple University Press, 1980.

Dick, Everett. *The Sod House Frontier, 1854–1860.* Lincoln and London: University of Nebraska Press, 1979.

Dickenson, Luella. *Reminiscences of a Trip Across the Plains in 1846 and Early Days in California.* Fairfield, Calif.: Galleon Press, 1977.

Dicker, Laverne Mau. *The Chinese in San Francisco.* New York: Dover Publications, Inc., 1979.

Dorson, Richard M. *American Folklore.* Chicago: University of Chicago Press, 1959.

Douglas, Ann. *The Feminization of American Culture.* New York: Avon Books, by arrangement with Alfred A. Knopf, Inc., 1977.

Drago, Harry. *Notorious Ladies of the Frontier.* New York: Dodd, Mead, 1969.

Drury, Clifford Merrill. *Elkanah and Mary Walker.* Caldwell, Idaho: Caxton Printers Ltd., 1940.

———. *First White Women Over the Rockies.* Vol. 1, 2, 3. Glendale, Calif.: The Arthur H. Clark Co. 1963.

Edgarton, Mary. *A Governer's Wife on the Mining Frontier: Letters from 1863 to 1865.* Salt Lake City: Tanner Trust Fund.

Faragher, John Mack. *Women and Men on the Overland Trail.* New Haven and London: Yale University Press, 1979.

Female's Practical Guide and Mother's Assistant. Bancroft Library, Berkeley: University of California, 1848.

Fischer, Christiane, ed. *Let Them Speak for Themselves: Women in the American West.* New York: E.P. Dutton, 1978.

Fitzgerald, Frances. *America Revised.* New York: Vintage Books, 1980.

Fraser, Mrs. Hugh. *Seven Years on the Pacific Slope.* London: T.W. Laurie, Ltd., 1914.

Goldman, Mimi. "Prostitutes on the Comstock." *Nevada Historical Quarterly.* (Summer, 1978).

Glanz, Dr. Rudolp. *The Jews of California.* New York: Waldon Press, Inc., 1960.

Hafen, Ann W. and LeRoy R. *Handcarts to Zion.* Glendale, Calif.: The Arthur H. Clark Company, 1976.

Heizer, Robert F., Alan F. Almquist. *The Other Californians.* Berkeley, Los Angeles and London: University of California Press, 1971.

Heywood, Martha. *Not by Bread Alone.* Edited by Juanita Brooks, Salt Lake City, Utah: Utah State Historical Society, 1978.

Hewes, Claire (Hofer). "Reminiscenses." 1898. MS. in typescript Special Collections Department, University of Nevada Library, Reno.

———. "The Fathering of the Clan." 1898. MS in typescript. Special Collections Department, University of Nevada Library, Reno.

Holder, Preston. *The Hoe and the Horse on the Plains.* Lincoln and London: University of Nebraska Press, 1970.

Hom, Gloria Sun. *Chinese Argonauts.* Santa Clara, Calif.: Foothill Community College, 1971.

Hutchinson, Alan C. *Frontier Settlement in Mexican California.* New Haven and London: Yale University Press, 1969.

Jeffrey, Julie Roy. *Frontier Women.* New York: Hill and Wang, 1979.

Johnson, Broderick H. ed. *Navajo Stories of the Long Walk Period.* Tsaile, Navajo Nation, Arizona: Navajo Community College Press, 1973.

Johnson, Charles A. *The Frontier Camp Meeting.* Dallas: Southern Methodist University Press, 1955.

Katz, Jane B. *I Am the Fire of Time.* New York: E.P. Dutton, 1977.

Keller, John E. ed. *Anna Morrison Reed, 1849–1921.* Letters. Lafayette, Calif.

Laing, Carl, Michiyo Laing, Heihachiro Takarabe, Asako Tokuno, Stanley Umeda, eds. *Issei Christians.* Pacific Synod, Sacramento: United Presbyterian Church, 1977.

Lapp, Rudolph M. *Blacks in Gold Rush California.* New Haven and London: Yale University Press, 1977.

Levenson, Dorothy. *Women of the West.* New York: Watts Press, 1973. Vol. IV, Nos. 1–4, Oct. 1971 to July 1972.

Levi, John Newmark Sr. "This Is the Way We Used to Live." *Western States Jewish Historical Quarterly.* Vol. IV, Nos. 1–4.

McDermott, John Francis. *Travelers of the Western Frontier.* Urbana: University of Illinois Press, 1970.

McNamee, Sister Mary Dominica S.N.D de N. *Willamette Interlude.* Palo Alto, Calif.: Pacific Books, 1969.

Marcy, Randolph B. *The Prairie Traveler: A Handbook for Overland Expeditions.* London: Trubner and Company, 1863.

Megquier, Mary Jane. *Apron Full of Gold.* San Marino: Huntington Library, 1849.

Mowatt, Anna Cora. *Autobiography of an Actress.* Boston: Ticknor, Reed, & Fields, 1853.

Michelson, Truman. *Narrative of a Southern Cheyenne Woman.* Smithsonian Miscellaneous Collections, 87:5.

Munkres, Robert L. "Wives, Mothers, Daughters: Women's Life on the Road West." *Annals of Wyoming.* (Oct. 1970) 191–224.

Myres, Sandra L. *Ho for California!* San Marino, Calif.: Huntington Library, 1980.

Newell, Linda King and Valeen Tippetts Avery. "Jane Manning James, Black Saint, 1847 Pioneer." *The Ensign* (Aug. 1979) 26–29.

Newmark, Rosa. "A Letter From Mother to Daughter." *Western States Jewish Historical Quarterly.* 5:1 (1972) 274–284.

O'Hara, Edwin V. *Pioneer Catholic History of Oregon.* Peterson, Oregon: Franciscan Monastery, 1939.

Olds, Sarah E. *Twenty Miles From a Match.* Reno: University of Nevada Press, 1978.

Paden, Irene D. *In the Wake of the Prairie Schooner.* New York: The Macmillan Company, 1953.

Parker, George F. *Iowa Pioneer Foundation I & II*. Iowa City: Iowa State Historical Society, Athens Press, 1940.

Platt, P.L., Nelson Slater A.M. *Travelers' Guide Across the Plains Upon the Overland Route to California*. San Francisco: John Howell Books, 1963, reprint of 1852 edition.

Pengra, Charlotte Emily Stearns. Diary. 1853. Eugene, Oreg., n.d. Reproduced by Lane County Pioneer Historical Society. Bancroft Library, Berkeley: University of California.

Pruitt, Ida. *A Daughter of Han*. Stanford, Calif.: Stanford University Press, 1967.

Read, George Willis. "Women and Children on the Oregon-California Trail." *Missouri Historical Review*. 39 (1944): 1-2.

Reinhardt, Richard. "On the Brink of the Boom: Southern California in 1877." *California Historical Society*. 52 (1973) 64-79.

Rideout, Mrs. Jacob Barzilla. *Six Years on the Border; Sketches of Frontier Life*. Philadelphia: Presbyterian Board of Publication, 1883.

Riley, Glenda. *Women in the West*. Journal of American Culture 3:2 (Summer 1980): 311-329.

Royce, Sarah. *A Frontier Lady*. Lincoln: University of Nebraska Press, 1977.

Rosenshine, Annette. "Life Is Not a Paragraph." Typescript. Bancroft Library, University of California,

Sandmeyer, Elmer Clarence. *The Anti-Chinese Movement in California*. Urbana, Chicago and London: University of Illinois Press, 1973.

Sanford, Mollie Dorsey. *Mollie: The Journal of Mollie Dorsey Sanford in Nebraska and Colorado Territories, 1857–1866*. Lincoln and London: University of Nebraska Press, 1959: Bison Books, 1976.

Scrimsher, Lila Gravatt. "The Diary of Anna Webber: Early Day Teacher of Mitchell County." The Kansas Historical Quarterly. 38:3 (1972): 320-337.

Shores, Sunset. *In Harvest Fields: The Work of the Sisters of Notre Dame on the Pacific Coast*. San Francisco: Gilmartin Company, 1926.

Solano, Isadora. Bancroft Interview. MSS transcript. Bancroft Library, University of California.

Somers, Sister Margaret. "The Beginnings of the Congregation of Notre Dame in the West." Master's thesis. Berkeley: University of California, 1922.

Sprague, William Forrest. *Women and the West: A Short Social History*. New York: Arno Press, 1940.

Starr, Kevin. *Americans and the California Dream, 1850–1915*. New York: Oxford University Press, 1973.

Stewart, Elinore Pruitt. *Letters of a Woman Homesteader*. Lincoln and London: University of Nebraska Press, 1961.

Stewart, Patricia. "Sarah Winnemucca." *Nevada State Historical Society Quarterly*. 14 (1971): 23-38.

Stratton, Joanna L., *Pioneer Women*. New York: Simon & Schuster, 1981.

Sunder, John E., ed. *Matt Field on the Santa Fe Trail*. Norman: University of Oklahoma Press, 1960.

Swallow, Joan Reiter. *The Women*. (The Old West: v. 23) Alexandria, Virginia: Time-Life Books, 1978.

Terrell, John Upton, Donna M. *Indian Women of the Western Morning*. New York: Anchor Press. 1st. ed., The Dial Press, 1974.

Tyler, Ronnie C., Lawrence R. Murphy. *The Slave Narratives of Texas*. Austin, Texas: Encino Press, 1974.

Thurman, Sue Bailey. *Pioneers of Negro Origin in California*, San Francisco: Acme Publishing Co., 1952.

Townley, Carrie Miller. "Helen J. Stewart: First Lady of Las Vegas." *Nevada Historical Society Quarterly*, 16:4 (Winter 1973) I; 215-239, *Quarterly*, 17:1 (Spring 1974) II: 3-8.

Unruh, John D. *The Plains Across*. Urbana, Chicago and London: University of Illinois Press, 1978.

Vorspan, Max and Lloyd P. Gartner. *History of the Jews of Los Angeles*. The Huntington Library, San Marino, Calif.: 1970.

Vuolo, Brett Harvey. "Pioneer Diaries: The Untold Story of the West," *Ms. Magazine*, 3:2, May 1975.

"Women of the Wild Frontier." *National Retired Teachers Association Journal* (March-April 1980), 61-64.

Wertheimer, Barbara Mayer. *We Were There: The Story of Working Women in America*, New York: Pantheon Books, 1977.

Williams, George III. Rosa May, *The Search for a Mining Camp Legend*. Riverside: Tree by the River Publishing, n.d.

Wilson, Carol Green. *Chinatown Quest*. Stanford, Calif.: Stanford University Press.

Wilson, Nancy Ross. *Westward the Women*. New York: Alfred A. Knopf, 1944.

Wilson, Luzena Stanley. *49'er*. Oakland, Calif. Mills College, Eucalyptus Press, 1937.

Woodson, Rebecca Hildreth Nutting. Photocopy of MS. Berkeley: Bancroft Library, University of California.

Ulric Ulman family, Round Valley, Nebr. 1886.

Mr. & Mrs. Davis on Clear Creek, Nebr. 1887.

Ira Watson family, near Sargent, Nebr. 1886.

Moses Speese family near Westerville, Nebr. 1888.

Unidentified couple in cornfield, Custer Co., Nebr. 1888.

Unidentified family, Custer Co., Nebr. ca. 1888.

Homestead east of Judith Gap, Montana.

Mr. Barnes (widowed in 1886), after rain-soaked roof collapsed, 1887.

Photographic Sources

Matilda Booth Thatcher, date unknown.

Jennie Metcalf, outlaw.

Mrs. Rose Bowen in her bedroom, Silver City, Idaho, 1890's.

Unidentified woman milking cow in Colorado.

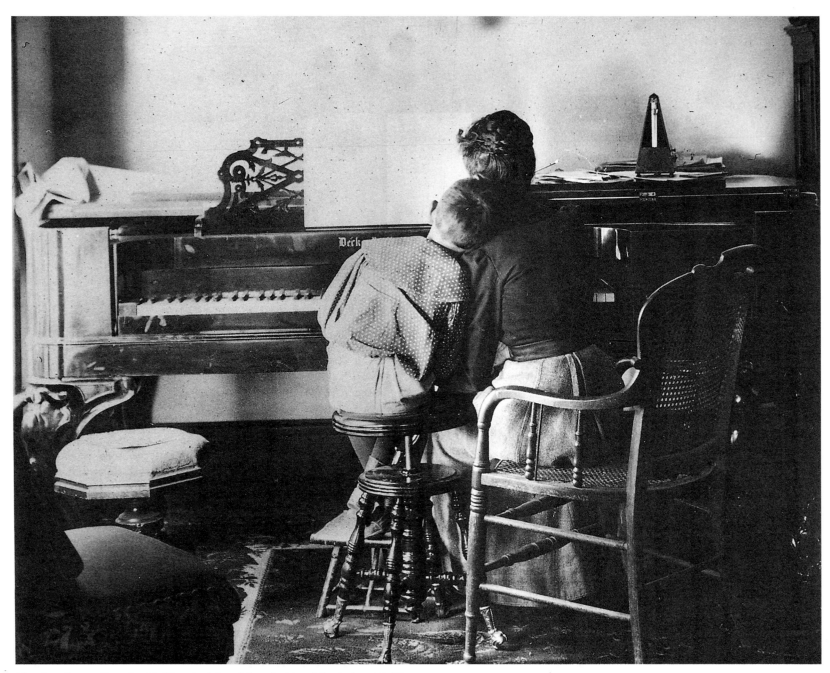

Teacher & pupil at the California School for the Deaf, Berkeley, Calif.

Acknowledgements

We offer sincere thanks to the following persons and institutions for making available to us the manuscripts, journals, documents, and general information necessary to produce this book: The Bancroft Library in Berkeley, California, for permission to use segments of the journal of Anna Harder Ogden, and for living up to the true meaning of scholarship by making its wealth of information so freely available to everyone; The New York Public Library for granting permission to reprint the letters of Pauline Williamson; The Daughters of the Utah Pioneers for permission to use the story of handcart pioneer Priscilla Merriman Evans; The Huntington Library in San Marino, California, for allowing us to reprint segments of the diary of Mary Richardson Walker; Houghton Mifflin Publishing Company for allowing us the use of Elinore Pruitt Stewart's letters; The Sisters of Notre Dame de Namur for granting us the use of Sister Mary Catherine's journal; the Nevada Historical Society for the use of Helen J. Stewart's day book and assorted letters; Mrs. Donald A. Belknap, heir to Keturah Belknap's manuscript, for granting us the use of the narrative.

This book would not have come to life half so well without the special cooperation and assistance of Sister Mary Justine McMullen, S.N.D.; Mr. Clinton E. Belknap; Diana Lachatanere, of the New York Public Library; Don Houser, of the Oakland Public Library; Glenda Riley; Susan M. Allen, of the Ella Strong Denison Library, Scripps College, Claremont, California; H. Gordon Frost, Professor of History, University of Texas at El Paso; Carrie Miller Townley; Paul Ogden; Tommie Clack; James T. deAbagian, Chancery Archives; and Mrs. Roberta Harband.

Special thanks for research assistance to Catherine Price, Janet and Victor Orange, Laura Black Bear Miles, Coralee and Myles Colligan, and Virginia Turner.

We would also like to acknowledge the primary research done by Carrie Miller Townley on Helen J. Stewart in her articles "Helen J. Stewart, First Lady of Las Vegas," Nevada Historical Society Quarterly, Vol. 14, No. 4 (Winter 1973) and Vol. 17, No. 1, (Spring 1974); by Dr. Clifford Merrill Drury, on the diaries of Mary Richardson Walker in First White Woman Over the Rockies, The Arthur H. Clark Company, Glendale, California, 1963; and by Elizabeth Fuller Ferris, who wrote the introduction to Letters on an Elk Hunt by a Woman Homesteader, by Elinore Pruitt Stewart, University of Nebraska Press, Lincoln, 1943. It is from these works that we obtained the biographical information on Helen J. Stewart, Mary Richardson Walker, and Elinore Pruitt Stewart.

We would like to thank the librarians and archivists of all those institutions listed in the Photographic Sources for their knowledge, helpfulness, and courtesy. They, and the women and men—past and present—who staff the libraries, archives, and historical societies of this country are the backstage heroines and heroes of this book. It is largely through their efforts that any visual or verbal record of the past remains to be shared.

We owe a special debt of gratitude to Billie Hobart for her helpful shaping of the direction of this book, and to the late Hilda Lindley for her invaluable encouragement in its early stages and for her demonstration of what excellence in the book business is all about.

Finally, we would like to thank R. Buckminster Fuller for his example of what it is to be a pioneer in the twentieth century—and perhaps even in the twenty-first.

Old William Marsh Homestead, 1886.

Book design by Carol Olwell. Typeset in Sabon and Baskerville by Thompson Type, San Diego. Production assistance from Harper & Vandenburgh, Oakland, and Hal Hershey, Berkeley. Mechanicals done by Jane Rockwell, Berkeley.

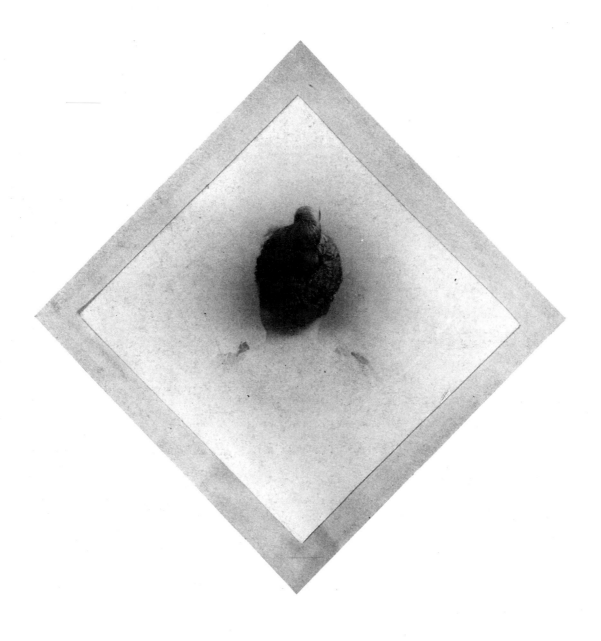